A Language of One's Own

Literary Arabic, the Palestinians and Israel

Ismail Nashef

EDINBURGH
University Press

Edinburgh University Press is one of the leading university presses in the UK. We publish academic books and journals in our selected subject areas across the humanities and social sciences, combining cutting-edge scholarship with high editorial and production values to produce academic works of lasting importance. For more information visit our website: edinburghuniversitypress.com

Edinburgh University Press Ltd
13 Infirmary Street
Edinburgh EH1 1LT

First published in hardback by Edinburgh University Press 2023

Typeset in 11/15 Garamond by
IDSUK (DataConnection) Ltd

A CIP record for this book is available from the British Library

ISBN 978 1 3995 1201 5 (hardback)
ISBN 978 1 3995 1202 2 (paperback)
ISBN 978 1 3995 1203 9 (webready PDF)
ISBN 978 1 3995 1204 6 (epub)

Major parts of this book are based on:

Ismail Nashef, *Arabic: The Story of a Colonial Mask*. Jerusalem: (Theory and Criticism in Context series, ed. Yehuda Shenhav), Van Leer Institute Press and Hakkibutz Hameuchad Publishing House, 2017 [In Hebrew].

Ismail Nashef, *The Arabic Language in the Zionist Regime*. Doha and Beirut: The Arab Center for Research and Policy Studies, 2018 [in Arabic].

Contents

Acknowledgements iv
Note on Transliteration v

Introduction 1

1 On Compulsiveness and Excessiveness: 'Arabic' 24

2 The Constitution of 'Arabic': Structural Beginnings and a Chain of Literary Events 55

3 The Mediation Position in 'Arabic': The Mimetic Mask 111

4 The Procedure Liberated: 'Arabic' in the Hands of Palestinian Experts 162

Conclusion: Narrating the History of the Non-historical 220

References 232
Index 249

Acknowledgements

I have been conducting my research on the sociolinguistic and literary fields in Palestine for several years now. Throughout the years, many people have been contributing to it in different, genuine and unexpected ways. I thank each of you friends, colleagues and comrades. At certain stages of this project, I published parts of it in Hebrew (Van Leer Jerusalem Institute and Hakibbutz Hameuchad, 2017) and in Arabic (Arab Center for Research and Policy Studies, 2018). Ami Asher translated the first raw Hebrew draft into English. I then added parts of the Arabic version to this translation, revised and rewrote parts of the chapters. The resulting version was then edited by Melanie Magidow, who also helped with translating parts of the Arabic version and provided language advice throughout the preparation of the manuscript. One of the anonymous reviewers' critical engagement with the manuscript helped me see parts of my arguments differently, and I thank them for their efforts and help. Finally, I am grateful to everybody at Edinburgh University Press who participated in preparing the manuscript for publication, especially Emma House, Louise Hutton and Isobel Birks.

Note on Transliteration

Following the house style, Arabic and Hebrew names and terms have not been transliterated in the main text. However, proper transliterations can be found in the endnotes and the references. I used the accepted spelling of the published authors' names in English. As for Hebrew transliteration, I have followed the Library of Congress guidelines.

For Duzan, Kinda and Neil

Introduction

The story of Arabic and its socially-produced forms under the Zionist regime represent one of the most fascinating aspects of the settler-colonial context that developed in Palestine in the twentieth century. It is an ongoing story, still unfolding with the intense drama that characterises other language wars of the modern era, such as French and English in Canada, and Arabic and French in North Africa. The history of Arabic via its socially-produced forms, while the events in question are still unfolding, is not always self-evident.[1] Perhaps therein lies the attraction of this research: letting developing events guide the study increases both insights and limitations. Rather than offering formal closure, this open-ended narrative describes the settler-colonial regime as a constitutive communicative event. It is a cluster of symbolic and semiotic interactions, derived from the sociopolitical order, while simultaneously contributing to reshaping it as it occurs.[2] This situation raises the following questions: What is the role of the narrator-researcher in relation to the story? How does the researcher structure the story as an intelligible research narrative?

Arabic scholars and speakers in the Arab World share a consensus on one major issue: Arabic is one of the main arenas in which speakers' identities are constituted in the modern era.[3] Because of its centrality, it has attracted socioeconomic, political and cultural forces that have tried to use Arabic to resolve various social contradictions that are not strictly related to issues 'internal' to language.[4] The history of these struggles is embodied in the structures of Arabic and its modes of usage, and it has accumulated into forms of linguistic operational rules of Arabic. For example, in spoken Arabic, certain dialects may be attributed to socioeconomic classes that are related to the distinction between living in rural or urban areas. In this sense, Arabic and its products are fertile ground for research: the living body of Arabic carries the social history of Arab societies in a manner similar to patterns of over-determination.[5] In spite of these generative positionalities of Arabic, the intersections between past and contemporary (neo)colonial regimes in the Arab World and Arabic and its products have not been addressed thoroughly. Only recently have scholars started to apply (post) colonial theoretical approaches to the study of Arabic and its products.[6]

Many anticolonial intellectuals have addressed the cultural sphere as a site of contestation between the coloniser and the colonised. Moreover, these intellectuals have laid the epistemological grounds for future academic research on the relations between the language of the coloniser and that of the colonised, as part of the contested cultural sphere of the colony as well as the metropolitan centre.[7] Historically, however, different types of relations have emerged between the languages of colonisers and colonised, depending on the specifc colonial context. Schematically, there have been three main types of these sociolinguistic relations in the colonies: 1) attempts at enforcing the language of the coloniser on the colonised and dismantling the infrastructure of the language of the colonised, as has been the case with Native American languages and English, Irish and English, or Arabic and French in colonial Algeria; 2) some sort of co-presence of the two languages that transforms both of them, as is the case with Indian languages and English, or Arabic, French and English in colonial Egypt; and 3) the emergence of new syntheses of languages, as has been the case with most of the Carribean pidgins and creoles. Unlike some other settler-colonial cases, such as the Native Americans' languages, the case of Arabic in Israel falls, roughly, within the limits of the second type that characterises classical colonial cases, especially the Indian one. Arabic and Hebrew are co-present in the Israeli sociolinguistic fields; both of these languages and their various registers have been reshaped due to the settler-colonial power relations between their respective communities. The trajectories of these settler-colonial hierarchical relations on Arabic and its products are our main focus in this book.

Since the inception of the Zionist regime, Arabic and its products have constituted a dynamic sphere in which opposing socioeconomic and political forces have been active in determing their course of evolvement.[8] With the establishment of the State of Israel in 1948, the treatment of Arabic has became institutionalised and taken the shape of a structural arena that since then has witnessed intense struggles: the construction of some identities as well as the destruction of others; and the maintenance or dissolution of others. From the point of view of the State of Israel which has brought this variation of the use of Arabic into existence, control over the language was supposed to secure the individual and collective subjugation of the Palestinians who became citizens of Israel – the so-called 'Israeli Arabs'. Similar to the Indian case, in order for this variation of Arabic to operate properly, both the apparatuses of the state and the Palestinian social forces operating within it had to translate their power into a certain form of Arabic and its products.[9] This translation is neither self-evident nor given *a priori* in the body of the language itself. The state organs had to mark the boundaries of this arena, and the Palestinians in Israel had to accept these boundaries, whether willingly or not.

Intervening in Arabic and its products in such a way that it articulates the position of sociopolitical power requires expertise and command of Arabic and its extensive history. Moreover, the intervention needs to be based on a kind of organising principle, a discourse understandable to the Palestinians in Israel, which allows the structuring of communicative events directed at them.[10] These conditions for building the arena of Arabic and its products were in place at the decisive juncture of the aftermath of the 1948 war. However, they did not grow out of the events of that war, but had been taking shape since the *Tanẓimat* of 1841 and, later, in the colonial realities of the British Mandate.[11] The *Tanẓimat* ignited processes of restructuring not only socioeconomic and political fields, but also cultural fields, particularly sociolinguistic sub-fields.[12] Changes in educational institutions were particularly prominent in this regard, including the new, modern governmental schools, as well as those established by Western Christian missionaries stationed in Palestine.[13] In addition to these local changes, the Palestinian communities were part of the *Nahda* taking place in Egypt and Greater Syria. By the end of the nineteenth century, Arabic was part of a thriving modern, multi-lingual Ottoman milieu.[14] The British Mandate reduced this field to three languages: English, Arabic and Hebrew. Moreover, it established particular institutional and administrative practices linking each language with certain communities, with Arabic for Palestinians and Hebrew for Jews. This is the prototype of institutional separation upon which the Zionist movement built during the Mandate period; Israel would later develop this prototype, among other state apparatuses, to manage its Palestinian citizens.[15]

As shown by multiple recent studies on the history of Arabic during the pre-statehood era in Palestine, the Zionist movement allocated resources and institutions to accumulate knowledge on different registers of Arabic, be it spoken or written.[16] For example, as early as 1926, the Institute for Oriental Studies was founded at the Hebrew University of Jerusalem, one year after its establishment. This institute generated Zionist experts on Arabic and its products, who moved into the organs of the Zionist movement, with some of them continuing to pursue this area of expertise after the establishment of the State of Israel.[17] The first public textual manifestation of these processes was *Haqiqat al-Amr*. This Arabic newspaper, founded by Histadrut in 1937, addressed a Palestinian readership.[18]

Conversely, textual and public activities in Arabic were central to Palestinian and Arab national revival.[19] Recent studies have indicated that, starting with the late Ottoman period and culminating in the Mandate period, a distinct field of Arabic and its products took shape using modern institutional infrastructure within Palestinian society.[20] This field encompassed newspapers, journals, prose and poetry, publishing houses and readerships, in addition to the official Ottoman and Mandate institutions. Some of the Palestinian intellectuals active during this time, whether locally or throughout the Arab World, also continued working with Arabic and its products after the establishment of the State of Israel. A conspicuous example consists of the Palestinian intellectuals who worked at *Al-Ittihad* prior to 1948 and thereafter, as well as other journals published by the Israeli Communist Party in the early 1950s.[21] The Zionist movement during the pre-statehood era coalesced with the Palestinian intellectual community after the establishment of Israel, within the arena of Arabic. The building of this arena of Arabic was initiated by the various state organs towards the end of 1948.

These processes of the social history of Arabic and its products form a significant layer in post-1948 developments. In what follows, I will examine the rewriting of that history by the State of Israel, which designated the arena for those who became its Palestinian citizens. As the empirical data of this study will show, this history has been rewritten by absenting it from the emerging structural position of Arabic in Israel. This book's main objective is to examine this new structural position of Arabic and its varied forms of communication and to understand its *modus operandi* throughout the period from 1948 to 2018, when the Israeli Knesset passed the Basic Law – The Nation State of the Jewish People.[22] This sociolinguistic arena has produced a certain type of textual and public action in Arabic, operating amidst the readership of Palestinians in Israel.[23]

More specifically, this book focuses on the modes of writing and reading of these texts. Writing and reading are actions of social agency, contesting the nature of the settler-colonial relationship that exists between Palestinians in Israel, as a collective, and the state, as well as the Zionist regime. The basic assumption is that these modes of literacy are the operatives that translate the socioeconomic and political forces into Arabic and its products.[24] They cast the social force into an exchangeable public textual form within the Palestinian readership. Once published, the text becomes a social force in its own right, operating according to internal rules; through the acts of writing and reading, it reshapes the literate Palestinian subject. This movement is not linear, although it is sometimes represented as such. Rather, it is a continuous movement in different directions, and our objective here is to extract its forms and patterns.

Unquestionably, the study of the social history of Arabic and its products in the State of Israel is a way of studying the settler-colonial context of the Palestinians in Israel.[25] Therefore, narrating the history of the social order in post-*Nakba* Palestine, through the narration of the history of Arabic and its products, relies on an analytical perspective of the settler-colonial sociopolitical order. As for the role of the narrator, in the process of structuring this research narrative, it is necessary to clarify my analytical approach to the aspects relevant to the present study, particularly in regard to the sociopolitical order and the way in which it relates to the Palestinian citizens of Israel. Contrary to some theoretical approaches, I argue here that a given sociopolitical order can relate to its subject groups in different and even contradictory ways.[26] In this case, Israel as a settler-colonial regime uses the same state apparatuses to treat Palestinians differently from the way in which it treats Zionist Jews. The duality of the use of the state apparatuses is inherent in the Israeli settler-colonial regime and is used as an organising bureaucratic principle to dominate and subjugate the Palestinian citizens.[27] It is important to note, at this early stage of this exposition of the duality of the state apparatuses, that its condition of possibility was the print capitalism of the post-World War II era. In the political sphere, this condition could materialise only via the nation-state format and its relevant apparatuses. Israel, as a settler-colonial regime, adopted this format and its bureaucratic logic of administering the populations under its control. But it has split its use according to hierarchical settler-colonial power relations – that is, whether it has been applied to the Zionist Jews or the Palestinians.

The Palestinians in Israel

Our baseline – namely, Israel is a settler-colonial state in its relation to its Palestinian citizens – requires further introductory elaboration through the prism of our current research. Despite the extensive literature on the Palestinians in Israel, the academic literature on their sociolinguistic field(s) has not yet used colonial or settler-colonial approaches.[28] To start with, Arabic and its products signify Palestinian-Arab national identity among Palestinians; they are also the infrastructure of this identity. This state of affairs is derived both from the history of Arabic among the Arab nations in the modern era and from the destruction of Palestinian material and social infrastructures in the 1948 war.[29] On the one hand, the revival of Arabic as part of the modern Arab project positioned it as the main sign of modern Arab nationality among Arab peoples, including the Palestinian people prior to 1948. On the other hand, the Palestinians who remained in Israel after the *Nakba* did so without the material and social basis that could provide for their needs on the material, symbolic and semiotic levels. All they had left was themselves in the context of the Israeli domination; and their collective identity was articulated in Arabic, its history and present-day products. Therefore, one of the main means used by the state apparatuses to deny Palestinian national collectivity in Israel has been the expropriation of the semiotic means of production of Arabic and its products from the collective ownership of the group of Palestinians in Israel.[30] In the chapters that follow, I will describe the concrete ways in which these expropriation processes unfolded, analyse the way in which these processes reflect the relationship between the State of Israel and the Palestinians within it, and suggest a conceptualisation of the social order that structures this relationship.

Citizenship is a mechanism of control and management that operates through modern bureaucratic registration. It applies not only to those included within its sphere, but also to its outgroups – those excluded and expelled from its sovereign territory.[31] Registering the Palestinians as Israeli citizens enabled their grouping, as well as their control and effective management. However, their separation as a group from the other citizens of the state has also enabled the reproduction of the collective identity of the Zionist Jews, the owners of the state and its semiotic – not only material – means of production. Nevertheless, despite this grouping of the Palestinians as a declaratively 'non-national' group, their nationality has only gained in strength over the years, in reaction to, among other factors, the settler-colonial state's institutional attempts to deconstruct the characteristics of their national collectivity.

Arabic and its products are an exemplary articulation of the complex relationship between the Palestinians in Israel and the State of Israel. Their expropriation from their owners in order to disassemble their collectivity has been achieved using settler-colonial practices, through the bureaucratic mechanisms of the nation-state, which decoupled the link between the Palestinians as a collective and the sign of this collective – Arabic.[32] Thus, the Israeli education system grouped the Palestinians in a separate sub-system, the Arab education system, where a certain Arabic was taught. In order for a Palestinian to create Arabic products, he or she had to integrate into the Israeli academic system. If we accept the assumption that we have here two national groups, one of which controls the other, then this is a variation on settler-colonial relations, much like the case of Ireland.[33] If we assume, however, that what we have is a constellation more complex than a relationship of one national collective controlling another, due to historical processes that bind the site of the struggle together with national and international socioeconomic and political sites, then we have here the Zionist regime as a settler-colonial project. The State of Israel is part of the broader socio-economic and political Zionist regime that has a material and institutional level of its own, managed by a certain organising principle that enables it to operate. To a significant extent, this regime maintains the State of Israel and its relationship to Palestinians, in general, and to its Palestinian citizens, in particular.

In the context of the arena of Arabic and its products in Israel, bureaucratically speaking it is the apparatuses of the State of Israel that maintain most of the textual and public activities in Arabic. However, patterns of Arabic literacy are derived from the more general superstructure of the Zionist regime; the state apparatuses are the procedural articulation thereof. For example, Chapter II will describe the literacy patterns of Zionists and Palestinians as well as the structural relationship between them. These patterns are not limited to the sovereign territory of the State of Israel, nor to the Jews as such, but are part of a Zionist regime that operates above state level – as a mechanism of sovereignty over a geopolitical territory.

For the purposes of this study, the sociopolitical order that regulates the relationship between the Palestinians in Israel and the State of Israel is considered a settler-colonial context, built upon the control of the Zionist movement over the Palestinians as a national collective, whether through state apparatuses or through the Zionist regime. These relations of control comprise various distinct but interrelated layers, one of which is Arabic and its products. Moreover, the state organs are the executive branch of the processes of controlling, dismantling and reorganising the national collectivity, and the Zionist regime is the general superstructure of the principles organising it. This framework of settler-colonial relations of control has been examined from multiple angles, but my analysis focuses on Arabic and its products. Therefore, we need to define the analytical frame used to study the products of Arabic and its structural arena as well as to examine their positions and roles in the sociopolitical order of Israel as a settler-colonial state.

The Sociolinguistic Field of the Palestinians in Israel

A society's sociolinguistic field(s) are inherent to its socioeconomic and political orders. A communicative event that takes place in society is derived from its socioeconomic and political order and translated into the organising principle of the sociolinguistic field(s). In order for such a communicative event to emerge, disseminate and reach its targets, several basic conditions are required, depending on the particular formations of each society in question. I will limit the present discussion to the conditions required for a communicative event in the nation-state format, with its national and settler-colonial versions, because it has been adopted by Israel. I will then assess the relevance of this discussion for the Palestinians in Israel and their sociolinguistic field, part of which is at the centre of this study.

In the national and the (settler-)colonial states, the working principle is the standardisation of social events occurring within its sovereign territory. These states are comprised of diverse individuals, groups and communities. Standardisation among them is therefore a prerequisite for the system to be able to operate vis-à-vis and within those individuals, groups and communities, as an imagined, homogeneous whole.[34] The standardisation of social events is achieved through bureaucratic mechanisms that specialise in the society's various domains of activity. For example, in the educational domain, the entire community is subjected to an array of bureaucratic procedures, such as division according to age groups. Such standardisation is also applied to language and its products, organising them as a distinct field within structural boundaries, subject to a cluster of internal working principles.[35] Accordingly, a specific material and institutional infrastructure must be maintained for the sphere of language and its products, in order for these standardisation processes to operate. The infrastructure includes standard grammar systems, a formal education system, an academy engaged in the standardisation of the (settler-)colonial or national language, mass media such as the printed and electronic press, and literary institutions: publishing houses, a literary canon, writing competitions, dictionaries and encyclopedias, and of course a readership.

Studies indicate that there is quite a significant variance across historical cases involving processes of constitution and construction of a material-institutional infrastructure of the language sphere.[36] The infrastructures are particular to their sociopolitical context. Their variance indicates the importance that needs to be attributed to the particular context under examination, proving that the relevance of the nation-state format needs to be reassessed, rather than automatically forcing it upon this case or the other. Moreover, colonial and settler-colonial histories are partly made up of initiatives by European national states to constitute the field of language and its products among the colonised and the natives, such as in India and partly in Egypt. The complexity of these historical cases requires analytical frameworks able to address this variance, as well as cases that challenge the nation-state format of language standardisation, such as Canada.

The sociolinguistic field among the Palestinians in Israel is part of the settler-colonial sociopolitical order that subjects them to state domination, as a colonised native group almost totally dependent on the coloniser-settler for its material and social existence.[37] The layers of this sociolinguistic field are constructed by the relations of control and management between the state apparatuses and the group of Palestinians. These relations operate in the context of the history and materiality of Arabic and its products, from the pre-colonial era and from their ongoing development in neighbouring Arab countries – one example being the above-mentioned multiple dialects among Palestinians and other Arabs. The intervention by settler-colonial state agencies in the sociolinguistic field varies with the history and materiality of the language and the interactions between them. For example, spoken Arabic has developed *vis-à-vis* Hebrew and its products through contact with government institutions and market forces, mainly in workplaces. Literary Arabic, however, has been consistently routed into other channels of subordination and standardisation, particularly the education system. In other words, unlike other cases, such as the British colonial administration in Egypt, the different state organs in Israel have not operated in the public sphere along the classical, central axis of Arabic – the diglossia of spoken and standard literary Arabic – and have not attempted to impose a certain register.[38] It may be argued that various mechanisms have operated on each register of the language, including both spoken and literary Arabic. What we have here is a reproduction of the structural split between language registers, with daily language as a mixture of dialects and registers.

This book focuses on events in the field of literary Arabic and its role as a sign of the national collectivity of the Palestinians in Israel. This role is central, given that literary Arabic has been a site for the construction of the collective identity of Arab secular nationality in the modern era and has stood for various types of collectivity in multiple periods in Arab history.

Note that the Israeli state mechanisms have accepted this role, allocating an operational arena to literary Arabic and working tirelessly to model it after the state's settler-colonial relations with the group of its Palestinian citizens.[39]

The focus on printed literary Arabic as a space in which Palestinians in Israel have been, and are being, constructed as 'Israeli Arabs' is inherent to the phenomenon under study. On the one hand, I examine the national language of that group, now subordinated to settler-colonial mechanisms, both of which operate according to the logic of a literary language in its printed format. On the other hand, the socioeconomic foundation of the settler-colonial state consists of print capitalism, which also operates as an organising super-principle.[40] This context means that, in order for the products of language to be exchangeable in the public social sphere, they have to be recoded in a printed format.

We also must take into consideration the literacy axis, which articulates a social agency derived from the context of print capitalism. As noted above, reading and writing enable the transition between various social and political spheres and the sociolinguistic fields. Accordingly, reading and writing represent key activities in the redesign of the settler-colonial and the national collectives – that is, the standardisation processes of these imagined communities. In what follows, I will focus on the public textual activities of the structural arena of literary Arabic in Israel as a site for dismantling and constituting, simultaneously, the collective Palestinian subject.

The public textual activities of this arena are extensive, covering a broad range of publication and distribution platforms, as well as genres that characterise this sphere in the (settler-)colonial and national states. These platforms include the Arab education system, the Academy of the Arabic Language, the Arabic language programs of the Israeli Broadcast Authority, publishing houses, daily newspapers, cultural and literary journals, academic journals, civil society organisations, conferences and literary competitions and awards. Textual genres include the news items in daily press and op-eds, essays, short stories, poetry, prose, sociocultural and literary reviews, essays on Arabic and its products, articles about political relations with the State of Israel and the national Arab project, scientific studies about Palestinian society and its various aspects including Arabic, and vision statements regarding the future of the Palestinians in Israel. The writers of these genres are not a homogeneous group; they include Palestinian intellectuals who survived the 1948 war, Arab Jews who immigrated to Israel, state officials, expert Israeli orientalists, Jewish and Palestinian scholars, writers, poets, politicians and public representatives. Together, they all have constituted the material and institutional infrastructure of the arena of Arabic and its products.

Importantly, this infrastructure is dynamic, having undergone significant changes throughout the period under study, 1948–2018. During that time, some platforms were more dominant than others. Consider literary criticism. During the first period, between 1948 and the late 1960s, cultural and literary journals were the dominant platform for disseminating this genre, which served as one primary sub-arena of the struggle over the nature of the relationship between the Palestinians in Israel and the state. The second period, from 1970 until the early 1990s, saw the academisation of literary criticism. The platform where the struggle took place was constructed by Palestinian academics who studied and worked in Israeli academia and published literary critical articles in Arabic for the Palestinian readership.

The centrality of the genre of literary criticism in this study requires clarification. This genre has played various roles in the modern era.[41] In (settler-)colonial and national states, particularly during the constitution of state institutions, literary criticism served as a mediatory educational tool, teaching the readership how to read and write literary and other texts. My argument is that reading and writing articulate a social agency that translates social forces into the text, and from it back to redesigning social forces and their struggles over the control and management of means of production. Thus, literary criticism may be used as a workshop for structuring the subject and its modes of operation in modern national and (settler-)colonial societies. It is therefore no surprise that, in the arena of Arabic and its products, the empirical materials collected for this study clearly indicate the important roles of the genre of Arabic literary criticism during the first period of this arena's constitution. Moreover, developments in the cultural and educational institutional spheres led to changes in the nature of literary criticism, particularly its academisation and conflation with other genres such as human rights discourse.

Israel applied the apparatuses of the settler-colonial state in order to create the material-institutional infrastructure of the arena of Arabic and its products. Operating by the principle of standardisation that allows the control and management of the imagined communities under its sovereignty, these mechanisms create a hybrid situation in the relationship between the Palestinians in Israel and the settler-colonial state. On the one hand, state apparatuses have acted to standardise literary Arabic, which is the foundation of the construction of the 'Israeli Arab' subject, thus symbolically eliminating the Palestinian native. On the other hand, the institutions of the structural arena have not been applied to the spoken language, unlike in other cases of (settler-)colonial states. Other state institutions, in order to split the Palestinians' national collective identity,[42] may have reinforced the dialects that separate various segments of the Palestinians in Israel.

This study examines the arena of literary Arabic and its social history through its public textual products. Some of them directly refer to Arabic's diglossia, particularly in relation to the sociolinguistic situation of the Palestinians in Israel. This reference, however, is not translated into material and institutional mechanisms that apply homogenising processes to the spoken registers of Arabic. This brief presentation of the social order, and the positioning of the arena of Arabic within it, will enable a more analytical formulation of the research phenomenon and question discussed in the following chapters.

Overview of the Book

This book addresses the positioning of Arabic and its products as a structural arena which has participated in the processes of reshaping the relationship between the Palestinians in Israel and the Zionist regime from 1948 to 2018. This social history of literary Arabic and its products in Israel is grounded in the view that both the Israeli state and the Palestinians now consider literary Arabic as a sign of the national collectivity of the Palestinians in Israel; whoever commands literary Arabic can design this collectivity. Therefore, I will address the products of literary Arabic that are produced by the different actors in that arena and consumed by the Palestinian readership in Israel. These products are exchangeable texts between state institutions and the Palestinians in Israel. Accordingly, the relevant social agency in this context lies in their modes of reading and writing.[43] In order to examine the main issues in this research, I will focus on the texts themselves in their public manifestation, as communicative events enabled by a particular way of performing literacy.

The book is organised around four main axes. The first chapter discusses the social history of the use of literary Arabic and its products among the Palestinians in Israel. It traces the structural conditions that enable reading and writing within that group following its constitutive event – the *Nakba*. The Palestinian catastrophe in 1948 created a situation whereby the Palestinians lost their ability to lose, denying them the possibility of constituting an independent collective. On the other hand, a mode of Zionist literacy characterised by excessiveness became locked in, whereby every event was reread and rewritten according to its relationship to the Zionist project. Conversely, these relations have led to the development of a compulsive Palestinian literacy – repetitive reading and writing closely attached to the body of Zionist excessive literacy, in order for the group of Palestinians in Israel to exist as a collectivity. The hierarchical relations between these two modes of literacy act as a blueprint for the entire sociolinguistic field in Israel. Moreover, they enable certain types of sociopolitical agencies that contribute to the reproduction of the settler-colonial *status quo*, while dismantling other more subverting sociopolitical agencies.

The structural relations between those two literacy modes – the excessive and the compulsive – are played out in the arena of literary Arabic and its products structured by the State of Israel through its settler-colonial institutions. This structural arena, henceforth referred to as 'Arabic', is built of three main layers organised vertically: 1) the material-institutional infrastructure; 2) the sign as an exchange value; and 3) the application of the sign as an organising principle in the form of a discursive formation in various communicative events that take place in the arena itself, or in reference thereto. On the horizontal axis, 'Arabic' is made up of various relational positions that claim multiple variations on the interactions of the Palestinians in Israel with the state. This network of positions produces the portrait of 'Arabic' in any given period.

Each of the next three chapters charts a distinctive portrait of 'Arabic' in a particular period of its social history. The second chapter paints the portrait of 'Arabic' in the period from 1948 to the late 1960s. In this first period in the public life of 'Arabic', three journals served as the main platforms for literary criticism, a genre that demanded a certain type of reading and writing in literary Arabic and called for a certain type of national collectivity among the Palestinians in Israel. During that period, literary criticism was divided into three main positions. One was the position of the state, articulated in the literacy of orientalist experts. It was mainly represented by *Al-Yawm*, a daily newspaper, but since the genre of literary criticism was then in the process of development by these experts, an 'educational' move also occurred in the *New Orient.* Already in the first issue of this journal, clear demands were presented to the group of Palestinians: a statement of minimal loyalty to the State of Israel and cutting off their sociocultural relations with the history and present of general Arab-Islamic culture. The second position was represented by *Al-Jadid*, the literary organ of the Israeli Communist Party. The discussion focuses on articles by Emile Tuma, one of the major Palestinian intellectuals active before and after the *Nakba.* According to Tuma, in order to redefine their national collectivity, the Palestinians had to return and reposition themselves in 'Arabic' as the owners of the semiotic means of production of literary Arabic. The third position was led by the periodical *Al-Mujtama*, whose founder and chief editor was Michel Haddad. Haddad and the group of Palestinians organised around him called for return and repositioning, accepting the Israeli terms of minimal loyalty and disconnection from Arab-Islamic culture by reproducing the Palestinian as 'a Child of Israel', as Haddad termed it. These three positions dialogued with one another during the first two decades after 1948, creating the continuum of 'Arabic', while the trichotomous dynamic among the various positions shaped this foundational stage of 'Arabic'.

The third chapter focuses on the period of academisation of literary criticism in Arabic for the Palestinian readership in Israel. Here I argue that these processes recreated the mediatory position within 'Arabic', thereby reshaping its internal dynamics and its relation to other state institutions. The historical carriers of these processes were Palestinian academics educated in the Arab education system and then in Israeli academia, some of whom were subsequently employed in permanent positions within it. A major figure in the academisation of Arabic literary criticism during this period – starting in the late 1960s – is Mahmud Ghanayim. I will examine his corpus of literary criticism that deals with Palestinian literature in Israel, designed to reach the

Palestinian readership through publications in literary journals that were part of the material and institutional infrastructure of 'Arabic'. Ghanayim studied in the Department of Arabic Language and Literature at Tel Aviv University, completing his MA and doctoral theses under the supervision of Sasson Somekh. A comparison of the bodies of knowledge of these two scholars indicates that Ghanayim represents a colonised mirror-image of the coloniser intellectual, particularly in regard to the modernisation of literary Arabic.

The fourth chapter focuses on the turning point of the early 1990s, manifested in multiple socioeconomic and political spheres, both global and local. In 'Arabic', two parallel processes emerged, characterised by the unprecedented claim by different actors to monopolise Arabic and its products in the State of Israel. The change began on the material-institutional level of 'Arabic', with a significant increase in the number of civil society organisations promoting projects designed to enhance the status of literary Arabic in Israel, particularly among its Palestinian citizens. At the same time, the academisation processes of the previous period led a group of Palestinian intellectuals to call, as early as 1989, for the establishment of an academy for the Arabic language. This process matured in 2007, when the *Supreme Institute of the Arabic Language* Law was enacted, mirroring the 1953 law for Hebrew. This led to the formation of a new range of positions in 'Arabic', each proposing a different route of return and repositioning *vis-à-vis* literary Arabic and its products. The dynamics that developed among these different positions in the 'Arabic' of our time relies on discursive formations of professional expertise that seek to monopolise the entire field of literary Arabic and its products, rather than a particular event or a series of communicative events, as in the previous periods. Some of the positions, such as the academic, claimed that monopoly through the compulsive mode, while others attempted to break free from the compulsiveness and the claim to own a Palestinian national excessiveness.

Having extracted the characteristics of these three periods in the social history of 'Arabic', the Conclusion analyses the general organising narrative of 'Arabic'. I will examine the analytical threads that tie the three periods together, with their respective portraits of 'Arabic'. My objective is not only to extract the narrative of the relations of the Palestinians in Israel with the settler-colonial state through the perspective offered by 'Arabic'. It is to do so without detracting from the importance of this historical narrative. Accordingly, I will also try to read and write through it the possibilities that it offers for transforming the structural quandary of 'Arabic'. This quandary of settler and native, of the excessive and compulsive agency modes, of an irresoluble contradiction in the ownership of the means of producing the collective is the organising core of the historical narrative.

In this introduction, I have begun telling the story of 'Arabic' by tracing the biographic outlines of a structural arena whose main role has been to contribute to the efforts of reshaping the relationship between the Palestinians in Israel and the settler-colonial state dominating and subordinating them. This journey through the biography of 'Arabic' will pass through four major milestones before reaching the fifth, which has yet to fully materialise. Here, we have to return to the position of the narrator or researcher. This position is articulated by a mode of literacy that negates the structural options offered by the state mechanisms to the group of Palestinians as a collective, a negation that constitutes the researcher. The analytical ability to negate, however, does not necessarily inhere a dialectics of liberation from the settler-colonial predicament – it only points to it.

Notes

1. Socially-produced forms include essays, declarations, novels, poems and literary criticism, among others.
2. In this book, I use the term 'settler-colonial regime' and particularly its variation of settler-colonial formation in the Palestinian territories occupied in 1948, in two major senses. The first refers to the sociohistorical phenomenon of a political group/state of European origin that colonises and settles in another land outside the European continent. The second sense is analytical, referring to the mechanisms of that regime and the ways in which they control and manage the colonised native society, on the one hand, and how socioeconomic and political groups within that society operate within and respond to these mechanisms, on the other. For more on these two senses, see Edward Cavanagh and Lorenzo Veracini (eds), *The Routledge Handbook of the History of Settler Colonialism* (London: Routledge, 2017); Robert Young, *Postcolonialism: An Historical Introduction* (Oxford: Blackwell Publishers, 2001), 1–69; Robert Young, 'Postcolonial Remains', *New Literary History* 43, no. 1 (2012), 12–42. As for the Palestinian

case, see Lorenzo Veracini, *Israel and Settler Society* (London: Pluto Press, 2006); Lorenzo Veracini, 'The Other Shift: Settler Colonialism, Israel, and Occupation', *Journal of Palestine Studies* 42, no. 2 (2013), 26–42; Nadim Rouhana and Areej Sabbagh-Khoury, 'Settler-Colonial Citizenship: Conceptualizing the Relationship between Israel and its Palestinian Citizens', *Settler-Colonial Studies* (2014), 1–21, https://doi.org/10.1080/2201473X.2014.947671

3. For an introduction to this issue, see Niloofar Haeri, 'Form and Ideology: Arabic Sociolinguistics and beyond', *Annual Review of Anthropology* 29 (2000), 61–87; Yasir Suleiman, *Arabic in the Fray: Language Ideology and Cultural Politics* (Edinburgh: Edinburgh University Press, 2013).
4. For more on the historical role played by Arabic in resolving sociopolitical contradictions in Egypt, see Al-Said Muhammad Badawi, *Mustawayāt al-ʿArabiyya al-muʿāṣira fī Miṣr: Baḥth fī ʿalāqat al-lugha bi-l-ḥaḍāra* [The Levels of Contemporary Arabic in Egypt: A Study on Language-Culture Relations] (Cairo: Dar al-Maʿarif, 1973).
5. See Louis Althusser, *For Marx*, transl. Ben Brewster (London: Verso, 1996), 87–128.
6. For further details, see Wail Hassan, 'Post Colonial Theory and Modern Arabic Literature: Horizons of Application', *Journal of Arabic Literature* 33, no. 1 (2002), 45–64; Wail Hassan, 'Postcolonialism and Modern Arabic Literature: Twenty-First Century Horizon', *Interventions* 20, no. 2 (2017), 157–73, https://doi.org/10.1080/1369801X.2017.1391711
7. Recently, new critical academic approaches have suggested seeing the case of Israel 'proper' – that is, the one established in 1948 – as a settler-colonial state rather than a classical colonial one. I will attend to the relevant debates on type(s) of colonial formations predominant in Israel in the first section of Chapter 1 below. See Veracini 'The Other Shift'; Rouhana and Sabbagh-Khoury, 'Settler-Colonial Citizenship'; Magid Shihade, 'Settler-Colonialism and Conflict: The Case of Israel and Its Palestinian Subjects', *Settler Colonial Studies* 2, no. 1 (2012), 108–23, https://doi.org/10.1080/2201473X.2012.10648828
8. In his study on the development of Israeli Arabic, Yonatan Mendel points to the centrality of Arabic's structural position in the history of the Zionist regime and elicits the modes of its usage by the mechanisms of that regime, particularly the security mechanism. Unlike Mendel's study, which focuses on the security mechanism and the Zionist Jews operating within it, the present book focuses on the arena allocated to the Palestinian citizens of Israel and its ideological mechanisms, such as the fields of literature and academia. See

Yonatan Mendel, *The Creation of Israeli Arabic: Political and Security Considerations in the Making of Arabic Language Studies in Israel* (London: Palgrave, 2014).

9. Bernard Cohen, *Colonialism and its Forms of Knowledge: The British in India* (Princeton: Princeton University Press, 1996).
10. For communicative events, see Dell Hymes, 'Introduction: Toward Ethnographies of Communication', *American Anthropologist* 66, no. 6 (1964), 1–34.
11. For the impact of the *Tanzimat*, see Butrus Abu-Manneh, 'Jerusalem in the Tanzimat Period', *Die Welt Des Islams* 30, no. 1/4 (1990), 1–44. For the British Mandate, see Jacob Metzer, *The Divided Economy of Mandatory Palestine* (Cambridge: Cambridge University Press, 2002).
12. On cultural changes, see Steven Sheehi, *Foundations of Modern Arab Identity* (Gainesville: University Press of Florida, 2004).
13. For the Ottoman schooling system, see Benjamin C. Fortna, *Imperial Classroom: Islam, the State, and Education in the Late Ottoman Empire* (Oxford: Oxford University Press, 2003). For missionary schools at the end of the nineteenth century in Palestine, see, for example, Hanna Abu Hanna, *Ṭalāʾiʿ al-nahḍa fī Filasṭīn: Khirījū l-madāris al-Rūsiyya, 1862–1914* [The Pioneers of the Renaissance in Palestine: Graduates of Russian Schools, 1862–1914] (Beirut: Markaz al-Dirasat al-Filastiniyya, 2005).
14. Faisal Darraj, 'Muthaqqaf ḥadāthī fī mujtamaʿ taqlīdī' [A Modern Intellectual in a Conservative Society], in *Tārīkh ʿilm al-'adab ʿind al-Ifranj wa-l-ʿArab wa-Fīktūr Hūjū* [History of the Science of Literature among Westerners and the Arabs and Victor Hugo], by Muhamad Ruhi al-Khalidi (Doha: Kitab al Dawha, 2013), 7–20.
15. Regarding Arabic in the British mandate, see Ami Ayalon, *Reading Palestine: Printing and Literacy, 1900–1948* (Austin: University of Texas Press, 2004). As for Hebrew, see Yael Reshef, *Ha'Ivrit biTḳufat haMandaṭ* [Hebrew in the Mandate Period] (Jerusalem: Ha-Akademiyah la-Lashon ha'Ivrit, 2015).
16. Gil Eyal, *Hasarat haḲesem min haMizraḥ: Toldot haMizraḥanut be'Idan haMizraḥiyut* [Disenchanting the Orient: The History of Orientalism in the Mizrahi Era] (Tel Aviv: Hakibbutz Hameuchad, Van Leer Jerusalem Institute, 2005).
17. Eyal, *Hasarat*, 44.
18. Mustafa Kabha, '*Itonut be'En haSe'arah: ha'Itonut haFalasṭinit keMakhshir le'Itsuv Da'at haḲahal, 1929–1939* [Press in the Eye of the Storm: The Palestinian Press as a Shaper of Public Opinion, 1929–1939] (Jerusalem: Yad Ben-Zvi, 2004). The Histadrut was the powerful Jewish trade union federation, which played a significant role in the Zionist nation-building effort.

19. 'Abd al-Raḥmān Yāghi, *Ḥayāt al-'adab al-Filasṭīnī al-ḥadīth: Mundhu bidāyat al-Nahḍa wa-li-ghāyat al-Nakba* [The Life of Modern Palestinian Literature: From the Beginning of the National Revival to the *Nakba*] (Beirut: Dar al-Afaq, 1981).
20. See for example, Ayalon, *Reading Palestine*; Ela Greenberg, 'Majjallat Rawdat al-Ma'arif: Constructing Identities within a Boy's School Journal in Mandatory Palestine', *British Journal of Middel Eastern Studies* 35, no. 1 (April 2008), 79–95.
21. For the history of this newspaper and its impact on Palestinian literature, see Saif al-Din Abu Saleh, *Al-Ḥaraka al-'adabiyya al-'Arabiyya fī Isrā'īl: Ẓuhūrhā wa-taṭawwurhā min khilāl al-mulḥaq al-thaqāfī li-jarīdat Al-Ittiḥād bayn al-sanawāt 1948–2000* [The Arab Literary Movement in Israel: Its Origin and Development Seen from the Literary Supplement of *Al-Ittihad* 1948–2000] (Haifa: Academy of the Arabic Language, 2010).
22. This law changed the legal status of Arabic in Israel from an official language alongside Hebrew to a secondary one. Thus, it changed the sociolinguistic field in Israel. For the English version of the law and its political and legal implications, see Hassan Jabareen and Suhad Bishara, 'The Jewish Nation-State Law: Antecedents and Constitutional Implications', *Journal of Palestine Studies* 48, no. 190 (2) (Winter 2019), 46–55.
23. On the processes of constituting the readerships of modern Arab societies, see Sabri Hafez, *The Genesis of Arabic Narrative Discourse: A Study in the Sociology of Modern Arabic Literature* (London: Al Saqi Books, 1993).
24. On the primacy of reading and writing in colonial Egypt, and its embodiment of socioeconomic and political forces, see Leila Ahmed, *Women and Gender in Islam: Historical Roots of a Modern Debate* (New Haven: Yale University Press, 1992), 144–68.
25. For comparison, see how Benrabah reads the colonial condition in Algeria by studying its sociolinguistic field: Mohamed Benrabah, *Language and Conflict in Algeria: From Colonialism to Post-Independence* (Bristol: Multilingual Matters, 2013), 21–50. For a comparison between the Palestinian and the Irish cases in this regard, see Joe Cleary, *Literature, Partition and the Nation-State: Culture and Conflict in Ireland, Israel and Palestine* (Cambridge: Cambridge University Press, 2004).
26. Veracini shows us, on the macro level, that Israel has different structural and institutional relations with the various Palestinian groups under its control. In this study, I look at the middle range level of the state apparatuses – for instance, the education system – in order to show that the same apparatus is built on a duality that stems from the settler-colonial nature of Israel. See Veracini, 'The Other Shift'.

27. Rouhana and Sabbagh-Khoury allude to the tensions in this duality through tracing the modes of Israeli citizenship that is granted to the Palestinians in Israel. See Rouhana and Sabbagh-Khoury, 'Settler-Colonial Citizenship'.
28. See for example, Azmi Bishara, *Al-'Arab fi Isrā'īl: Naẓarah min al-dākhil* [The Arabs in Israel: A View from Within] (Beirut: Markaz Dirasat al-Wihda al-Arabiyya, 2000); Veracini, 'The Other Shift'; Rouhana and Sabbagh-Khoury, 'Settler-Colonial Citizenship'.
29. Wail Hassan refers to the symbolic capital of Arabic and its literary products as part of 'cultural memory', which is crucial in resisting the (neo)colonial regimes in the Arab World. See Hassan, 'Post Colonial Theory and Modern Arabic Literature', 53–56.
30. These systematic acts of expropriation are in line with Partick Wolfe's analysis of how the native is materially and symbolically eliminated in the settler-colonial contexts. See Patrick Wolfe, 'Settler Colonialism and the Elimination of the Native', *Journal of Genocide Research* 8, no. 4 (2006), 387–409, https://doi.org/10.1080/14623520601056240
31. For a general discussion of the legal system in colonial settings see Samera Esmeir, *Juridical Humanity: A Colonial History* (Palo Alto: Stanford University Press, 2012). For more on the Palestinians' Israeli citizenship and its roles in shaping their relationship to the state, see Ismail Nashef, 'Ḥal al-tawāṭu" [On Complacency], *Jadal Mada* 12 (February 2012), 1–10; Rouhana and Sabbagh-Khoury, 'Settler-Colonial Citizenship'; Lana Tatour, 'Citizenship as Domination: Settler Colonialism and the Making of Palestinian Citizenship in Israel', *Arab Studies Journal* 27, no. 2 (2019), 8–39.
32. On the relationship between the colonial and the modern in colonised societies, see, for example, Timothy Mitchell, *Colonising Egypt* (Berkeley: University of California Press, 1991). As for the relations between the settler-colonial cases, see Patrick Wolfe, *Settler Colonialism and the Transformation of Anthropology: The Politics and Poetics of an Ethnographic Event* (London: Cassell, 1999); Veracini, *Settler Colonialism: A Theoretical Overview* (New York: Palgrave, 2010).
33. On the relation between language literature and settler colonialism in Ireland, see, for example, Terry Eagleton, Fredric Jameson and Edward Said, *Nationalism, Colonialism and Literature* (Minneapolis: University of Minnesota Press, 1990); Barry McCrea, *Languages of the Night: Minor Languages and Literary Imagination in Twentieth-Century Ireland and Europe* (New Haven: Yale University Press, 2015), 20–46.
34. For the nation-state, see Benedict Anderson, *Imagined Communities: Reflections on the Origins and Spread of Nationalism* (London: Verso, 1983); for the colonial state,

see Ranajit Guha, *Dominance without Hegemony: History and Power in Colonial India* (Cambridge, MA: Harvard University Press, 2011).

35. For more on language in the nation-state as a distinct and organised social field, see John B. Thompson, *Studies in the Theory of Ideology* (Berkeley: University of California Press, 1984), 44–72. For the colonial state, see, for example, Benrabah, *Language and Conflict in Algeria.*
36. See, for example, the cases of Egypt, France and India in ʿAbd Al-Munʿaim Al-Dasūqi Al-Jumaīʿ, *Majmaʿ al-lugha al-ʿArabiyya: Dirāsa tāʾrīkhiyya* [Academy of the Arabic Language: A Historical Study] (Cairo: Al-Hay'a al-ʿAmma Lil-Kitab, 1983); James S. Allen, *In the Public Eye: A History of Reading in Modern France, 1800–1940* (Princeton: Princeton University Press, 1991); Cohen, *Colonialism and its Forms of Knowledge.*
37. For different approaches on this matter, see Muhammad Amara, *Al-Lugha al-ʿArabiyya fi Isrāʾīl: Siyāqāt wa-taḥaddiyāt* [The Arabic Language in Israel: Contexts and Challenges] (Umm al-Fahm, Israel: Markaz Dirasat wa-Dar al-Huda, 2010); Hanna Herzog and Eliezer Ben-Rafael (eds), *Language and Communication in Israel* (New Brunswick: Transaction Publishers, 2001); Yasir Suleiman, *A War of Words: Language and Conflict in the Middle East* (Cambridge: Cambridge University Press, 2004); Camelia Suleiman, *The Politics of Arabic in Israel: A Sociolinguistic Analysis* (Edinburgh: Edinburgh University Press, 2018). For more recent studies that focus on specific Palestinian communities, see Muhammad Amara, *Arabic in Israel: Language, Identity, and Conflict* (London: Routledge, 2017); Nancy Hawker, *Palestinian Israeli Contacts and Linguistics Practices* (London: Routledge, 2018).
38. On diglossia and Arabic as a prime example of diglossia, see Charles Ferguson's classic article, 'Diglossia', *Word* 15 (1959), 325–40. On the 'contempt' of British colonial officials towards classical Arabic see Haeri, 'Form and Ideology'.
39. The term 'arena' is borrowed from Volosinov's theoretical model. It has been further developed by Williams, who discussed the sign as part of real lived social processes, and by Bourdieu as a 'field'. See V. N. Volosinov, *Marxism and the Philosophy of Language*, transl. Ladislav Matejka and I. R. Titunik (Cambridge, MA: Harvard University Press, 1986); Raymond Williams, *Marxism and Literature* (Oxford: Oxford University Press, 1977); Thompson, *Studies*, 42–72.
40. Anderson, *Imagined Communities.*
41. For the social history of literary criticism, see Rafey M. A Habib, *A History of Literary Criticism and Theory: From Plato to the Present* (London: Blackwell, 2007).
42. For more on the splitting of the Palestinians into smaller, non-national groups, see Ahmad Sa'di, *Thorough Surveillance: The Genesis of Israeli Policies of*

Population Management Surveillance and Political Control towards the Palestinian Minority (Manchester: Manchester University Press, 2013).

43. I use 'mode' here based mainly on Guha's idioms of power and subordinations in *Dominance without Hegemony*, 23–59, and Cohen's investigative modalities in *Colonialism and its Forms of Knowledge*, 5–15. For further elaboration and discussion of 'mode', see Chapter One below.

1

On Compulsiveness and Excessiveness: 'Arabic'

Embarking on the study of Arabic and its products in Israel demands several contextualisation processes not usually found in the study of national languages in relation to their nation or colonial or settler-colonial states. On the one hand, Israel uses typical nation-state sociolinguistic field apparatuses to administer its settler-colonial regime *vis-à-vis* its Palestinian citizens and their Arabic, such as education systems, media outlets and the Academy of the Arabic Language. On the other hand, the entire Arabic sociolinguistic field is subordinated to the Hebrew one and ordained by its apparatuses, which in turn (re)produces certain modes of reading and writing in Arabic as well as in Hebrew. As a result of the catastrophe of 1948, these modes of reading and writing became, and to a large extent still are, one of the main tools for the Palestinians in Israel to survive (and, at times, to overcome) the Israeli settler-colonial management practices concerning them.

Moreover, in order to understand and explain critically these dynamics, one has to bring into the analyses the context of print capitalism and its different stages of transformation over the last several decades. As I will argue, Israel and the Palestinians have differed in their use of the tools and apparatuses offered by print capitalism. I will deconstruct their reading and writing modes according to the rules of printed mass communication.

The aim of this chapter is to set the stage for the interrelated historical and theoretical frames of analyses that will be used in the next chapters to explore how Arabic has been used by Israel and its Palestinian citizens in the context of print capitalism. More specifically, this chapter will provide analytical tools capable of uncovering the interrelations between instances of reading and writing in Arabic by and for the Palestinians and the Israeli institutional environment that enables certain manners of these literary practices while curbing others.[1]

The unique case of the Palestinian citizens of Israel is that they have a national language, Arabic, but as a community they do not have a nation-state or the modern apparatuses to administer their Arabic in relation to their collectivity. Since their subordination to Israeli settler-colonial rule in 1948, there have been incessant attempts by the State of Israel to disconnect the Palestinians from Arabic, as part of dismantling and eliminating the national aspect of the Palestinian community. The major attempt was an institutional subordination of Arabic to Hebrew and its modern apparatuses – that is, 'modernising' Arabic based on the modern revitalisation of Hebrew.

These attempts resulted in three interconnected levels of operations in order to recreate a version of literary Arabic as a non-national language that reproduces the settler-colonial power relations between the Palestinian community and the State of Israel. Built on the model of specialised national and colonial state apparatuses, the first level includes an institutional infrastructure, an education system, publishing houses, newspapers, literary magazines and other apparatuses. The second level is an organising set of codes determining how to attribute meanings to communal events, memories and a sense of belonging, as Arab-Islamic culture and history were systematically devalued, forcing Palestinians to distance themselves from them. The third level is a discursive formation which organises the interactions between the community and the state. These interactions aim to 'modernise' the community properly, maintaining its loyalty and submissiveness to the dominant settler-colonial power configuration.

As a result of establishing these levels, a new 'Arabic' emerged as the language of communication between the state, the community and among the Palestinians themselves. I will focus on the written form of this communication in the public sphere, comprising books, essays and news items, as it reflects most clearly the national settler-colonial matrix of relations.[2] This chapter will start by laying out these levels and their interrelations, as they will constitute our frame of reference throughout the book. However, solely laying these out would fail to bring forth a deeper understanding of the settler-colonial regime in Palestine. For that purpose, I will try to contextualise this case within the larger settler-colonial and capitalist circles of analysis.

The argument that there is a structural history of the use of Arabic in the Zionist regime is based on the particular nature of that regime and its interactions with its various subject groups. The organising principle of the material and institutional infrastructure of the Zionist project – the pre-statehood Jewish community in Palestine, the State of Israel and other, international institutes – is a dichotomous classification according to the categories 'Jews' and 'non-Jews'. These two categories contain identity continuums organised according to Zionist hierarchies. This dichotomous structure is not given *a priori*; rather, it is part of the processes of constituting the regime, which are structured from the application of the organising principle. The outcome of such application is the construction of the group of 'non-Jews', which includes primarily the Palestinians, as the negation pole of the group of 'Jews'.[3]

Accordingly, in order to trace the Zionist mechanism of negating the group of Palestinians, I will consider Arabic and its literary products as one of the main representational platforms of the group of Palestinian citizens of Israel in the age of print capitalism. I will examine both the Zionist mechanism of negating Arabic, along with its various written outlets, developed by the Palestinians from their position as 'negatees' under the Zionist regime. Since the present research addresses the social and political evolution of the use of Arabic since 1948, I will focus on the corpus of literary Arabic texts produced during this period. The basic assumption is that this textual corpus contains, subject to its internal laws, the field of the regime's irresolvable contradictions: that of organising the interactions between the settler-colonial state and the natives, and that of processing their contradictions through its unique literary formalisation.[4]

In addition to defining this corpus and those involved in its publishing and reading, I will also define the processing and formalisation movement – that which transfers and embodies the sociohistorical forces onto Arabic. Because of these embodiments, I will focus on reading and writing rather than other aspects of the language system. What lies at the basis of this movement in the modern era is a social agency embodied in the very act of reading/writing. Therefore, the present chapter's goal will be to trace the relations between the Zionist regime and the Palestinians through their practices of reading and writing Arabic literary products.

It is well known that (settler-)colonial oppressive relations involve bidirectional dependency between coloniser and colonised. The history of reading and writing in Arabic under the Zionist regime, and by extension the sociolinguistic interactions among Palestinians themselves in Israel, are embedded in this bidirectional dependency. By studying these histories, I contend that I will be able to demonstrate the ways in which social and political forces are transferred onto Arabic linguistic materials. Based on the data gathered for this research, our baseline is that the process of transfer takes two basic forms: excessive literacy on the Zionist side and compulsive literacy on the Palestinian side.[5] These are two different positions operating within the same settler-colonial power structure of domination and symbolic elimination; therefore, they must be considered expressions of a single settler-colonial sociolinguistic field.

Theoretically, excessiveness could be divided into three main levels and the movement between them. First, there is the excess owned by the settlers, in the Marxist sense of accumulating material and symbolic surplus value in the colonies.[6] Second, excessiveness – in the sense of excess, a term coined by Georges Bataille to refer to the logic of creative work – is used here to indicate the formative processes of the accumulated surplus value in the colonies.[7] Third, we have saturation, following the secular version of the term developed by Jean-Luc Marion to refer to the 'saturated phenomenon', which is here not subject to the rules of subjective perception, but only to its own rules. The implication of this reading of a 'saturated phenomenon', for our context, is that the circulated forms of the surplus value determine how they will be perceived by various individuals and groups under its settler-colonial domination and subordination.[8]

I argue that the Zionist mode of literacy produces excess: every sociohistorical event is rewritten in Zionist terms. This pattern leads to an enormous accumulation of meanings that require the new owners to invest in productive work, reconstructing these meanings as Zionist. Moreover, this state of excess and saturation requires continual maintanence. This means continually investing in the state apparatuses that generate and manage reading and writing practices. At the same time, the resulting excess and saturation block the subject's access to other not-yet-Zionised sociohistorical instances, blinding the subject to them.

Conversely, compulsiveness, a Palestinian literacy mode, combines those three theoretical levels in a dynamic of lack and loss that is imposed on the Palestinian collective in its attempt to survive the Zionist excessiveness mode. The basic condition of existence that brings about compulsiveness is the loss of ownership of the semiotic means of literacy, and with it the loss of the ability to read or write sociohistorical events as their owner. This non-accumulation of meanings creates a large void that requires repetitive acts of reading and writing that could reopen the possibilities for reclaiming the means of producing meaning and excess – but this is impossible in this settler-colonial field, hence the compulsive nature of this mode of literacy. This void prevents the subject from seeing other sociohistorical instances. In this case, however, this blocking is due to the excessiveness of the void, the saturation of loss. This type of loss predetermines how the subject will perceive other phenomena unrelated to her predicament.

As in any other sociohistorical phenomenon, there are conditions of possibility, in the sense developed by Bourdieu, out of which these two modes of literacy have grown and developed in the settler-colonial Zionist regime.[9] Major among these is the janus face of modernity/coloniality and its socioeconomic base, the capitalist order. Particularly, as I will contend, it is the constellation of these two conditions in the form of print capitalism, as an overarching operational logic, and their materialisation in a settler-colonial formation, which have enabled these two modes of literacy to grow, to develop and to operate as a part of the Zionist regime. For the purposes of this study, this operational logic is composed of two parts. First, there is a homological relationship that organises the commodification of social and cultural events, as one of the central principles of the capitalist order. Second, modern modes of reading and writing are partially subordinated to this homological relationship, which renders it critical for the understanding of the dynamic of settler-colonial literacy relations in Palestine.[10] I will conclude this chapter by outlining these homological relations as our point of departure for the following chapters.

The Settler-Colonial Condition of Arabic in Israel

Settler-colonial regimes succeed at that moment when they are perceived by themselves and by others as 'regular' – or, better yet, 'natural' – nation-states.[11] The processes by which they could achieve this success vary according to time, place and the context of its imposition. Still, one common characteristic holds in most modern cases of settler-colonial regimes, and that is the structural determinant of eliminating the native as a pre-condition of such a success.[12] The elimination of the natives could take various shapes, from the literal physical to the symbolic dismantling of them as subjects with agency. In the case of Israel, the elimination of the Palestinian native, as individuals and as collectives, took place at the physical level in the war of 1948.[13] For different historical reasons, by the end of the war some 150,000 Palestinians, who composed 18 percent of the population under the control of the new State of Israel, remained in their villages, towns and cities. In its relations with this community of Palestinians, Israel has been developing and using different tools and practices of elimination, physical as well as symbolic, in order to subjugate them and remould them according to settler-colonial power relations. In this context, Arabic and its products, as a marker of a national collectivity and a carrier of cultural memory, have been one of the main native sites to be eliminated. The processes of the material and symbolic elimination of Arabic have taken place by applying modern apparatuses and tools that are usually part of the repertoire of the nation-state format of modern polities.

During the war, the material and technological infrastructure of Arabic – such as libraries, publishing houses and printing machines – were either destroyed, looted, or annexed by different Israeli institutions and agencies.[14] Probably, except for the Israeli Communist Party, which included Palestinians and Jews, nothing in this infrastructure of pre-1948 was left intact, or owned by Palestinians. And already by the end of 1948, one could observe a new material technological infrastructure in place, producing Arabic products, mainly newspapers, for the Palestinian readership in Israel. This nascent infrastructure has been developing since then; as we will see in the following chapters, it is mainly owned by Israeli settler-colonial apparatuses.

The symbolic elimination of Arabic and its products has taken a less clear and homogeneous path. Israel has imposed a hermitic isolation on the Palestinians, disconnecting them from their Arab-Islamic cultural centres, such as Egypt, Lebanon and Syria.[15] Institutionally, it has placed Arabic as an attachment to Hebrew, to be fostered anew and remoulded according to the settler-colonial regime of sensibilities, symbolically reproducing the hierarchical power structure. If the Palestinians could not resist, at least not directly, the dismantling of the material and technological infrastructure of Arabic, they have had a large margin of resistance to the symbolic elimination of Arabic and its products. For in addition to being the last refuge of collective identity after the war of 1948, Arabic and its products have also been acting as the main force and carrier of Arab-Islamic cultural memory. In light of these positionalities of Arabic, one could understand the investment of the Israeli state apparatuses in the processes of its elimination and reappropiation.

As a settler-colonial regime, Israel has kept the Palestinian community outside the settlers' one using different tools to maintain the separation.[16] However, Israel did not only operate at the level of dominance *vis-à-vis* its Palestinian citizens. It has worked to produce and sustain the degree of hegemony that is necessary for administering its Palestinian citizens. In contrast to the colonial state with its condition of dominance without hegemony, as described by R. Guha, as a settler-colonial state with genocidal practices, Israel is an illegitimate dominance for the Palestinians. Hence, the Israeli settler-colonial apparatuses have been imposing a deep erasure of one version of Arabic and violently inserting another one. Put differently, the symbolic elimination of Arabic and its products as the marker of the national collectivity, as well as the fostering and remoulding of a version of Arabic subordinated to Hebrew, have constituted main processes for disseminating a settler-colonial hegemony.

The main challenge of this double move of elimination and reappropriation is that it must be done on the material levels of Arabic, and not on the ideological one only, as with other similar cases. This means that the Israeli state apparatuses have to acquire systematic native (as well as academic) knowledge of Arabic, so as to be able to produce a settler-colonial version of Arabic. Since the pre-state era, and more systematically after its establishment, the settler-colonial regime in Palestine has been investing in building institutional infrastructure aimed at acquiring and producing knowledge on and in Arabic. These knowledge and institutional infrastructures have been crucial for constructing the settler-colonial version of Arabic as the only linguistic medium of communication in Arabic between Israel and its Palestinian citizens.

On the practical level, these dynamics of symbolic elimination and reappropriation have been conducted via reading and writing practices, as proper to print capitalism's dominant mode of communication. A settler-colonial mode of reading and writing could not but own any tools of producing meaning, as the cases of Australia, the USA and Canada exemplify the elimination of the natives' languages.[17] Similarly, the reading and writing mode of the Israeli settler-colonial regime has developed to own any symbolic and semiotic tool of production in Palestine, coupled with incessant attempts to redefine events by their relations to the settler's community only. But the particularity of the Israeli case in this regard is the reappropriation of the Palestinians' language, literary Arabic, as part of the symbolic dismantling of their collectivity. This reappropriation has led to the necessity of purging the national version of Arabic and reinstituting a new version of settler-colonial literary Arabic among the Palestinians. For the Palestinians, these processes have severely aggravated their losses from the war of 1948. But paradoxically, reinstituting the new settler-colonial version of literary Arabic has provided a language for the Palestinians to partially express their losses. The new version of Arabic was meant to consolidate the losses as a defining element for the Palestinians' new status as 'the natives' of the Israeli settler-colonial regime. As a derivative of the power configuration that resulted from the war of 1948, this language of almost total loss depended on the language of almost total ownership of any tools for meaning production in Palestine. The mode of reading and writing this language of loss is based on the incessant drive/desire to regain meaning, in order to survive as a collective, with the acute awareness of its impossibility in this settler-colonial setting.

These early dynamics of the settler-colonial regime in Palestine have shaped the sociolinguistic field under study in this book. Specifically, I will focus on the languages of loss and ownership via their modes of reading and writing, the compulsive and excessive, respectively. My aim is to explicate the processes of their inception, development and transfomations across the periods covered in this study.

'Arabic': Infrastructure, Sign, Discourse

The structural history of the use of excessive – and compulsive – reading and writing is deeply rooted in the more general history of the material and institutional infrastructure of the Zionist regime. As we have seen, these modes of literacy are part of the *modus operandi* of the regime, as well as its maintenance across time. In this section, I will demarcate the uses of reading and writing with two aims in mind. Such demarcation will clarify the structure of use along the diachronic time axis, defining the boundaries of the corpus of textual and public activities and their material and institutional dimensions to be empirically examined in the following chapters. I will start with defining the material and institutional infrastructure; then I will describe this infrastructure in the context of excessiveness and compulsiveness as the main modes of literacy under the Israeli settler-colonial regime.

The format of the modern nation-state, as used by settler-colonial regimes, operates by domains of specialisation. Each domain – be it social, economic, cultural, or otherwise – operates according to the institutions of the state, the market and civil society that specialise in its management. The domain of spoken and written language – in its printed, broadcast, or any other form – is managed by an array of government, market and civil society institutions, and it is affected by their interrelations. These institutions constitute the material infrastructure of the domain of language in the nation-state. Since language is present in every social activity, the domain of language here is specific to institutions dealing with language itself by producing, marketing and consuming its products. In its traditional form, this infrastructure includes the education system, national language academy, broadcast media, publishing houses, dictionaries and encyclopedias, literary institutions, the readers and so on. These are deployed in a network of institutions interrelated in a hierarchic structure. Together they determine which language is the language of the nation-state, or the settlers, as in our case, who owns its symbolic and semiotic means of production, and how its products may be consumed so as to reproduce the existing structure of production relations.[18]

Various factors intervene to determine the individual's positioning within this sociolinguistic infrastructure – class, gender, ethnic identity, race, age and the like – according to the history of the particular social order. However, the individual's position is enabled by their belonging to the national identity of the nation-state, or the settlers' identity in the case of settler-colonial states. Whoever does not belong to this identity cannot be positioned by these factors and is subjected to a different classification system, such as the settler-native one. The variety of positions of social groups, within the material-institutional infrastructure, leads to conflicts over controlling the infrastructure and its means of production, as well as conflicts between the groups and the coercive mechanisms of the infrastructure itself.[19]

This conflictive arena constitutes a kind of systemic site that spreads beyond the specific event of the dominant language and its products. In the State of Israel and the Zionist regime in general, this is a central site in constituting and maintaining the settler-colonial project, where the above-mentioned Zionist excessive literacy processes occur.[20] After the material and institutional infrastructures of the Palestinian society were dismantled and destroyed in 1948, Israel created a specific sub-site where the compulsive literacy mode of the group of Palestinian citizens of Israel occurs. It is comprised of institutions that focus on Arabic and its products, which the state has initiated and built from the dynamic of the relations of managing the colonised natives and exploiting them, thereby producing added value. For example, in October 1948 the state began publishing *Al-Yawm*, an Arabic-language daily intended for the Palestinian readership in Israel. It also created an Arab education system which, although being formally a part of the general education system, operates separately – a sub-system whose *modus operandi* is derived from the settler-colonial relations as they operate in the Israeli sociolinguistic and educational fields.

This newspaper and the Arab education system, as well as other institutions, construct the exchangeable Palestinian subjectivity in the Zionist regime – or what is known as an 'Israeli Arab'. The state has separated the domain of Hebrew and its products from that of Arabic and its products, based on settler-colonial affiliation, and created a sub-system for the latter within the former's institutional system. The relations between the two are ones of strong dependency, where the sub-site of Arabic operates according to its structural subordination to that of Hebrew; it is a subordination that is practised and instantiated in the two modes of literacy of excessiveness and compulsiveness. The present study focuses on this sub-site of Arabic and traces its textual and public performances and instantiations since 1948.

However, the distinction made here between the material-institutional and the ideological spheres, between the education system and the content it teaches, is an analytical one designed to highlight the characteristics of the material-institutional sphere. In order for this sphere to exist in a settler-colonial regime and to serve as an infrastructure for a certain activity domain, it is organised at the time of its construction according to a set of codes, to be utilised as a working principle.[21] The sub-site of Arabic and its products, which operates according to a compulsive mode of literacy, was established simultaneously with the construction of the logic of compulsiveness. Without this institutional ideological apparatus, the learning materials of the Arab education system would be strictly educational. Similarly, a piece in *Al-Yawm* about the desirable relationship between spoken and literary Arabic would be no more than an opinion about the diglossia of Arabic. This raises analytical questions: How is the material-institutional arena of language framed and expressed in the settler-colonial state? How is its organising working principle articulated? How are these framings, expressions and articulations applied in the sub-site of Arabic and its products in the State of Israel? And in particular, how is its organising principle of compulsiveness framed, expressed and articulated? Answers to those questions will equip us with the theoretical and methodological tools for examining the textual and public activities in this sub-site.

My point of departure will be the observation that the organising working principle of the domain of language in the format of nation-states, as adopted by settler-colonial states, is a sign in the semiotic sense, a mechanism of generating meaning in a certain manner.[22] This sign is only made possible out of the material-institutional infrastructure of the domain of language in such states. In its operation, it is not a sign that hovers over the social or political processes, but it is rather inherent to these processes, reorganising their sequences of events. Consider for instance a Palestinian teacher, who is a citizen of Israel, explaining to his students the relationship between Arabic and their national identity in Israel. Here, the sign acts as a discursive formation as it operates in real lived social processes.[23]

Thus, we have three operational analytical levels that will allow us to examine the sub-site of Arabic in Israel. The first is the material-institutional infrastructure, such as schools, publishing houses and the Ministry of Education. The second is its working principle, which may also be understood as a set of codes for generating meaning – that is, the semiotic sign. However, these codes are applicable in the reorganisation of textual and public events only when they act as discursive formations. That is, the sign at that moment when it is used by real social agents – such as journalists, poets, critics and academics – occurs at the third level. I refer to this conceptualisation of the compulsive literacy mode of the sub-site of Arabic and its products in Israel as 'Arabic'.

The sign 'Arabic' indicates the structural systemic sub-site, or, better yet, a dynamic arena, initiated by the State of Israel to manage, reorganise and produce its Palestinian citizens and maintain them on a long-term basis in the structural position of colonised natives. 'Arabic' is the event and the space of compulsive literacy, whose activities enable its empirical manifestations on the textual and public levels. On the level of material-institutional infrastructure, 'Arabic' is constructed of a network of institutions built by the parent institutions of the domain of Hebrew and its products: the Academy of the Arabic Language in Israel, radio and television stations, daily newspapers, literary journals, publication houses, prose and poetry competitions, civil NGOs and more. These institutions have been built to operate according to the compulsive mode of literacy. Due to this nature of the institutions of 'Arabic', they contain various positions that, although subordinated to the mode of compulsive literacy, express different relationships between the groups of Palestinians in Israel and the Zionist regime and its state. One of the main axes of this research is the examination of the nature of these positions, their interrelations and the changes that have occurred in them since 1948. These dynamic interrelations paint the portrait of 'Arabic' at a given moment. In this study, I have located three such portraits of 'Arabic' that have developed since 1948. Each of the following three chapters will focus on one of them, describing its variation on the mode of compulsive literacy of the groups of Palestinians in Israel.

In this section, we have seen that the excessive and compulsive modes of literacy occur in particular sites in the institutions of the State of Israel, its market and civil society. The structural sub-site which I have called 'Arabic' includes three levels that operate together as one unit: the material-institutional level, the organising principle as a sign with an exchange value and the discursive formation, which is a translation of the sign that organises the various events occurring in 'Arabic'. I argue that, in order to extract the structural history of the use of the compulsive literacy mode, one needs to trace the history of 'Arabic', beginning from the moment of its constitution as a sub-site in 1948. We must examine the textual and public interventions within or through 'Arabic', as they pertain to the relations between the group of Palestinians in Israel and the Zionist regime. The settler-colonial relations between this group of Palestinians and the Zionist regime have a conflictive history, culminating in the War of 1948. They also have a larger socioeconomic context, print capitalism, the combination of which resulted in the shape of the empirical level I have delineated here. In order to fully grasp the deep-seated power relations and their actualisation in the two modes of literacy that this study examines, an initial introduction to them through the prism of reading and writing is required.

The History of the Loss of Literacy

How can you read and write the history of reading and writing? And how are these social actions to be performed in the case of a catastrophe – a final and total cataclysm?[24] One way of narrating the history of literacy in Palestine is by exploring the introduction and institution of settler-colonial, in the guise of modern, practices of reading and writing and their infrastructure. It entails the presentation of the three consecutive regimes that have controlled and managed the Palestinians from the mid-nineteenth century until today: late Ottoman rule, the British Mandate and Israel. Each regime initiated concrete processes to incorporate colonial, settler-colonial and modern literacies as part of its regime-maintenance mechanisms.

During late Ottoman rule, the *Tanzimat* restructured the socioeconomic order, modernising the cultural sphere, including education.[25] Ottoman Turkish and Arabic were the languages of instruction in the new government schools. Other European languages and Russian were the languages of instruction in missionary schools. Hebrew was taught in Jewish religious institutions and, later, in the Israeli Alliance school (*Alliance israélite universelle*).[26] This multilingual scene under the umbrella of the Ottoman administration was part of a general Ottoman identity and was not based on the nation-state model of a standardised national language for all.[27] The issue of Arabic as an expression of Arab national identity started in a nascent form only with the rise of the Union and Progress party to power after the coup of 1908.[28] The Great War period did not see a major shift in this regard, but the institution of the British Mandate coincided with the rise of an Arab-Palestinian national articulation of Arabic.

The Mandate authorities reduced the multilingual scene to three official languages – English, Arabic and Hebrew – with a clear power hierarchy between them in favour of English. More importantly, the Mandate authorities linked Arabic and Hebrew with the Palestinian and Jewish communities, respectively.[29] The official and institutional assigning of a language to a community and separation of communities were enforced by laws, institutions and policies. The Palestinian and Zionist Jewish communities each developed their own ideological apparatuses so as to reinforce this separation on nationalist ground.

As many recent studies have shown, by the 1930s the communal and institutional segregation processes were almost complete.[30] Arabic and Hebrew each had their own field within a proto-nation-state format for a community with its own material, institutional and ideological infrastructures. This final institutional separation between the two groups of people included hierarchical power relations to determine their interactions. The separation and closure in turn led to the beginnings of the Zionist mode of excessive literacy. The operative skeleton of this mode of literacy relied directly on print capitalist apparatuses, which were in place and operating in the Yishuv by then. These beginnings took a rather intensified institutionalisation towards 1948 and thereafter with the establishment of the State of Israel, as the culmination of the settler-colonial Zionist movement.

Following the war of 1948, the Hebrew field became the core of Israeli state apparatuses, while the Arabic field was dismantled, its remaining parts of the infrastructure taken as war 'booty' by Israeli state organs.[31] From the Israeli point of view, the war of 1948 resulted in Arabic being a branch of the Hebrew field in Israel. It had to be dismembered from its near past and more distant memory. As for the Palestinians in Israel, after they lost the pre-1948 material, social and political orders, Arabic became their last refuge in articulating their collectivity amidst the new settler-colonial realities. Unfortunately, this symbolic and semiotic collectivity contained no socio-material base, except for the Palestinians themselves, and their collective memories as shaped by the late Ottoman rule, the British Mandate and the tragic events of 1948. A major part of the institutionalisation processes of the new modes of literacy – that is, excessiveness and compulsiveness – was the liquidation of the option of writing by the Palestinians in Israel. This occurred through the literal dismantling of print capitalist apparatuses owned by Palestinians, destroying printing machines and forbidding the importation of books and newspapers from the Arab World. The systematic actions by Israeli institutions to disconnect Arabic from the Palestinians as a group rest on the understanding that, in order to be a nation, one needs to own a national language. If Palestinians did not have a national language, then they could not be a nation. Israel's dismantling of Palestinian ownership of Arabic led to structural relations of dependency that intensified the engraving of the new modes of literacy onto the Palestinian as well as the Israeli Jewish communities.

This almost chronological relaying of the history of literacy in Palestine presents it from the point of view of the three consecutive sociopolitical regimes: late Ottoman rule, British Mandate, Israel. A different, but related point of view to approximate the history of literacy in Palestine could be presented by excavating the forces that shape its positionality in the collective memory of the Palestinian community in Israel. Three major forces can be located operating in this collective memory that pertain to the sociolinguistic field under examination here: Palestinian local history, Arab-Islamic tradition and modernity, usually in its colonialist and settler-colonial manifestation.

Local Palestinian history is a socioeconomic framework that has emerged as a way of life which has made it unique in its own eyes and in relation to its different Others, including both Arabs and non-Arabs.[32] The main characteristic of this location is the complex relationship between two axes. The first axis represents the types of movement of people, goods and ideas between the southern, central and northern parts, on the one hand, and between the villages and the cities, whether along the coast or across the mountains, on the other hand. The second axis is that which crosses locality and ties it together with Egypt, the Levant and beyond, to the rest of the world.[33] These two axes have required different modes of reading and writing, for they have rested on different modes of economic, social and political activities. The owning and/or use of certain modes of reading and writing has been contingent on movements in and between these different layers that built the locality of Palestine. Beyond the owning and use of a certain mode, however, the marginality of the Palestinians' contribution to Arabic literacy is evident, particularly when compared to neighbouring literacy centres such as Egypt and Syria.

The second force operating in the Palestinian sociolinguistic field is old and new Arab-Islamic languages and literatures – an ocean of ink one may choose to jump into or try to avoid, but the immanence of whose constitutive forces and their material manifestations one cannot ignore.[34] What is interesting in our context is that different parts of this Palestinian field have had different relationships to this literary corpus and have usually not denied their very locality, allowing a considerable extent of local manoeuvring with reference to the modes of literacy of this tradition.

The third force is modernity, embodied first in the practices of late Ottoman rule, then in the British colonial regime and its various aspects, and finally in the Zionist settler-colonial regime. Literacy is integral to the bodies of these three regimes, their presence and the logic of their oppressive practice, as well as their processes of producing themselves and their Others.[35] Note that the coercive, symbolic and semiotic involvement of the modern, the colonial and the settler-colonial projects is so total that it often seems to cancel out the other historical layers.

The latter two forces, Arabic literature and (settler-)colonial modernity, operate very differently in relation to the Palestinian locality. In the case of Arabic literature in Arab-Islamic history, the Palestinians are rather marginal in terms of their presence as a distinct collective, as manifested in their writings/readings. The emphasis here is on different normative systems of classification and evaluation of reading and writing that are positioned in the Arab-Islamic religious-governmental body. In the case of (settler-) colonial modernity, the British and Zionist mechanisms of literacy became institutionalised, from their very beginning, as a negation of the Palestinians, their Arab identity, their Islamic identity and their Eastern positionalities. The Palestinian sociolinguistic field draws upon these two traditions, becoming saturated by signs, contents and forms, which are then internalised in the acts of reading and writing that it allows.

Being positioned between and within these two traditions, the Arabic literature and the (settler-)colonial modernity projects, has created modes of literacy that distinguish the Palestinians mainly as readers, whereas the sociohistorical importance of their writing is minor. This is because the Palestinians were incapable – whether collectively or individually – of surviving the power structures that began taking shape under late Ottoman rule, continued in the British Mandate period and were fully constituted through the establishment of the State of Israel. For example, in the nineteenth century, unlike Egyptian society, Palestinian society did not create a modern infrastructure of production separate from the Ottoman government body. Had it created such an infrastructure, it could have relied on it in the face of the British and Zionist settler-colonisers.[36] An opportunity for initiating the construction of such a modern infrastructure, together with the other infrastructures mentioned above, was offered by the intensive contact with Turkish nationalism in the early twentieth centry and, later, with colonialism in its various forms.

The position of the Palestinians within these hierarchic power structures, and subsequently under the Zionist settler-colonial regime, as mentioned above, led to a mode of compulsive literacy among the Palestinian citizens of Israel. Being a product of a settler-colonial power system, this is not a particularly surprising mode, since the oppressed tend to read the oppressor as an effective survival technique in various contexts.[37] Nevertheless, it appears that Palestinian compulsive reading and writing do have unique characteristics: traces of Zionist writing present in the act of Palestinians' reading, and at the same time an acute self-awareness of this act. The uniqueness of this acute awareness is derived from the interrelations between excessive and compulsive literacy modes that entail intense clashes, mergings, dialogues, denials, thefts and sometimes the physical erasure by the new ruler of the Arab-Islamic literary traditions. The structural lines of oppressed-oppressor relations are realised in, among other domains, the practices of writing and reading, but it is the spectrum of these dynamic layers of histories that together enable the appearance of the Palestinians in Israel in the shadow of the Zionist project, against and within it.

These dynamic histories culminated in the *Nakba* of 1948, and they have continued to play major roles in the post-*Nakba* era as raw materials for the Palestinian sociolinguistic field in Israel. As for the sub-site of literacy in this field, the post-*Nakba* era is a kind of castrating saturation of excess and a void of meanings and their manners of circulation. It operates as an arena of contradictions that actively and continuously draws into it processes of constituting a collective Palestinian identity. But it does so in the broad historical context of the impossibility of that collectivity.

Compulsiveness and Excessiveness

The imposed and coercive encounter with the Zionist regime constituted a screen through which Palestinians came to see the world. This encounter began institutionalising in the early 1930s, with the founding of establishments that deconstructed and reconstructed the social, material and historical landscape of Mandate Palestine.[38] Inevitably, this institutionalisation led to the total disassembly of the Palestinian social and political order in 1948. In that year, the space, time and reading and writing tools necessary for the Palestinian community to exist and operate were dismantled. In this sense, the main consequence of 1948 was an enormous void filled with written Zionist discourses. To this day, the Palestinians have been preoccupied with interjecting a written discourse into it, with no apparent success.[39]

The Zionist closure of this enormous void operated as a process of reproducing the written excess, which constitutes private, ahistorical ownership of the modern moment in its reconstruction in the Palestinian site. For the Palestinians in Israel, the dismantling of their literacy and saturation with an excess of Zionist writing forced them to internalise modern Zionist reading tools to survive the new structure, which recoded their place in the world as one that was not theirs.[40] For the Jews, the Zionist surplus writing/reading mechanisms required practices of tremendous expenditure. Producing the surplus meaning required material, social and symbolic resources to maintain the new material and semiotic structures.

The colonised natives are reconstructed as a void, by dismantling them in direct proportion to the degree of excess and expenditure. The new position of the Palestinians in Israel is unique – it is a one-lane, one-way highway. It represents a route into the heart of the external in the written body – the act of reading. Therefore, the Palestinians in this structure can be found only in the traces, or more precisely the ruins, that result from the dynamics of gaining excess via expenditure. In order to track the Zionist practices, one must observe the real and the imagined body of the Palestinian community. Its topography is the result of the encounter with the Zionist physical and textual excess. The Palestinians in Israel are unique in their relation to the Zionist project and its written excess in their role as the shadow of the Zionist written body, its compulsive readers.

The compulsiveness of the Palestinian reading of the Zionist text is not derived from the internal structure of what is written. Nothing in reading this text requires, denies, or prevents a certain mode of performance. The act of reading is flexible, easily reshaped into a new and unfamiliar form whenever it is approached anew. This quality is the result of the unending potential of renewed contact between the reader and the act of reading, which materialises as an event in an accumulating and formalised history that stretches the past into the future.[41] The Palestinian reading of the Zionist body of surplus writing is performed by observing the traces of the inscription left by Zionist writing on the Palestinian body, within it and beyond it. This observation is from up close, like a shadow shadowing a shadow, since it is an eye that examines its own wound. In performing this reading, it seeks what has not yet been inscribed or seized by the Zionist excessive writing machine. Palestinian reading may be likened to a remapping of the Palestinian body, which is unable to do anything but remap itself with each reading act. The problem does not lie with the isolated act of reading, but in the time and space sequences formed through multiple and accumulating acts.

In terms of Zionist textual excess, every possible domain is written endless times in countless Zionist forms.[42] The main characteristic of the Zionist corpus of writing is the content excess of possible forms, on the one hand, and the excess of forms for every possible content, on the other. Every social and historical form of life can exist only by providing Zionist content for its formalisation. In addition, for every possible form, some appropriate Zionist content lies in wait. That is the excess. There is no form that can escape its Zionist content, nor can there be. At the same time, every content or meaning of any sociohistorical existence can only exist by virtue of having been born out of Zionist form, and such forms are endless – and that is excess. Palestinian readers face this structural complexity, and in an attempt to survive the excess, they develop tactical survival techniques. I argue that due to the power structure and the particular manners of closure of the settler-colonial field of contradictions – that is, dismantling the material and symbolic infrastructures previously owned by the Palestinians – the synthesis of these survival techniques is the compulsive reading mode.

If the argument about Zionist excess is not in and of itself excessive, we must return to the particular history out of which and towards which we are speaking. I will now turn to examining two interrelated points: the excess, and the history that enables us to see it. How can we examine the theory that an excess is not an excess, but the defining aspect of a particular structure? And what about the case of the Zionist settler-colonial regime discussed here? On the one hand, we have the excess that is the result of the accumulation of meanings and their forms of communication. On the other hand, we have the excess required by the structure of a collectivity, in order for it to reflect upon itself, to see itself through it. Usually, it is a desirable excess that does not necessarily exist, but that produces a general horizon which allows the members of the collectivity to understand their behaviours, feelings and thoughts in certain ways. The Zionist settler-colonial regime is not only this or that – it appears to be both and something else as well.

Losing the Ability to Lose

Most Palestinians experience the *Nakba* as an event of loss. Historically, this loss transformed the ways in which the Palestinian collective produced and reproduced itself, its immediate environment and its position in the world.[43] Structurally, we can argue that the one-time historical event of loss is synchronic: the site of loss exists wherever and whenever the Palestinian collective exists, and it is part of the ongoing construction of that collective. Therefore, in order to examine the modes of reading and writing of the *Nakba* and of the era that followed it, we must first position it in the context of loss as a historical event and a structural site. Both of these, the event and the site (and their interactions), are key determinants in the dynamics of constituting the Palestinian communities.[44]

On the collective level, the *Nakba* is a moment of repetition, a temporary visit to a beginning that is already gone. The return to the trope of the *Nakba* is compulsive; its repetitiveness is a constituent part of any other movement of the collective.[45] This is because the Palestinian collective has failed in its attempts to traverse the black hole that resulted from the events of 1948, in the memory sequences of the story of its constitution. This failure is one of the distinct characteristics of the ways in which the *Nakba* is represented in the collective Palestinian memory. As such, it gives birth to, shapes and formalises the Palestinian collective's work – that repetition inherent to every Palestinian collective movement. Being unable to traverse the black hole means the inability to lose – that is, everything was lost in the *Nakba*. What we have here is a kind of double step of a first-order image that meets itself as a second-order image.[46] The Palestinian collective does not meet in itself the loss of the ability to lose, despite the fact that this is its main characteristic, but it is highly aware of its formative practices of non-traversal. As a result of this dynamic, in the life of Palestinians today we can identify two axes of space-time – that of the ongoing daily life and that cut short in 1948, in a manner that pushes the Palestinian repeatedly to the moment where time stood still. The Palestinian life-cycle relies on the interactive link between those two axes and is the product of the movement of the two forces: the quotidian that pushes forward linearly, and the other, which pushes inwards, to the moment of interruption and loss.

There are many types of loss, some of them very difficult and even unbearable on both individual and collective levels. One of them, which we may call total loss, is unique in that it is followed by the subject losing the ability to lose any more, thereupon ceasing to be a subject. The loss of the ability to lose is the ultimate loss, charting the boundaries of our humanity. Humans may be defined as social entities according to their ability to lose, but when they lose the ability to lose, they are no longer defined as part of society. They are invisible. Therefore, in cases of almost-total loss, individuals and groups usually struggle – sometimes to the death – to retain the ability to lose. In many respects, this dynamic of total loss is the inversion of private ownership relations as the dominant form of identity construction in the era of capitalism.[47] We must therefore ask: What is the meaning of the (in)ability to lose? What causes it? What shapes it? Does it transcend particular societies and histories? And is the *Nakba* a case of losing the ability to lose? If it is, what makes it unique? And perhaps just as important, will we be able to better understand total loss by studying the unique case of the *Nakba*?

Today, most of the historical and social literature on the war of 1948 and its results focuses on details and rhetorical questions regarding the intentions of historical subjects active in the events of that war. Nevertheless, most historians are in agreement as to the main result of the war: it reorganised the field of conflicts of the previous period, in a way that led to the dismantling and destruction of the previous balance between the main contradictory forces of the British colonial regime in Palestine. It also created a system of balance that ushered the colonial regime into a new era, in the incarnation of the Israeli settler-colonial state.[48] Therefore, destroying and dismantling one of the historical subjects that represented a major polarity in the equation of the previous British colonial order – the Palestinian collective – was crucial in order for the new configuration of the settler-colonial regime to emerge. Hence, the dismantling and destruction of Palestinian collectivity were almost total, to the point of its losing the ability to lose – that is, to the point of its return to a zero level of sociality. Structurally, the settler-colonial regime cannot see and imagine itself in a real intersubjective context. It must therefore destroy the social, material, human (as in both the individual and the collective bodies) and any other collective basis upon which the Palestinian subject could act. Put differently, at the *Nakba* of 1948, the Palestinian collective lost its ability to lose because the settler-colonial regime had literally destroyed and dismantled everything that could be lost, with nothing left to lose.

One of the main results of the almost total loss of 1948 is the dispersal of Palestinian society into different fragments, according to the geopolitical location in which Palestinians resettled. These various fragments of the Palestinian collective have complex relations with the Zionist settler-colonial regime.[49] On the structural level, we may argue that all fragments maintain the same relationship with the Zionist settler-colonial regime; but on the individual level, each of the fragments of the Palestinian collective treats the regime differently. Each fragment's position varies along the time and space axes; accordingly, the relationships between each fragment and the regime vary as well. This complexity is expressed in the ambivalent relations between the Palestinians and the post-1948 settler-colonial regime. On the one hand, having a relationship with the settler-colonial regime could help a particular Palestinian fragment to regain the ability to lose. On the other hand, this would mean depending on the regime that had denied it in the first place. The ability to lose, enabled by the settler-colonial regime for Palestinian fragments, is unique: it requires the subject's fragmentariness as a condition for its temporary social existence. As for the group of Palestinians in Israel, which is a fragment of the Palestinian collective, we must ask: How does its fragmentariness operate in the context of the mode of compulsive literacy, which is the main modality for reproducing this fragment's collective temporary social existence? Conversely, how has the Zionist mode of of excessive literacy sustained its ability to inscribe the loss of the ability to lose onto this Palestinian fragment's void and loss? What kinds of relations exist between them?

So far, we have been delimiting and describing analytically the modes of reading and writing, in the context of the settler-colonial order, that developed between the State of Israel and its Palestinian citizens. At this stage, and in order to deepen our critical understanding of this dynamic of reading and writing, I want to introduce a larger circle of analysis: the conditions of possibility that have been enabling the Zionist regime to grow, develop and operate according to the structures I have described thus far. Specifically, I will claim that modernity/settler-coloniality (and its foundation of the socio-economic capitalist order) promoted print capitalism as an operational logic of the settler-colonial state. The operational logic overarches homologically the two domains of commodification and of reading and writing. It thus produces circulatable and consumable literary products within the boundaries of the settler-colonial state. This circle of analysis sheds new light on the empirical manifestations of the modes of literacy dominant in the Zionist regime, the excessive and the compulsive. Moroever, the empirical data collected for this research span the transitional moment into the late capitalist order, which took shape among the Palestinians in Israel in the early 1990s. This moment had direct and lasting impacts on the operational logic of commodification as well as reading and writing. This requires further development of our tools of analysis. In the following section, I will elaborate on the two moments of print capitalism, the classical and the late, and the analytical tools thereof that I will use in the later chapters of this book.

Print Capitalism: Commodifying Reading and Writing in a Settler-Colonial Context

One of the challenging issues raised by this study is the development of analytical frames and tools that could capture the complexities of settler-colonial literary relations in Palestine. The academic literature on this topic has hitherto followed conventional disciplinary boundaries. Linguists study the linguistic aspect of Arabic in Israel, while scholars of literature are confined to exploring different literary genres of the Palestinian literary canon.[50] At times, political scientists utilise a poem or a scene from a novel as an anecdote for supporting their analyses. I propose to deviate from this academic tradition because it falls short from critically understanding, let alone explaining, the unique complexity of settler-colonial literary relations in Palestine. Instead, I offer the political economy of language and (settler-)colonial literary relations as an entry point, based on the data collected for this study.[51]

The previous sections have delineated the institutional infrastructure of 'Arabic'. It is a typical network of institutions characteristic of print capitalism as an operational logic of the nation-state format, as applied to (settler-) colonial states.[52] As operational logic, print capitalism relies on two homological domains: commodification as well as reading and writing. Usually, in the context of nation-states, the two domains are separated by different mediatory institutions, mainly the market and the legal system, concealing the subordination of reading and writing to commodification.[53] In the settler-colonial context in Israel, there is a different variation on these homological relations between commodification and reading and writing. There are no mediatory institutions between the two domains for the Palestinians citizens of Israel as a community. What we can observe in this case-study is a collapse of the homological relations typical of modern nation-states or colonial states.[54] What does it mean that there is a direct, unmediated commodification of reading and writing?

The settler-colonial order in Palestine must be profitable in order for Israel and the Zionist regime to sustain themselves.[55] In the process of their transformation into a productive force within the settler-colonial order, the community of Palestinians in Israel must consent to the new order, or to use the Israeli discourse, become 'loyal' to the state. A 'loyal' Palestinian is the only exchangeable commodity, as both manual and intellectual labour, possible in Israel. To manufacture loyalty, beyond the usual direct repressive state apparatuses, Israel has used among its Palestinian citizens mass communication, mainly in printed formats.[56] At this intersection, reading and writing became crucial, as tools for decoding the Palestinians and recoding them as 'loyal' colonised natives. The State of Israel monopolised the modes of reading and writing and their means of production, with settler-colonial institutions having authority over the sociolinguistic field of Arabic in the Palesinian community. This monopoly means that, in contrast to nation-states and colonial ones, Israel owns the material as well as the symbolic and the semiotic means of production in relation to its community of Palestinian citizens. In such a case, the homological relations between commodification and reading and writing become redundant; the state does not need homological relations to administer its colonised native subjects because it monopolises both domains and manufactures loyalty in the form of a commodified literary product.

As for the Palestinians in Israel, they experienced a deep split in their relationship to Arabic. They could use reading and writing, but they were not the owners of the institutions responsible for reproducing Arabic as exchangeable symbolic capital on the collective level. The imposed commodification of reading and writing in Arabic, decoding the Palestinians and recoding them as 'loyal' colonised natives, created a set of literary practices that are far from being merely 'exchangeable' in terms of loyalty to the state. These settler-colonial literary practices will be my entry point of discussion in the following chapters, only to trace through them the larger circles of analyses, the direct settler-colonial context and print capitalism as an overarching context.

The late capitalist era brought with it drastic changes in print capitalism as an operational logic of nation-states and (settler-)colonial states.[57] In the context of the Palestinians in Israel, these changes started to manifest in the early 1990s. The most relevant change has been the transformation in the type of monopoly ownership by the State of Israel of the material as well as the symbolic and semiotic means of production in regard to the Palestinian community in Israel. This transformation opened the door for Palestinian non-governmental organisations (NGOs) to claim at least some type of shared ownership of these means of production with the state. The premises of these claims by the new sociopolitical agents, NGOs, rely on professional and legal discourses, in contrast to the Palestinian national ideologies of the previous stage. These changes and claims have far-reaching implications for settler-colonial literary practices and relations within the Palestinian community. We will address these changes in the last chapter of this book.

Conclusion

The aim of this chapter is to set the frames of analysis that will be used as a point of departure in our exploration of the settler-colonial literary practices and relations among the Palestinian citizens of Israel. To a large extent, these frames were conditioned by the results of the war of 1948 and their implications for Israel and its Palestinian citizens. I adopt a multidisciplinary approach, using several circles of analyses based on homological relations between them. I have pointed to three main frames of analysis: the institutional infrastructure through which Israel administered Arabic and its products, the modes of literacy and the context of print capitalism as an operational logic in the settler-colonial states.

The data collected for this study show three distinct periods, each with its own dominant variation on practising reading and writing within the excessive and compulsive modes of literacy. Each of the following three chapters will focus on one of these historical periods and its economic, social and political contexts, as they pertain to these particular variations. The following chapter will present the first portrait of 'Arabic' that became established with the moment of structural closure of the settler-colonial Zionist regime in 1948. I will trace the processes of constituting 'Arabic' as an arena by analysing the textual and public activities of various groups, of both Palestinians and state representatives. This first period in the life of 'Arabic', I will claim, sealed the structural relations between Arabic and Hebrew in Israel.

Notes

1. For an attempt to contextualise the Palestinian sociolinguistic situation, see Suleiman, *A War of Words*, 137–217. As for the nation-state and its national language, see Anderson, *Imagined Communities*, 67–82. For a political economy model of language in capitalism, see Ferrucio Rossi-Landi, *Language as Work and Trade: A Semiotic Homology for Linguistics and Economics* (New York: Praeger, 1983). For a historical and theoretical account of the imperial and colonial contexts in which culture, in general, and language and its products, in particular, constitute prime sites in which the power relation are played out, see Edward Said, *Culture and Imperialism* (New York: Vintage, 1994); Walter Mignolo, *Local Histories/Global Desgins: Coloniality, Subaltern Knowledges, and Border Thinking* (Princeton: Princeton University Press, 2000), 217–311.

2. See the Indian case for a comparative perspective: Cohen, *Colonialism and its Forms of Knowledge*, 16–56.
3. For a detailed analytical description of this classification system, see Gil Anidjar, *The Jew, the Arab: A History of Enemy* (Palo Alto: Stanford University Press, 2003).
4. See Althusser, *For Marx*.
5. The concepts of 'excess' and 'compulsion' are borrowed here from different intellectual genealogies. It is important to state that I use them here as analytical tools without the psychopathological shades that they might have had in their previous usages.
6. On the concept of surplus in Marx's thought, see Samir Amin, *Three Essays on Marx's Theory of Value* (New York: Monthly Review Press, 2013).
7. Georges Bataille, *The Accursed Share: An Essay on General Economy*, vol. 1: *Consumption*, transl. Robert Hurley (New York: Zone Books, 1991).
8. Jean-Luc Marion, *In Excess: Studies of Saturated Phenomena*, transl. Robyn Horner and Vincent Ber Bronx (New York: Fordham University Press, 2004).
9. Pierre Bourdieu, *Outline of a Theory of Practice*, transl. Richard Nice (Cambridge: Cambridge University Press, 1977), 72–78.
10. There is an extensive literature on the political economy of language and literary practices. See, for example, Rossi-Landi, *Language as Work*; Norman Fairclough, *Critical Discourse Analysis: Critical Study of Language* (London: Routledge, 2010); David Block, *Political Economy and Sociolinguistics* (New York: Bloomsbury Academic, 2018).
11. Lorenzo Veracini, 'Understanding Colonialism and Settler Colonialism as Distinct Formations', *Interventions* 16, no. 5 (2014), 615–33, https://doi.org/10.1080/1369801X.2013.858983
12. Wolfe, 'Settler Colonialism and the Elimination of the Native'. For a comparison between the Palestinian case and the Native American one in this regard, see Steven Salaita, *Inter/Nationalism: Decolonizing Native America and Palestine* (Minneapolis: University of Minnesota Press, 2016).
13. Ilan Pappe, *The Ethnic Cleansing of Palestine* (Oxford: Oneworld Publications, 2006); Rouhana and Sabbagh-Khoury, 'Settler-Colonial Citizenship'.
14. See, for example, Geish Amit, 'Salvage or Plunder? Israel's 'Collection' of Private Palestinian Libraries in West Jerusalem', *Journal of Palestine Studies* 40, no. 4 (2011), 6–23.
15. Rouhana and Sabbagh Khoury, 'Settler-Colonial Citizenship', 5–6.
16. Veracini, 'The Other Shift'.
17. For a comparative perspective on these and other settler-colonial ones regarding owning the tools for producing meaning, see, for example, Annie Coombes (ed.),

Rethinking Settler Colonialism: History and Memory in Australia, Canada, Aotearoa New Zealand, and South Africa (Manchester: Manchster University Press, 2006).

18. For more on the domain of language and its characteristics, see Thompson, *Studies*, 42–72.
19. For more, see Volosinov, *Marxism*.
20. For more, see Herzog and Ben Rafael, *Language*.
21. See Pierre Bourdieu, *Language and Symbolic Power*, transl. Gino Raymond and Mathew Adamson (Cambridge, MA: Harvard University Press, 1991).
22. For more on the sign, see Ferdinand de Saussure, *Course in General Linguistics*, transl. Wade Baskin (New York: Columbia University Press, 2011).
23. For more on the discursive formation, see Michel Foucault, *The Archeology of Knowledge*, transl. A. M. Sheridan Smith (London: Routledge Classics, 2002); Michel Foucault, 'The Order of Discourse', in *Untying the Text: A Post-Structural Reader*, ed. Robert J. C. Young (London: Routledge, 1981), 48–78.
24. See, for example, Maurice Blanchot, *The Writing of the Disaster*, transl. Ann Smock (Lincoln: University of Nebraska Press, 1986).
25. See Abu-Manneh, 'Jerusalem in the Tanzimat Period'; Alexander Scholch, *Palestine in Transformation, 1856–1882: Studies in Social, Economic, and Political Development* (Washington, DC: Institute for Palestine Studies, 1993).
26. See Fortna, *Imperial Classroom*. For missionary schools at the end of the nineteenth century in Palestine, see, for example, Abu Hanna, *Ṭalāʾiʿ al-nahḍa fi Filasṭīn*.
27. For more details on the cultural scene in late Ottoman Palestine, see Michelle Campos, *Ottoman Brothers: Muslims, Christians, and Jews in Early Twentieth-Century Palestine* (Palo Alto: Stanford University Press, 2011).
28. To capture this early formation of national identity via Arabic, see Darraj, 'Muthaqqaf ḥadāthī'.
29. Ayalon, *Reading Palestine*; Reshef, *Ha'Ivrit biTkufat haMandaṭ*.
30. Sherene Seikaly, *Men of Capital: Scarcity and Economy in Mandate Palestine* (Palo Alto: Stanford University Press, 2015); Metzer, *The Divided Economy*; Deborah Bernstein, *Constructing Boundaries: Jewish and Arab Workers in Mandatory Palestine* (Albany: State University of New York Press, 2000).
31. See, for example, Amit, 'Salvage or Plunder?'
32. See, for example, Beshara Doumani, *Rediscovering Palestine: Merchants and Peasants in Jabal Nablus, 1700–1900* (Berkeley: University of California Press, 1995).
33. See, for example, Salim Tamari, *Mountain against the Sea: Essays on Palestinian Society and Culture* (Berkeley: University of California Press, 2008).

34. See, for example, Zakariyya Muhammad, *Qaḍāyā fī l-thaqāfa al-Filasṭīniyya* [Issues in Palestinian Culture] (Ramallah: Muwatin, Palestinian Institute for the Study of Democracy, 2002); Ayalon, *Reading Palestine.*
35. For different perspectives on this, see Ayalon, *Reading Palestine*; Esmail Nashif, 'Isn't It Good to Be Literate?' *Mediterranean Historical Review* 21, no. 1 (2006), 105–14.
36. For the Egyptian case, see Mitchell, *Colonising Egypt.*
37. The literature on this subject is quite extensive. See, for example, Homi K. Bhabha, *The Location of Culture* (London: Routledge, 1994); Frantz Fanon, *The Wretched of the Earth*, transl. Richard Philcox (New York: Grove Press, 1967).
38. The processes that matured in the 1930s are still not completely documented, but several studies have already suggested their existence and institutionalisation. See, for example, Roza El Eini, 'The Impact of British Imperial Rule on the Landscape of Mandate Palestine, 1929–1948' (PhD diss., The Hebrew University of Jerusalem, 2000); Patrick Wolfe, 'Purchase by Other Means: The Palestine Nakba and Zionsim's Conquest of Economics', *Settler Colonial Studies* 2, no. 1 (2012), 133–71, https://doi.org/10.1080/2201473X.2012.10648830
39. On these dynamics and processes of writing and emulation attempts as an echo of the 1948 event, see Ismail Nashef, *Mi'māriyyat al-fuqdān: Su'āl al-thaqāfa al-Filasṭīniyya al-mu'āṣira* [The Architecture of Loss: The Question of Contemporary Palestinian Culture] (Beirut: Dar al-Farabi, 2012).
40. Obviously, this process is not linear and has involved several levels. That which is described here is the most central and dominant.
41. Much has been written on the special role of the reader. See, for example, Roland Barthes, 'The Death of the Author', in *Image Music Text*, transl. by Stephen Heath (London: Fontana Press, 1977), 142–48.
42. For descriptions of historical events derived from this structure, see Geish Amit, *Bet haSfarim haLeumi vhaUniversiṭayi 1945–1955: Mif'al Ha'varatam shel Sifre Ḳorbanot haSho'ah, 'issuf haSifriyot haFalasṭiniyot beMilḥmet 1948, ve'ssuf Sifre Mehagrim miArtsot haIslam* [The National and Academic House of Books 1945–1955: The Project of Gathering the Books of the Holocaust Victims, Collecting the Palestinian Libraries from the War of 1948 and Collecting the Books of the Immigrants from Islamic Countries] (PhD diss., The Hebrew University of Jerusalem, 2011).
43. Many argue that this event has not yet been told, and that we must seek to retell it by telling most, if not all, of the events that comprised it. It is an attempt to deal with the loss through narrative, an attempt that will naturally

fail due to the nature of the relation between the event and its representation. Recently, there have been published two books worth mentioning in this regard. Kassem tries to retell the story of the women who experienced the *Nakba* of 1948. Azoulay tries to conceptualise the visual representation of the *Nakba* of 1948 in photography. Fatma Kassem, *Palestinian Women: Narrative Histories and Gendered Memory* (London: Zed Books, 2011). Ariella Azoulay, *'Alimut Mekhonenet, 1947–1950: Gene'alogiyah Ḥazutit shel Mishṭar veHafikhat ha'Ason le'Ason miNkudat Mabaṭam* [Constituent Violence: Visual Genealogy and the Turning of the Catastrophe into a Catastrophe in Their Eyes, 1947–1950] (Tel Aviv: Resling, 2009).

44. Recently, some studies have attempted to untangle the relations between the present-day Palestinian identities and the *Nakba.* See, for example, Ahmad Sa'di and Lila Abu-Lughod (eds), *Nakba: Palestine, 1948, and the Claims for Memory* (New York: Columbia Unversity Press, 2007).
45. Gilles Deleuze, *Difference and Repetition*, transl. Paul Patton (New York: Columbia University Press, 1995).
46. See Roland Barthes, 'Myth Today', in *Mythologies*, transl. Annette Lavers (New York: Farrar, Straus, & Giroux, 1972), 109–64.
47. For comparison with a different view on total loss, see Giorgio Agamben, *Homo Sacer: Sovereign Power and Bare Life*, transl. Daniel Heller-Roazen (Palo Alto: University of Stanford Press, 1998).
48. See, for example, Nur Massalha, *The Politics of Denial: Israel and the Palestinian Refugee Problem* (London: Pluto Press, 2003); Benny Morris, *The Birth of the Palestinian Refugee Problem Revisited* (Cambridge: Cambridge University Press, 2004).
49. Note that there is no single body of research that discusses all Palestinians and covers all their fragments, created following 1948. Most studies, be they books or articles, focus on one fragment or another. We may infer from this that the existing research corpus accepts the political and military reality created after 1948. Some of the studies that try to examine all Palestinian fragments do not refer to them analytically as a single group, but as each fragment existing in its own right. A prime example is Baruch Kimmerling and Joel S. Migdal, *Palestinians: The Making of a People* (Cambridge, MA: Harvard University Press, 1998).
50. For linguists, see, for example, Hawker, *Palestinian Israeli Contacts.* For literary scholars, see Bashir Abu-Manneh, *The Palestinian Novel: From 1948 to the Present* (Cambridge: Cambridge University Press, 2016); Refqa Abu-Remaileh, 'Three Enigmas of Palestinian Literature', *Journal of Palestine Studies* 48, no. 3 (Spring 2019), 21–25.

51. I am relying on theoretical developments by several scholars here. However, I am remoulding their interventions in a certain manner, according to the case study at hand. See Volosinov, *Marxism*; Williams, *Marxism*; Fredric Jameson, *The Political Unconscious: Narrative as a Socially Symbolic Act* (Ithaca, New York: Cornell University Press, 1981); Bourdieu, *Language*; Aimé Césaire, *Discourse on Colonialism*, transl. Joan Pinkham (New York: Monthly Review Press, 2001); Ngugi wa Thiong'o, *Decolonising the Mind: The Politics of Language in African Literature* (Nairobi: Heinemann, 1986); Cohen, *Colonialism and Its Forms of Knowledge* ; Guha, *Dominance without Hegemony*; Wolfe, *Settler Colonialism and the Transformation of Anthropology*; Veracini, *Settler Colonialism: A Theoretical Overview*.
52. For further details, see Anderson, *Imagined Communities*; Guha, *Dominance without Hegemony*.
53. Louis Althusser, *Lenin and Philosophy and other Essays*, transl. Ben Brewster (New York: Monthly Press Review, 2001), 127–88; Monica Heller, and Bonnie McElhinny, *Language, Capitalism, Colonialism: Toward a Critical History* (Toronto: Toronto University Press, 2017).
54. Ahmad Sa'di gives vivid examples of this pattern of the collapse of homological relations between different domains in the settler-colonial context in Israel. See Sa'di, *Thorough Surveillance*.
55. Shlomo Swirski, *Mḥir haYohorah: haKibush – haMḥir sheIsrael Meshalemet* [The Price of Vanity: The Occupation – The Price that Israel Pays] (Tel-Aviv: Adva Center and Mapah, 2005).
56. Israel uses many apparatuses to manufacture 'loyalty' among its Palestinian citizens. Here we only focus on those relevant to the present discussion.
57. Ernest Mandel, *Late Capitalism*, transl. Joris de Bres (London: Verso, 1998).

2

The Constitution of 'Arabic': Structural Beginnings and a Chain of Literary Events

One of the main processes resulting directly from the 1948 war was that the Palestinians had to adapt to the new settler-colonial realities in order to survive as individuals and as a community. What makes these processes crucial is that this community of Palestinians in Israel did not exist before the war of 1948. In a sense, the community had to invent itself within a context of dire circumstances. One part of the adaptation processes that the community underwent was the repositioning of itself in relation to the old and new institutions, memories and collective identities at their disposal. One example of this repositioning is the community's new attitudes and feelings toward Arab-Islamic cultures, as part of a bygone past, in contrast to the alarming realities of the present. I argue that, because of the total loss experienced by these Palestinians, the idea and practice of symbolic returning to the lost collective self became a major discursive formation in the building of the new community. Arabic played multiple roles in rebuilding the community. First and foremost, from well before 1948, Arabic represented the collective identity of the Arabs. In the settler-colonial context, a new role developed: Arabic acted as the main mediator to the collective self of Arabness, reconstructing the collective self through acts of reading and writing. In the process of rebuilding the community, 'Arabic' was thus repositioned. It was reframed as the central object of desire and over-invested, or recharged, with collective feelings and energies, at times even erotic ones. In this chapter, I will detail these acts of repositioning and recharging Arabic, as it was performed by the Palestinians and the new Israeli establishment.

In the post-1948 socio-material context, the Palestinians were subjected to expropriation and closure by the Israeli regime.[1] In addition to the destruction of material and social infrastructures and their implications, the mechanisms of the new government expropriated the space-time infrastructure. Villages and neighbourhoods in cities were under military rule, with imposed curfews and restricted movement of residents. In addition, Palestinians were forbidden any contact with Palestinian and Arab communities outside of Israel.[2] Control of space-time was maintained mostly, but not exclusively, through the mechanisms of the Military Government.[3] The regime also operated through committees that determined population management, expropriation and closure policies and applied them to new spheres, such as education.[4]

As in the case with other Palestinian groups, the initial stage of the constitution of the Palestinians remaining under Israeli rule as a collective occurred with the partial displacement of their sociopolitical agency to the field of the Palestinian-Arab culture, with Arabic at its core.[5] On the one hand, we may read this dynamic of displacement to the cultural sphere on the level of a historical event and argue that it represented a regressive move of return to what was left after the war and the ensuing catastrophe. On the other hand, we can see this dynamic as part of a structural move by the Palestinians to constitute their new collectivity. And it was achieved by the processes of charging the new collective object of desire, Arabic, with new meaning.[6] Both of these readings require an in-depth examination of the processes of return and repositioning, and of the way in which this process has profoundly redefined and transformed the Palestinians' symbolic capital. Above all, I will demonstrate that it was not the entirety of Palestinian-Arab culture that was selected by the Palestinians as the cultural property to return to – Arabic was chosen, particularly literary Arabic. Returning to this cultural property was a constitutive act of coping with the Israeli rule.

It was no coincidence that literary Arabic was selected as an object for repossession by the emerging collectivity. In addition to the specific context that took shape after the 1948 war, Arabic was a quintessential cultural asset during the rise of modern Arab nationalism, becoming one of the pillars of national revival from the mid-nineteenth century onwards.[7] Even before that time – indeed, throughout history – Arabic had been the jewel in the crown of Islamic-Arabic identities. In that sense, literary Arabic was always seen as both the most authentic Arab space and the Arabs' most significant contribution to other world cultures.[8]

This preeminent status of literary Arabic was articulated in the cultural endeavours and writings of many members of the Palestinian intellectual elite prior to the 1948 war. Since the late nineteenth century, Palestinian intellectuals had participated in the pan-Arab discourse on the role of Arabic in processes of national revival and resistance to Western colonialism and the Islamic Ottoman regime.[9] After 1948, this tradition became a major asset in the symbolic capital of the group of Palestinian intellectuals who remained, and it was used as a bridge upon which to return to 'Arabic' and reposition oneself within it. This group included educators such as Hanna Abu Hanna, lawyers such as Hanna Naqara, writers such as Najwa Qawar-Farah, intellectuals such as Emile Tuma and politicians such as Emile Habibi.[10]

However, literary Arabic and Palestinian culture in general were not uniquely Palestinian objects of desire. From the very start of the Zionist settler-colonial project, its relations with the Palestinian language and culture were mediated by the proto-state Yishuv's mechanisms of supervision and control, and it co-opted them by way of gentrification.[11] These mechanisms produced a knowledge corpus, institutional practices and means of supervision and control that served the post-1948 regime in its expropriation and closure practices, which extended into the spheres of language and culture. For example, the regime established a segregated education system for Palestinians, with separate teacher seminars. In addition, there existed separate Arabic newspapers, magazines, publishing houses and so on.[12] These institutions processed the language's historical materiality and produced a particular type of Arabic that detached the so-called 'Israeli Arabs' from Arab nationalism and, subsequently, also Palestinian nationalism. In this chapter, I argue that the version of Arabic which died in 1948 was resurrected as a 'dead' Arabic in terms of its national associations. The Palestinians' return to and repositioning in Arabic, now considered an impregnable fortress for Arab nationalism, produced a constantly renewing arena of conflictual relations between the coloniser-settler and the colonised native, in turn producing an array of intensive mixed and tense emotions, ranging from the sense of the *heimlich* to the *unheimlich*.[13]

The complexity of the 'Arabic' arena in Israel is evident mainly in the types of activities, products and discourses that developed around it, whether among the Palestinians or among various officials in the state mechanisms assigned to develop and maintain it.[14] This chapter focuses on the processes of formalisation of the arena of 'Arabic'. This formalisation included building the mechanisms that would carry out the acts of representing the collective identity and, at the same time, operating as a mediator to reconstruct it. These mechanisms inculcated a certain structure of feeling in this collectivity, as constituted by both Palestinian intellectuals and non-Palestinian orientalists, some of them government officials, in the first decade after the 1948 war.[15] These two groups, Palestinians and Zionist officials, interacted dynamically in constituting this arena. The processes of formalising 'Arabic' took place in speech, reading/writing, intellectual and artistic associations, and the establishment of sociopolitical institutions. I contend that the two groups practised their sociopolitical agencies through certain modes of reading and writing. Reading and writing were directly connected with the processes of formalising 'Arabic', due to the context of print capitalism and its dominant forms of mass communications, such as newspapers, magazines and books, among others. Reading and writing were the concrete set of activities through which the positions of the two groups, regarding the building and the controlling of the new Palestinian community in Israel, were articulated. In the previous chapter, I have named the Palestinian set of activities the compulsive mode and that of the Zionist regime the excessive mode. Here I will try to trace them through the activities of reading and writing of particular historical subjects who participated in setting the stage for the Palestinians to read and write in the new settler-colonial context in Israel.

The present analysis opens with an examination of the arena's sub-categories of actions, products and discourses. The empirical data of 'Arabic' can be divided into three major sub-spheres: sociocultural criticism, literary criticism and relations with the State of Israel. Although these sub-spheres operated separately, they saw intensive cross-movement of intellectuals and experts, as well as their products and discourses. There are distinct patterns of mobility suggesting, at the very least, the presence of a distinct speech/literary community.

In the first decade after 1948, Arabic prose and poetry represented the major public site not subject to direct control by Israeli government mechanisms. This facilitated direct political action against the State of Israel through literary practices. Most Arabic writings were published in the daily press and literary journals. Between 1948 and 1970, the field of Arabic prose and poetry played roles that exceeded its conventional role in the Western nation-state.[16] It was used as one of the major strategic platforms for returning and repositioning within 'Arabic', reconstructing the new Palestinian collectivity. Different groups among the Palestinians in Israel and the group of Zionist experts and officials had been seeking ways to control, manage, rechannel and, at times, suppress expressions of the reconstruction of the Palestinian collectivity and national identity. Palestinian and Zionist-orientalist literary criticisms developed together, as did literary and poetic writings. They were published in the same outlets, and they steered the movements of return and repositioning, acting as a meta-language out of which strategies, tactics and modes of operation were derived in 'Arabic'.

To set the stage to present and analyse the data of literary criticism texts, we need to describe the material, institutional context. The establishment of this context has enabled the symbolic, textual and discursive production of these texts. I will begin by investigating the moment of the structural constitution of 'Arabic', as textually understood by Israeli officials. Then I will examine three major sub-spheres or sites within 'Arabic' by exploring their textual corpus. It is important to note that each of the three sites maintained a relative independence on the material and institutional levels. The first site is the Israeli Communist Party and the group of Palestinian intellectuals active within it.[17] The literary criticisms that they published form the empirical material in the focus of this investigation.[18] The main figure and, to a large extent, the leader of this site was Emile Tuma, and this study will therefore concentrate on his literary-critical corpus.[19] The second site was comprised of the group of orientalist experts who among themselves discussed how to construct 'Arabic' in order to manage its inhabitants in a way well-suited to the nascent settler-colonial state and its mechanisms. This group was dominated by Eliyahu Khazzoom and Shmuel Moreh, who laid out and articulated the discursive rules of order, *à la* Foucault, of the criticism of Palestinian literature published in Israel.[20] The third site was the group of Palestinians who had accepted the role of 'Israeli Arabs' and built a material institutional infrastructure that produced Arabic literature and literary criticism in order to educate the Palestinians as such. The mover and shaker of this group was Michel Haddad, who founded the main publication in this site, *Al-Mujtama*.[21] I argue that these infrastructures formed the material-institutional basis for 'Arabic'.

A fundamental issue arises regarding the nature of the interrelations among these three sites and between them and the state mechanisms of expropriation and closure. In the previous chapter, I have discussed the structural relationship between Palestinian and Zionist reading/writing, suggesting that the former was affected by the inability to lose and embodied in a pattern of compulsiveness, whereas the latter was embodied in a pattern of excessiveness and constituted part of the control mechanism of those who monopolised the ability to lose.

This chapter addresses the diachronic level of these structural relations, as sets of reading and writing activities, but the relationship between the two levels is not obvious and does not represent a traditional dichotomy of structure-event. It would appear that the strategies of expropriation and closure used by Israeli state mechanisms straddle the boundary between what is permanent and what is passing. The aim of this straddling is that the expropriation of space and time, as well as the closure imposed on what cannot be totally expropriated (in this case, the mere presence of the Palestinian collectivity in Israel), will block the kinds of dynamics that can develop between the Palestinian event and the settler-colonialist structure of excessiveness or compulsiveness. I will test this hypothesis by expanding the critical discussion of the spatiality and temporality of those parts of the Palestinian event of reading and writing that the settler-colonial apparatuses proved unable to contain.

On Literary Criticism and the Literature of Life

In the first decade after the establishment of the State of Israel, the arena of 'Arabic' was constituted as the space and temporality of a struggle over the definition and design of Palestinian collectiveness in Israel. It operated mainly through the Arab education system and Arabic-language publishers and texts. These social fields did not exist independently as designed and structured fields. The parallel fields in the pre-statehood period had undergone processes that redesigned them and even spawned new sub-fields. Education, the press and literature were not distinct and separate, but interacted and interrelated, whether in terms of the individuals active in all three of them simultaneously, the ideas that moved across them, or the material and symbolic infrastructures provided by each to the others. Most Palestinian literature, for example, was published in the local press, and some of it was included in formal curricula. The material and symbolic infrastructure of all three was 'Arabic'.

The education system and most of the Arabic press were controlled by the state, but the unique characteristics of the literary field made it difficult to subordinate it directly to state mechanisms. It therefore served as a drainage basin for conflicts that could not be directly articulated in the education system and the newspapers controlled by the government, Histadrut, or Zionist political parties. The literary field, however, was not provided; it had to be constructed.[22] First, it was necessary to determine what the relevant literature was, how to write and read it, what its aesthetic structure should be and, especially, how it related to the reality from which it would emanate and in which it would operate. This, in turn, necessitated writing *about* literature – literary criticism that would deal with life and position literature within it. I will now examine the opening position of the Israeli state establishment that enabled the arena of 'Arabic', see how the arena narrated itself, and how it educated its agents to adopt its desirable aspects.

Michael Assaf: What Should Be Done with the 'Arabs' in Israel?

In the first years after the establishment of the State of Israel, the status of the Palestinians and their relationship to the state became an arena where several sociopolitical, military and national forces interacted – both old and new.[23] The discourse about these forces was a major topic among the orientalist experts and bureaucrats of the new regime, and it took place in several spheres.[24] The organ of the Israel Oriental Society, *The New Orient*, was one of several public sites where this discourse was constituted and conducted. The first article that shed light on the structural constitution of 'Arabic' was published by Michael Assaf in the first issue of *The New Orient* in 1949.[25] Titled 'The Integration of Arabs in Israel', it referred to the status of Palestinians in the State of Israel and the nature of their relationship to the state. According to Assaf, integration meant turning 'the Arabs into citizens who have a minimal sense of loyalty to the State of Israel; and that is the first stage'.[26] Listing the various spheres of life, Assaf explained to his learned readers which factors were facilitative and which were obstructive to the processes of achieving the desired integration. After presenting the housing, Military Government and employment factors and describing the benefits to the Palestinians by their very contact with state institutions, he delved into education and the press, praising the Ministry of Education and Military Government:

> Particularly beneficial is of course the activity of the Ministry of Education. Over 75% of the Arab children in the (approximately) hundred villages and six towns inhabited by Israeli Arabs are already studying in schools provided and supervised by the state. The Israeli authorities – and the military governors deserve special commendation in that regard – have gone to great lengths everywhere to open the schools on time, or as soon as possible.[27]

Assaf described the state mechanisms as positive factors in that they promoted the integration of the Arabs, fostering their loyalty to the State of Israel. Conversely, obstructive factors were related to the Palestinians' recent past. Assaf indicated two such factors. The first remained from the pre-statehood period: (pedagogically, mentally and 'politically') inept teachers and inappropriate textbooks. The second factor was the shortage of Jewish Hebrew teachers able to educate the Palestinian students according to the Jewish educational doctrine. This factor was developed as a strategy to address the first factor: Jewish teachers would enable a 'corrective' education to offset the Palestinian teachers and Arabic textbooks.[28] The pre-statehood textbooks were tangible, textual remains of the type of education, the mental-political capacity and 'familiar attitude' that was to be eliminated. Through the strategy described by Assaf – Hebrew studies and contact with the Jewish education system – the Palestinian would be redefined as 'Israeli Arab', with at least the minimal required loyalty to the State of Israel. Hebrew, and the Arabic textbooks written or edited by the education system, were the points of departure for defining the arena of 'Arabic'. The nature of the

'Arabic' that these points are meant to design consists of some, if minimal, identification with the State of Israel.

In Assaf's article, the Arabic-language press received special attention. When describing the Histadrut's efforts to promote the integration of the Arabs in Israel, he referred to the founding of the weekly *Haqiqat al-Amr* as early as 1937 and the fact that it was printed almost continuously during the intermediate period, despite its upheavals. He went on to summarise the situation of the Arabic press in Israel:

> After the abolition of the Ministry of Minority Affairs [in 1949], the budget for *Al-Yawm* – a newspaper published in Arabic in Jaffa by a group of orientalist scholars – became the responsibility of the Ministry of Education. The newspaper is generally informative, in small format, and has been published continuously since September [October] 1948. Its daily circulation is about 1500. The newspaper is edited by Jews, but Arab writers contribute to it regularly.[29]

The mechanisms of government considered the 'Arabs' a group that had to be reeducated, and the Arabic press was one of the main means to that end. The orientalist scholars could understand the 'Arabs' in a 'methodical and scientific' manner, and their knowledge could be converted into an effective educational tool. *Al-Yawm*, with Assaf as chief editor, became the main conduit through which the establishment provided 'general information' to the Palestinians in Israel until 1968, when it was replaced by *Al-Anba*. Assaf underscored the fact that it was edited by Jews and regularly contributed to by Arabs, thereby indicating the desirable hierarchy within 'Arabic'.

To illustrate the type of 'general information' through which the newspaper educated the 'Arabs', the following is a passage from an article by Ovadia Levi, *Al-Yawm*'s correspondent in the Acre area, which referred to the Military Government and its 'positive' aspects:

> It is no secret that peacemaking in this region, and maintaining homeland security in the transition period, as well as the desire to lay the foundations of labour and welfare, are the reasons for the establishment of the Military Government. We believe the implications of the Military Government must not be reduced to the military offices that seek to enforce military regulations. First and foremost, it should be seen as a mediator between the citizens and

> population [on the one hand] and the authorities and various government ministries on the other. And at the same time, these offices represent the source of the most reliable information about the condition of the citizens and their requests [. . .] The fact that most citizens are not familiar with the legal means that can help them exercise their rights gives the military offices priority in serving the public.[30]

Whereas Assaf explained to his orientalist readers how to conduct the interface between the Palestinians and the education system so as to lead them to integration grounded in loyalty, Levi moved from theory to practice: he instructed his Palestinian readers to accept the Military Government and redefined the positive roles played by the regime. Levi could not ignore the practices of oppression, domination, expropriation and closure, however, and therefore had to argue that they were of secondary importance. The 'Arabs' must realise the great benefits of the Military Government and its offices – that is, know how to depend on government institutions and thereby integrate better. This was the formula that Assaf bequeathed to the orientalists and applied as the chief editor of *Al-Yawm*: more contact with the establishment, more reeducation and greater loyalty.

The Arab education system and Arabic press served as the main mechanisms established by the Israeli government early on in order to channel the 'Arabs' into integration. As it was articulated by Assaf, integration was meant to deconstruct their collectivity and redefine it according to Zionist forms of meaning – loyalty – which exemplified the mode of excessive reading and writing then and now. At this point in the development of the relationship between the state and the Palestinians under its control, both Hebrew and Arabic could be used as the communicative infrastructure of both mechanisms. Either of the two languages could be used in communication events between the government and the 'Arabs'. It appears, however, that these two options played distinct roles in the integration processes, with the hierarchic structural relation between them dictating the superiority of Hebrew speakers and the dependency of Arabic speakers on them, reflecting European colonial projects.[31]

For their part, the Arabic speakers made no attempt, at this point, to claim ownership of Hebrew, initiating a struggle over the definition of 'Arabic' as a collective asset in their interactions with state mechanisms. However, being interlocked in a particular settler-colonial power hierarchy meant returning to the set of repetitive activities of reading and writing Arabic as a way of re-claiming it – that is, the compulsive mode of reading and writing. This sociopolitical situation required a change in 'Arabic' and, therefore, also a change in the type of collectivity and the question of whose asset it was.[32]

Emile Tuma: The Palestinian Critic

In the early 1950s, the Military Government directly dominated the Palestinians and applied both spatial and temporal expropriation and closure as two of its main tools. The Arab education system and state-sponsored press also applied expropriation and closure to the symbolic framework of belonging to the Islamic collectivity and Arab nationality, in order to reeducate the Palestinians for integration – that is, loyalty. Opposite those systems, and as part of the dynamics they generated, Palestinian intellectuals who had survived the 1948 war and its consequences initiated the construction of alternative positions within 'Arabic'.[33] Most prominent among them were the journalists of *Al-Ittihad*, who realised that there was an urgent need to create a literary and cultural journal to protect Arabic culture and language against its dispossession by the new press and education system sponsored by the state. Moreover, it would reinforce the Palestinians' particular national identity, while emphasising the importance of Jewish-Palestinian cooperation. Indeed, in 1951, such a journal was published as a supplement of *Al-Ittihad*, but the authorities banned it, claiming that it was a separate title that required its own licence. The later issues were published under the title of *Al-Ittihad*. This cat-and-mouse game with the authorities continued until 1953, when lawyer Hanna Naqara under his name obtained a licence for an independent monthly called *Al-Jadid*.[34]

The publishers of *Al-Jadid* tried to recruit writers from among the surviving Palestinian intelligentsia, but most of these attempts failed, and initially the monthly suffered from a significant shortage of writers. The desk workers of *Al-Ittihad* provided the texts, with some of them using several *noms de plume* to form the impression of multiple writers. Emile Tuma, for example, wrote several articles in every issue – under his own name as well as the pseudonym Ibn Khaldun and others.[35] Be that as it may, within a few years *Al-Jadid* became the main cultural platform in Arabic, independent of state or Histadrut mechanisms and their extensions; it retained this status for at least two decades.

In an editorial evaluating the journal's contribution, on the tenth anniversary of its founding, Tuma described its early days and subsequent development:

> The *Al-Jadid* family expanded and grew in both quantity and quality [. . .] *Al-Jadid* opened its gates to the young and gifted who had survived the Catastrophe and been strengthened by its fire. They unified the Arab nation's campaign for freedom from injustice. These included Issam al-Abassi, Hanna Abu Hanna, Hanna Ibrahim, Tawfiq Ziad and Issa Loubani. They all composed fascinating, picturesque poems of struggle [. . .] Two of them, Tawfiq Ziad and Hanna Ibrahim, composed poems and wrote short stories [. . .] They were joined by a second wave that overcame all attempts to make them ignorant and deviant and was influenced by *Al-Jadid*, including Mahmoud Darwish and Salem Jubran.[36]

The main distinction here is between those who had survived the 1948 war and those who were 'edified' by the Israeli education system and survived it. The second group not only survived, but also decided to openly join the fray. Conversely, Tuma described writers of another kind:

> Some have chosen to use pseudonyms and would not identify with *Al-Jadid*, neither explicitly nor implicitly at the present time [. . .] But whoever seeks to evaluate their writings will find that their publications in *Al-Jadid* were the finest among them [. . .] Nowadays, new pens grace the pages of *Al-Jadid* [. . .] but the fear of the terror of the tyrannical dictatorship still keeps many pens at bay or away from their natural home.[37]

If we position the founding of *Al-Jadid* within the reclaiming of 'Arabic' while it was being constructed, then the historical events described here suggest interrelations among various patterns of return and repositioning. The first is that of the group who initiated *Al-Jadid*, characterised as we have seen by its open and explicit work, its return to 'Arabic' and its positioning in that arena. The *Al-Jadid* founders' group forged a collective sense of ownership and constructed a shared structure of feeling of reconnection through 'Arabic'. A second group was composed of later writers using pseudonyms: its members also promoted return and repositioning on the collective level, but on the individual level were still unable to return 'home', either because they developed a home-not-home nexus, or because the expropriation practices of 'Arabic' and its closure by the regime made for a personally-ambivalent *unheimlich* experience.[38] A third group never returned to reposition itself within 'Arabic' on the declarative collective level; as Tuma wrote, their fear 'still keeps many pens at bay or away from their natural home'. This group may be divided into two sub-groups with distinct patterns of return and positioning. The first is made up of those who avoided publishing what they could write, and the second is located 'away from its natural home', meaning those Palestinians who wrote in state-sponsored newspapers and journals. The members of both sub-groups could feel 'at home' in 'Arabic' without having a sense of ownership over it.

These four patterns of return and repositioning – the overt, the covert and the two 'landlordless' patterns – articulate different positions within 'Arabic'. They claim collective ownership of 'Arabic' in different ways, in the face of the regime's structural position as described by Assaf – integration that means loyalty. As a literary critic, however, Tuma did not settle for mapping the positions within 'Arabic'. Together with the other founders, he carefully detailed the operational dynamics of each position with reference to reality, in order to bequeath to the Palestinians, or rather 'educate' them, according to an ideal model – that of a 'Palestinian' in the Israeli settler-colonial context.

An interesting case, illustrative of a return and repositioning pattern, was that of writer Najwa Qawar-Farah, as represented in two critical essays by Tuma. The first was published in *Al-Jadid* in 1956, titled 'Abiru sabil' [Passers-By], on the short-story collection under the same title by Najwa Qawar-Farah. The second was published a year later as 'Durub wa-masabih' [Lanes and Lanterns], also titled for a work by Najwa Qawar-Farah.[39] Qawar-Farah belonged to the group of Palestinian writers and intellectuals who survived the *Nakba* and continued their writing and sociopolitical activism after 1948. She was not identified with any particular political current; however, given her public standing as a writer and prominent figure with influence on the community, both the authorities and the *Al-Jadid* founders' group tried to affect her path of return and to determine the site of her repositioning within 'Arabic'. Her volume of collected stories, *Passers-By*, was published in Beirut and reached the Arabic readership in Israel with the authorities' approval.[40] Nevertheless, the context of the publication in Beirut and the book's path to the local Palestinian readership are unclear, since at that time there was no (official) traffic of people and goods between the Palestinians in Israel and the Arab world.

At the beginning of his critique, Tuma wrote that Qawar-Farah was one of those who wrote both before and after the war. Tuma then moved on to clarify what, on the face of it, seemed contradictory in these stories:

> [Even though] the themes of these stories may sometimes seem far removed from the current affairs of the Arab minority, they essentially discuss the instances of our present lives. And nevertheless, most of her [literary] paintings depict a bygone period and a society torn by the tragedy that affected the Arab people in Palestine and uprooted it. This, however, does not diminish from [the stories'] importance or that of their message.[41]

Uncharacteristically, Tuma expressed a rather lenient view of Qawar-Farah as he sought to include her in the group that articulated the first pattern of return and repositioning. He went on to argue that . . .

> Najwa in these stories is a revolutionary [*thaira*], albeit in a quiet and gentle manner. She takes revenge, albeit by way of religious piousness [*al-wara*]. And her protagonists, who discuss life, are characterised by quiet and gentle rage toward the society of the wealthy and their values, and their faith is characterised by noble social ideals [. . .] Najwa detests injustice and corruption, abhors the lives of the 'westernising' rich, sings the praise of honest living, and tends to the safety of rural life.[42]

This reading by Tuma presented the desirable common denominator between him and Qawar-Farah in terms of their basic views on the social order: a structure of feeling that repudiates the injustice of the lives and values of the wealthy. According to Tuma, Qawar-Farah positioned herself at the side of the exploited, against the exploiters and their coalition with the 'West'. But while they shared the structure of feeling, Tuma argued that this was insufficient:

> In her hate and love she seems as though standing by the roadside, looking on as the caravan of life marches on, without being able to affect or stand up

> to it [. . .] And perhaps her choice of title was an accurate reflection of what she felt and what she wanted to convey to her reader.[43]

In support of his position that calls to intervene in the caravan of life and transform it rather than describe it from a gentle and sensitive bird's-eye view, Tuma presented the stories' main theme: interpersonal relations between fathers and sons, women and men, and marital issues. Here, too, Tuma claimed that Qawar-Farah's literary account was lively: she stood by the bereft and oppressed, but the account was 'top-down, shallow more than profound, imaginary more than realistic'.[44] And then Tuma made a *volte-face* and stated:

> We have no right to comment on the ideological tendencies or emotions of the writer Najwa, but these tendencies have congested some of her stories with a mystical [*ghaybiyya*] outlook and sudden drama, which have weakened the structure of some of the stories [. . .] One last word about the style of the writer Najwa: [. . .] it is rightly said that the content determines the style, which in turn adjust itself thereto. This is what leads the style of the writer Najwa to match the contents of her stories. And it is a generally subdued and gentle style, sometimes dramatic and imaginary. This style makes it easier for the reader to accompany Najwa gradually, until she relates that which she wishes to relate.[45]

In this passage, Tuma made interesting analytic moves with regard to the writer, but also in terms of the process literary criticism can lead. First, he emphatically used the title of 'writer' (*adiba*, or female writer in the original) as a recurring prefix to her first name. He then made a distinction between her writing and her personal opinions and feelings, until these infiltrated her literary structure. In Tuma's view, at this point the critic must intervene. Here Tuma pointed to the thematic and stylistic characteristics of the writer, taken from her ideological and emotional world, and highlighted the structural link between them. In doing so, he identified the type of prose used by Qawar-Farah, who could not but adopt the stylistic characteristics of mysticism and imaginary drama. Tuma's moves beg the question: What is the problem with identifying with the exploited and bereft and rising against the rich who exploit and dispossess them? Moreover, what is wrong with mysticism and drama?

Tuma used Arabic terms borrowed from a discourse that may be called 'pre-scientific' – a religious morality discourse which he assumed, probably rightly, to be prevalent among his and Qawar-Farah's readers. Tuma's objective was to channel these moral sentiments into a rational position, one that is the opposite of mysticism, and to lead a pro-active change in the 'caravan of life' rather than describe it in dramatic colours. With this in mind, Tuma concluded his article as follows: 'In this volume, [Qawar-Farah] has positioned herself with the forces that follow light and life, even though her qualified positioning is forced upon her, given her religious thinking and tendencies'.[46] Religion – in this case, Christianity – placed the Palestinian in a position of being unable to intervene in and transform life. Instead, she relied on mysterious superpowers that would suddenly bring about miraculous salvation. Tuma charted a different path for his readers – a return to and repositioning in 'Arabic', that collective symbolic capital whose repossession would lead to rational agency and pro-active change.

A year later, Tuma published another critical article in *Al-Jadid*, about the writer's new book *Lanes and Lanterns*, in which she discussed the Palestinian refugee problem and Arab-Jewish relations.[47] Tuma considered these contents a positive development for the writer, as she turned from a passive onlooker on the struggles of life to a full-fledged partner. However, so Tuma argued, this transition was far from smooth and betrayed doubts and ambivalence that articulated the field of conflicts she inhabited. Tuma described the contradictory forces that shaped her creative process as follows:

> Najwa's development from her position as an observer on life to the position of a combatant in a campaign occurs under conditions of ideological conflict, [. . .] and it appears this conflict is particularly salient in Najwa's introduction to *Lanes and Lanterns*, which may be seen as an honest and truthful credo. In this introduction, Najwa emphasises [that] 'the author's mission is to sometimes paint life and chart, in many cases, a better path for it'. But then she retracts, and here the conflict seems intense, and states [. . .] after recalling that the author may find himself obliged to criticise and show the way: 'And perhaps here, should [the author] rather criticise and chart the path, he would not find the story to be the best instrument, and perhaps his instrument is the poem or the essay. His first duty in the story is to paint the people and society as they are, and there is no room for his direct intervention'. We believe that

> the intensity of the ideological conflict in Najwa's prose derives from the vestiges of mysticism to which she still clings.[48]

According to Tuma, the conflict was not problematic in itself, but it was a constitutive part of a developmental process. Then Tuma's critical knife cut through the implications of these dynamics for the position developed by the writer and her positioning in what he called 'the desert of abstraction' that resulted from her mysticism. Qawar-Farah declared that, had she been asked to choose whether to belong to the group of victimisers or that of the victimised, she would have picked the latter. In Tuma's opinion, this blurring of the identities of master and slave, in the context of Palestinian realities, reproduced power relations and conveyed acceptance of 'reality'. Tuma concluded that 'Najwa's prose is one that projects confusion and anxiety, and such prose cannot be as strong as we would like and as alive as it could be'.[49]

After Tuma had found the grounds to justify his claim by analysing passages from the stories in *Lanes and Lanterns*, he expanded his front and attacked the other forces operating in 'Arabic'. In particular, he suggested that some literary critics who had praised the volume were representatives of the governmental site within that arena:

> These people have done Najwa and her prose ill service, motivated and inspired by a reactionary line that calls for giving in to injustice and even extols the injustice and the acceptance of pain as 'the path to salvation'. [. . .] Those who have sung her praises in *Al-Yawm* and other newspapers have done so in order to call upon the Arab minority in Israel to surrender to the national oppression and accept the oppression as something that makes them human. [. . . They] used an expression by [Qawar-Farah], outside the frame of one of her depictions, pulling an opinion out of a complete canvas that paints a specific issue. Najwa, however, helped them in that by selecting the expressive style and content that is part of a struggle between different intellectual currents.[50]

Tuma exposed and denigrated what the authorities made of Qawar-Farah's prose, through their newspapers, to normalise the current state of affairs and naturalise a particular form of 'Arabic'. He situated her return and repositioning in 'Arabic' as a position that accepts the emotional and religious structure as part of the legitimate tradition, but, by itself, is insufficient to deal with the new settler-colonial context. Moreover, Tuma considered Qawar-Farah a test-case of the struggle over the character of the emerging collective, a struggle waged between the mechanisms of power and the forces that resisted them among the Palestinians. Therefore, in concluding his article, he adopted Qawar-Farah and included her in the forces struggling over the nature of the collective:

> Perhaps our criticism expresses a sharp and assertive position towards Najwa, but this stems from our appreciation of the importance of her literary work [. . .] And we do not feel she needs to be addressed gently, since her prose is powerful enough and in no need of defending. Her writing is a developing tree that does not require protection from the vicissitudes of the weather. What it needs is pruning and polishing.[51]

These words positioned Qawar-Farah as an established writer, for whom literary criticism suggested ways of leveraging her work to more 'literary' directions. According to Tuma, the more she delved into the Palestinians' reality and positioned herself within it, the better her literary forms would become. At the same time, delving into life – as opposed to looking at it from the side of the road or from a bird's eye view – would necessarily lead to a sociopolitical and literary position that would oppose the regime in a rational way, able to lead to a pro-active transformation of life.

According to Tuma, literature is part of the construction of Palestinian life, and literary criticism determines the nature of literature and therefore of life itself. The analysis presented here gives the impression of immediacy, affinity to the point of blurring the modern normative distance between the literary text – both prose and its criticism – and other spheres of life. It appears that the transitions between them evince a dynamic of acuteness and urgency of the formative moment of the arena of 'Arabic'. Most probably, this is due to the initial stage of reconstructing the community and the centrality of the literary sphere in these processes. That is to say, there were no mediatory institutions, at this point, between the different spheres of social activities and the literary sphere. This condition made reading and writing the prime tools available to be used as mediators for the Palestinians to reconstruct their collectivity in Israel. But acuteness and urgency shaped it, as we saw in Tuma's essays, with certain characteristics of compulsiveness.

Reading and writing became repetitive activities for re-owning 'Arabic' as a community with no ability to have losses. Below, I will need to explain the displacement of the settler-colonial field of contradictions into the literary sphere in more detail and in relation to the set of activities of excessiveness as practised by Israeli officials. In what immediately follows, we will see how acuteness and urgency are clearly apparent in the position of the regime, articulated in the literary criticism written by orientalist experts on the field of Palestinian literature that emerged in front of their eyes.

Two Israeli Critics: The Orientalists

Literary criticism was also used by the orientalist experts employed by the state in order to channel the Palestinians' return and repositioning within 'Arabic'. In the immediate aftermath of the 1948 war, *Al-Yawm* and occasionally also the Histadrut-sponsored *Haqiqat al-Amr* published literary reviews for the Palestinian reader. Early into the first decade after statehood, additional journalistic platforms were established, serving the regime and its mechanisms in shaping 'Arabic' and the various positions within it. One of them was the Israel Oriental Society's journal *HaMizrah HaHadash* [The New Orient], which served as a site for activities by government officials and others active in the Israeli orientalist community, and it was certainly familiar to a fairly broad Israeli readership. It may therefore be seen as an arena where orientalist experts presented their views, studied, discussed and analysed their colleagues' views and – most importantly for our purposes – developed discursive and dominative strategies towards the Palestinians in Israel. In what follows, I will examine reviews published in the first decade after 1948. I aim to understand the discourse about the Palestinians within this community of experts, designed to develop strategies for the shaping of a particular kind of 'Arabic' – that is, integration through minimal loyalty to the State of Israel and the constitution of that contradiction in terms called 'Israeli Arab'. Such strategies represent the major activities of the mode of excessiveness in that period.

Expert discussion of the Palestinians in Israel was present in *The New Orient* already in its first issue in 1949, as we have seen, for example, in Michael Assaf's article. The contributors to the journal dealt with a variety of subjects – educational, socioeconomic, religious and others – but the discussion of post-1948 Palestinian literature, as a field in itself, began in earnest in the mid-1950s. The first experts to write about this topic included Eliyahu Khazzoom, Jacob M. Landau and Shmuel Moreh. Khazzoom and Landau played various roles in governmental systems, including intelligence agencies, while Moreh was a prominent orientalist familiar to the Israeli public.

Eliyahu Khazzoom

In 1956, in Issue 3, Vol. G of *The New Orient*, the literature section first included the category 'Israeli Arabic Literature', with two reviews by Khazzoom. One was about Najwa Qawar-Farah's stories. The second, titled 'Arabic Poetry in Israel', was about a poetry collection edited by Michel Haddad, as well as a book by Jamal Qawar.[52] Khazzoom opened this review by describing the main characteristic he attributed to Arabic poetry: stagnation. He argued that Arabic poetry only changed through contact with a different, superior culture. Khazzoom explained that, for generations, the format of Arabic poetry had remained unchanged, without significant development, the poets rejecting any foreign influence.

This pattern was broken only when young Arabs immigrated to the US, where they became liberated of their spiritual isolation and acquired different concepts concerning the art of poetry and the intellect.[53] According to Khazzoom, not only do the Arabs need to come in contact with another culture, but also emigrating to the more developed culture and planting roots in it frees them of their cultural stagnation and spiritual isolation. In the case of the Palestinians, he believed, a similar process took place: they were cut off from Arab culture, planting roots in Israeli society, and thereby becoming free of their stagnation. However, as Khazzoom cautioned, this process was still in its infancy: 'To a degree hitherto much lesser – albeit not insignificant – the Israeli environment has influenced the Arab youth growing in Israel, and the books before us are somewhat reflective of this influence'.[54]

The comparison Khazzoom made between *al-Mahjar* ('Diaspora') poets – a group of poets active among the Arab migrant communities in the Americas in the second half of the nineteenth century – and the Palestinian poets under Israeli rule is intriguing, not only in that it conveys his view of the Palestinians as exiles.[55] It is also intriguing in that the transformation is irreversible – the migration and the change in poetic conventions are profound. These activities of cutting off the Palestinians from Arab culture and planting roots in Israeli society were to become the prime acts of the excessive mode of reading and writing, for they gave the Zionist forms meaning, a monopoly on their settler-colonial subjects.

Khazzoom went on to describe the new and special elements of the poetry collection edited by Haddad:

> The first [book] is an anthology edited by Michel Haddad, editor and founder of the journal *Al-Mujtama*, published in Nazareth. Seventeen Israeli poets are represented [in this anthology], four of them Jewish immigrants from Iraq. Note that we do not find here the conventional subjects of Arabic poetry, and not even the traditional metres. Although new and broad horizons have yet to open up for these youngsters, the shift towards a new path in Israeli Arabic poetry is nevertheless clearly evident.[56]

It is well known that anthologies are political moves in the literary field, defining literary groups using extra-literary boundaries as distinct from other, similar groups. Khazzoom actually declared the emergence of Israeli Arabic poetry by making a clear distinction between it and general Arabic poetry and, indirectly, between it and Israeli poetry in Hebrew. Compared to Arabic poetry, Israeli Arabic poetry began to develop and make progress, but compared to Hebrew poetry (and modern Western poetry in general), it was still in its infancy.

According to Khazzoom, these dynamics were reflected in the contents and metres of the poems:

> Although the themes are mostly dreams, longing and incessant cravings – the lights and shadows of youth as Longfellow calls them – the innovation lies in the lack of selfish preoccupation of the poet with himself and the absence of the non-pragmatic tendency of so many of the Arabic poets in all eras. And it is precisely in the poetry by the younger poets, such as Ahmad Tawfiq Said (actually, almost all of these poets are around the age of twenty) that we find a humane tone that is absent from Arabic poetry, with the exception of the Mahjar / diaspora poets.[57]

Khazzoom's description of Arabic poetry in Israel in the anthology he reviewed was grounded in two discursive axes: age and content. In terms of age, if most contributors were in their early twenties, this meant that they had, by this time in 1956, been educated in the Israeli education system. In terms of content, Khazzoom noted that it was free of what he called 'the selfishness and non-pragmatism' of other Arabic poets; instead, he identified indications of a 'humane' tone. This description suggests a process of purifying the Arab-ness of the group members, on the one hand, and constituting an Israeli Arab-ness on the other. However, that Israeli Arab-ness was lacking and incomplete, was still in its youth, to use Khazzoom's terminology, and therefore must keep growing as far as Khazzoom's readership was concerned. It could do so by pruning and planting; and the new trees were already starting to bring forth fruits in the figures of the Israeli Arab poets included in the anthology.

At this point in his review, Khazzoom mentioned Jamal Qawar as an example for the success of the process he discussed; he reread and rewrote him in the excessive mode. Whereas the poets in the anthology were in their early stages of development according to Khazzoom's standards, Qawar was almost a graduate of the pruning and planting:

> Jamal Qawar's rebellion is even more daring and far-reaching, since in addition to the subject of his poetry (Jubran-style protest against forced marriages), he has cut off all ties to the traditional Arabic poetry form.[58] His style of poetry is that which is called *vers libres* in French literature: some rhymes remain, albeit irregularly, whereas the metre is free – as in poems written in England mainly in the nineteenth century. Qawar also does not hesitate to use words from the spoken language and colloquial terms, which has incurred the wrath of Arab critics in Israel.[59]

Thus, Qawar had undergone a purification. Uprooted from Arabic poetry, his work was comparable with modern traditions of Western poetry from the nineteenth century, since he had adopted parts of them. He was not truly modern yet, however; he was still up to his knees in the previous century. Khazzoom posited to his expert readers that, in fact, the Israeli Arab would complete his purification only by turning his back completely on Arab culture and adopting Western (such as French or English) traditions, to reshape his poetry and thereby his culture.

In these reviews, Khazzoom mapped for his readers the position of Israeli Arabic poetry and the dynamics that should be reproduced in order to shape and reposition it within the structure of expropriation and closure: it must be expropriated from the Arab cultural space and enclosed as an addendum to the Israeli Hebrew culture construed here as representative of Western modernity. We have to assume that Khazzoom was aware of the status of poetry as the main pillar of Arabic culture. Poetry is not just another sub-field of 'Arabic', but a working model of the general arena. Therefore, what Khazzoom was aiming at was to disconnect 'Arabic' from its Arab-ness and recharge it with aspects of modern Western culture as embodied in Zionist Hebrew culture. This path of return and repositioning within 'Arabic' was charted for orientalist experts and public officials, the readership of *The New Orient*; it taught them how to read and write Palestinian events excessively.

Shmuel Moreh

In his reviews, Eliyahu Khazzoom focused on two examples of 'Israeli Arabic literature' on different levels. Two years later, in 1958, the same journal published an article by Shmuel Moreh: 'HaSifrut baSafah haAravit beMedinat Israel' [Arabic Literature in the State of Israel].[60] Moreh sought to map the entire field of local Arabic literature. This was the first contribution to *The New Orient* that addressed Arabic literature in Israel as a distinct field with clear boundaries. Unlike Khazzoom, Moreh presented variety in the positions of the field, but like him, he used the same discursive formations of pruning and planting, thus enforcing a Zionist monopoly on the redefinition of Palestinian literary events. Moreh was not satisfied with the purification of Arabic prose and poetry. Nor did he feel that the adoption of elements of Western Zionism had gone far enough. Instead, he argued that Arab nationalism must be purged, including all its aspects, and hence he had taken the excessive mode of reading and writing to new dimensions.

Moreh opened his article by demarcating the field of Arabic literature in Israel. The first boundary he charted was the disconnecting of the field's present from its recent past, prior to Israeli statehood. The second was delineated by excluding the Iraqi Jewish writers from that field, after years in which they had been considered part of it, side by side with the Palestinians. Moreh repositioned them in the field of Hebrew and considered them liaisons in translation between Hebrew and the Arabic field. The first boundary was grounded in the claim that, in the days of the British Mandate,

Palestinian Arabic literature had been deficient. Whoever had been active in that field had left the country with the establishment of the state; even if they had they stayed behind, this would not have been enough to develop the field:

> At the time of the British Mandate of Palestine, Arabic literature was not of high quality. It lacked originality and depth and concentrated on the Palestinian question and the fight against Zionism and the Jewish national home [. . .] With the establishment of the state, the nationalist writers left the country and continued their literary activities abroad.[61]

Here, Moreh marked the year zero of Arabic literature in Israel. He argued that pre-1948 literature was irrelevant to the field's development, as it did not meet quality criteria and focused on 'the Palestinian question', while the writers themselves 'left' the country. Thus, he marked a starting point of a literature free of Arab nationalist elements. This year zero of local Arabic literature overlapped with the year zero of statehood, and it was the latter that had shaped the former in its present form, thus redefining it via Zionist forms of meaning. To further underscore this line of argument, Moreh went on to write:

> The massive flight by the country's Arabs has turned the Arab community into a minority made up mostly of villagers. The few writers who remained hardly wrote anything, because they wanted to wait and see what the future would bring. Both astonishment at the course of events and various psychological motives have paralysed their activity. Therefore, in the first years after statehood, it seemed as though Arabic literature in Israel was a thing of the past.[62]

Moreh proceeded to prune this field in a triple move. First, there was a massive flight, as he put it. Second, those who remained were villagers, disconnected from the urbanity that mediates or enables literature. Third, their condition was so traumatic that they stopped writing. This way, Moreh cleared the field of past remains, marked the boundary between it and the present and thereby delineated the field of Arabic literature in Israel as, in fact, a Zionist one.

As mentioned above, the second boundary charted by Moreh involved the exclusion of Arab Jews, particularly those who emigrated from Iraq, in the field of Arabic literature. Here too Moreh's argument was grounded in the twin concepts of pruning and planting, albeit with a twist. He wrote:

> With the massive immigration of Jews from Arab countries, and particularly the Iraqi Jews in 1950–1951, the Iraqi Jewry constituted the seed for the revival of Arabic-language literature. Among the Iraqi immigrants were many experienced and renowned poets and authors. Their main literary platform was the weekly literary section of *Al-Yawm* newspaper, which began appearing in 1948, and to a certain extent the weekly *Haqiqat al-Amr*. The younger of the Iraqi immigrant poets brought with them 'free verse', which took its present form under the influence of Iraqi poets Badr Shakir al-Syyab and Ms Nazik al-Malaika.[63]

According to Moreh, it was the combination of Iraqi Jews and the organs of the Zionist establishment that planted the first seed of Arabic literature in Israel. He described the young immigrant poets as carrying with them the seed of progress and made an intra-Zionist distinction between the old and the new generations. Moreh pointed to two specific poets as leading the dramatic change in modern Arabic poetry; unlike Khazzoom, he seemed not to consider Arabic poetry as a monolith. Be that as it may, he argued that the Palestinian writers could not 'revive' Arabic literature in Israel by themselves, but that they needed the help of the young Zionist poets to introduce them to recent developments in modern Arabic poetry.

Apparently, however, this group of Iraqi writers had a task more important than reviving Arabic literature. In the first years following their immigration to Israel, they used their symbolic Arab(ic) capital to integrate in state mechanisms, but it seemed they too had to undergo a process of pruning and replanting. After Moreh mentioned the scarcity of Arabic books published by Iraqi Jews following their immigration and their focus on literary writing published mainly in the establishment press, he began to mark the second boundary of the field:

> These Iraqi Jewish writers had to devote their entire energies to learning the Hebrew language in order to integrate into the country's life spiritually, socially and economically and make a living; [. . .] and their Arabic literary activities became secondary [. . .] Today they are mainly occupied with translations from Arabic literature into Hebrew and vice versa.[64]

Moreh channelled the Iraqi Jews into a process different from that of the Palestinians in Israel in terms of their attitudes to Arabic literature and Arab culture in general, thereby excluding them from the arena of 'Arabic'. These Arab Jews must undergo a process of shedding and purifying 'Arabic', instead planting a national Hebrew seed. Although Moreh claimed that the Iraqi Jews' involvement with 'Arabic' was secondary, as translators they nevertheless formed a bridge between 'Arabic' and Hebrew and therefore were not yet completely 'cleansed'. Their status remained a kind of intermediate position between the two collective linguistic arenas. This move by Moreh drew an additional boundary for 'Arabic' in Israel and sought to structure an overlap between national and linguistic belongings. The demarcation of these two boundaries – the temporal boundary of the field and the overlapping of nationality and language – cleansed 'Arabic' and prepared it to be planted in Israeliness. It framed an Arabic literary field that operated according to the logic of the Zionist regime; it was formed as an adjunct to the Zionist project and it functioned within Zionism's national-temporal boundaries. In this manner, Moreh widened the scope of excessive reading and writing set by Khazzoom, the temporal boundary of the field, to reread and rewrite the Arabic literary field as a Zionist project *per se*, without any remains of Arab nationalism.

After delineating the external boundaries, Moreh moved on to describe the internal boundaries. To a significant extent, the latter derived from the former, since Moreh measured them in reference to Israel's year zero and to the degree of overlap between nationality and language in the settler-colonial context. He went on to argue that the internal space of the field of Arabic literature in Israel was divided into two main categories: communist and non-communist. The former was presented as a monolithic entity, while the latter was divided into secular and religious (Christian). The communists did not meet the two basic criteria suggested by Moreh since they had begun their activities prior to the Israeli year zero and did not accept, at least in principle, the Gordian knot he tied between language and nationality. As for the non-communists, their two sub-groups met Moreh's criteria, each in its own ways. The secular sub-group was formed in the Israeli year zero, accepting the language-nationality nexus, but due to that year zero, their nationality was Israeli rather than Palestinian. The sub-group of religious Christians, on the other hand, was made up of Christian sects, in Moreh's terminology, that did not claim a particular national identity and that, according to Moreh's Zionist view, were located outside the national space-time.

Moreh presented these three groups in terms of forces, spheres of activity and subjects. According to Moreh, the infrastructure of the field of Arabic literature was divided into four parts: 1) the state infrastructure, mainly *Al-Yawm* and *Haqiqat al-Amr*; 2) the communist infrastructure, made up of *Al-Ittihad* and *Al-Jadid* and the circles active around them; 3) the secular infrastructure that revolved around Michel Haddad and the journal *Al-Mujtama*; and 4) the infrastructure of the religious Christians with their publications, particularly *Ar-Raid*. Moreh's description indicates that these four positions are separate and do not intersect. If we follow the names of these writers and their reviews, however, we will find that they are not as discrete as Moreh posited. The material and institutional infrastructure and the discourse community are a single phenomenon with different aspects: material (that is, they inhabit the same cities and villages); institutional (namely, they work in the same schools and newspapers); and discursive (they are involved in the same communicative events).

In analysing the infrastructure of the Arabic literature field, Moreh ignored the interrelations between the various positions within it, but his presentation of the themes that preoccupy this literature is more complex. In doing so, he referred to a single distinct group he called 'the secular writers'. In reading their themes, he marked an internal thematic-emotional boundary that combined the two above-mentioned external boundaries – the boundary of time and that of identity – invested with emotional binaries of the 'good'/'bad' type. This boundary was then used to measure the writers and their subjects. A typical Zionist orientalist, he began as follows:

> Arabic poetry in Israel is more flourishing than other genres, such as the story or play. However, this poetry is also still deficient in its ideas and form. This is suggested by 'letters to the editor' in the various journals. The results of the Arabic-language literary competition held by the Histadrut [. . .] together with the Ministry of Information also attest to that.[65]

Apparently, Moreh found support for his argument regarding the deficiency of the poetic genre in letters to the editor and a competition held by the

Zionist establishment. The average reader and the settler-colonialist regime are not experts on poetry and cannot attest to its quality. However, these supports are appropriate since they articulate the thematic-emotional equator mechanisms mapped by Moreh within 'Arabic'. When Moreh went on to describe the nature of the deficiency he found in the genre, it turned out that he meant its 'political' aspect – that is, Palestinian poetry that deals with the collectivity of the Palestinians from a national Arab perspective and hence does not abide to excessive reading and writing. The distinction he made, informed by the national-political Palestinian-Arab theme, was not purely thematic, but included relations of belonging and identification.

The socio-linguistic activity of 'literature' was seen by Moreh as articulating the overlap between 'Arabic' and Palestinian-Arab nationality. This overlap re-positioned the Palestinian writer outside the bounded 'Arabic' of Moreh. The poetry was unrelated to the Zionist year zero and negatively related to the Zionist structure; in particular, it did not overlap with the Israeli Arab-ness. These discursive calculations were made by Moreh as part of the classification system with the binary thematic-emotional scale: the 'good' non-political poetry versus the 'bad' political one. In this manner he detailed the inner mechanism of excessive reading and writing, as well as its structure of feelings toward various Palestinian events.

To blaze his own trail among literary texts and mark the internal thematic-emotional boundary, Moreh pointed to two modes of literary work. The first mode deals with individual themes of love and longing for the past, mimicking the form of classical Arabic poetry. The second mode deals with contemporary political events; its form is reminiscent of 'shouts and curses', as he put it.[66] According to Moreh's standards, both these modes failed. The first does not refer to the Israeli year zero. As a result, the way in which it addresses the relation between language and nationality alludes, albeit indirectly, to a nostalgia for an Arab national tradition. As for the second mode, when he sought to draw the second boundary accurately and in a manner that would seem as neutral as possible, he marshalled Palestinian literary criticism. He relied on an article by poet Rashid Hussein on the state of Palestinian poetry:

> The poet Rashid Hussein warned against this phenomenon [of political poetry] in the monthly *Ar-Raid*, in an article titled 'Our Poets', where he said:

> 'I do not deny that poets need to write political poetry, but there is no need for all that they write to be politics. Most of our poets in Israel are currently waiting for some tragedy or political event in order to write a poem about it'. The rush to write political poems seeking to address events so long as the readership takes an interest in them has turned poetry into a shallow, journalistic-like genre. And this is what Rashid Hussein says in the same article: 'Poets may write political poetry, but they must realise that political poetry is not expressed in shouts and curses. They must begin digesting things and express them later in an artistic and moderate form'. A similar opinion has been voiced also by Ms Najwa Qawar-Farah.[67]

The heated discussion of poets, writers and critics of Palestinian literature on Palestinian political poetry and its reference to contemporary tragedies and events was presented here by Moreh from a seemingly literary perspective. His quoting of Hussein is intriguing. He mentioned the distinction between the various genres, particularly that between journalistic writing and poetry. Moreh chose to emphasise that 'rushed' poetry, one that responds to the present, was not only inappropriate but rather superficial and reminiscent of journalism. But what is that present to which Palestinian poetry 'rushes' to respond to? What is the present for which it must wait and which to digest properly before expressing it artistically and 'moderately'? Moreh rushed to answer this question by presenting a split in the temporality of the thematic-emotional boundary.

He described two types of present: that of literary time, which is derived from the structure of the Zionist year zero and the overlap between 'Arabic' and Israeli Arab-ness, and a second literary time, which is derived precisely from the negation of the Zionist year zero and the overlap between 'Arabic' and Palestinian-Arab nationality. At this point, Moreh turned to structuring the first type of present and detailed its contents, forms and inherent possibilities. The second type was not described in detail but presented as a position of general negation. In this classification system, what is not read and written in the excessive mode becomes noise, or 'shouts and curses', simply meaningless and without form. It does not qualify as a literary event.

As suggested, Moreh referred to two literary modes: works on romantic subjects that mimic classical Arabic poetry and those that deal with current affairs in vulgar form. The Israeli year zero transformed the themes of Arabic literature. Moreh elaborated:

> Since 1956, the poets began dealing with subjects that are more relevant to the lives of Arabs in Israel, and above all the problems of peace between Israel and the Arabs, the problem of Arab refugees, the situation of the Arab minority, the Military Government, the development of the Arab village, description of the lives of villages and peasants and love of the land. Even the nationalist awakening in the Arab world and the uprisings in Algeria and Lebanon are echoed in this poetry. This change in the subjects of poetry has come about thanks to the expansion of the educational network throughout the country. The rising standard of living among the peasants and the development of Arab villages, particularly the expansion of the road network, have brought them into closer contact with the well-informed and active Jewish society and with the outside world.[68]

These subjects in Arabic poetry were taken from the local experience of Palestinian poets under Israeli rule. To a significant extent, these poets were bound by the practices of the settler-colonial mechanism and its activities, as well as their responses derived from it. The Military Government and other organs of power set the pace of quotidian life and what could be changed in it.

This matter was further clarified through the relationship Moreh suggested. He identified a cause – the Israeli year zero. The effect is socioeconomic changes that have mediated the literary transformation – the contact of 'peasants' with the 'outside world'. This means that the Palestinian events were read and written via the Zionist institutions and were monopolised by them to be events, which is the typical excessive mode. After establishing the causality, Moreh made another step in shaping the thematic-emotional boundary. He presented a living model of these processes – poets who had undergone processes of pruning and planting in Israeliness and were now sub-agents of such processes:

> However, the most urgent problem for the poets is that of the peace between Israel and the Arab countries. The Arab countries and Israel must forget the bitter past and the quarrels and start a life of peace and tranquillity for the sake of the region and the common people who fell victim to the aspirations

> of the Arab rulers. The young poet Rashid Hussein [. . .] who graduated from high school after the establishment of the state and also began writing poems in the Arabic language, is the leading writer about the subject of peace.[69]

It now turns out that the problem lies not in political poetry itself, as Moreh claimed previously, but in the poet's political orientation. Moreh wrote about what he called 'the problem of peace between Israel and the Arab countries', thereby reformulating and redefining the events and tragedies of that year zero, 1948. His formula suggests that, as part of the purification process, he sought to erase the identity of the Palestinian collective, since he referred to Israel and to Arab countries but not to that collective, which simply did not exist. The planting in Israeliness had borne fruit in the figure of Hussein, the 'Israeli Arab', a new category resulting from the excessive mode, which substituted the erased Palestinian Arab category. Hussein was a kind of rural Arab raw material that had successfully undergone the processes of pruning and planting, and now had an Israeli genealogy – and lo and behold, he desired peace.

This article by Shmuel Moreh delineated the boundaries of Arabic literature in Israel from the point of view of the authorities. Using the model he presented, Moreh explained to his readers how the field of Arabic literature and other 'Israeli Arab' fields were supposed to operate and position themselves in the Zionist settler-colonial structure, after having been read and written according to the Zionist excessive mode. Moreh followed in Eliyahu Khazzoom's footsteps by displacing expropriation and closure from the military, political and socioeconomic spheres to the sphere of language and literature. He expropriated Arabic from its historical cultural space by cutting it off from its pre-1948 roots and, subsequently, also by framing it within the national language, turning it into an arena designed for Israeli Arabs.

Particularly interesting is the synthesis between those two external boundaries, leading to the cleansing moves, and the internal boundary, which produced planting in Israeliness. 'Arabic' was planted in local issues of the Palestinians living in the settler-colonial regime, and collectively, it was adjunct to the settler-colonial structure. This was the internal grammar of the *modus operandi* of the arena of 'Arabic', as Moreh presented it to his readers. In this way, Moreh formalised 'Arabic' as a tool of mass communication in Israel.

He applied to it the three premises of excessive writing and reading: temporal boundary, identity and a structure of feeling. These three premises operate via the pruning of what happened before 1948, the Arab national identity and any political solidarity with the Palestinian national collective. And they plant the zero time of the Palestinian community at the establishment of Israel. The realities of Israel created the community and its identity – and accepting the 'zero time' frame leads to subordination by the Zionist regime.

This raises a fundamental question: What is the position of the 'Israeli Arab' within 'Arabic'? How have the strategies suggested by Moreh operated among the Palestinians who have supposedly adopted them? As the following section will demonstrate, the position of the 'Israeli Arab' within 'Arabic' dialogued with other positions in that arena.

Michel Haddad: The Israeli Arab Critic

One autumn evening in 1951, Michel Haddad sat in Nazareth and entertained the idea of founding a journal on cultural affairs. He wrote that he considered several possible titles for such a journal: *Life*, *Youth*, *The Voice of Youth*, *New Alliance*, *New Society* and *Society*.[70] In order to better feel their sounds, he began to say the names aloud. His little daughter, then lying in bed, heard him and asked, almost asleep: 'Daddy? What's with you, daddy? Who are you talking to?' He turned his gaze on her and saw her rubbing one eye with her hand, staring at him with the other: 'Where is your society, daddy?'

This is how the founder of *Al-Mujtama* (Society) described the journal's birth.[71] The narrative of a sociocultural entrepreneur who raises an idea, puts it into practice and manages to bring about significant sociocultural change is a common one, at least since the beginning of the Arab renaissance during the second decade of the nineteenth century. But what is particularly interesting in the story of the founding of *Al-Mujtama* is the following:

> I asked for a licence to publish *Al-Mujtama* and met Mr Sharet in his visit to Nazareth, to tell him about my idea and ask him to help me expedite the licensing process. He answered, 'If you remain resolute in achieving what

> your heart desires and run into difficulties, call me again'. It was as if the Prime Minister had the gift of prophecy.[72]

If Prime Minister Moshe Sharet was supportive of Haddad and his project, this meant that *Al-Mujtama* was a top Israeli national priority. This anecdote may be interpreted in different ways, but particularly noteworthy are the space and temporality that Haddad established between his daughter and the Prime Minister of Israel. Haddad structured this site as empty of any sociocultural or political actor who could have mediated between his family and the state. It was *Al-Mujtama* that – from the very moment of its inception – was supposed to mediate between the group of Palestinian individuals and the state mechanisms. It was the journal that was supposed to present the state to the Palestinians and vice versa.

This mediation was performed by *Al-Mujtama* in several ways, but mainly through an intensive preoccupation with literature. The journal reconstructed Arabic literature in Israel as a highly distinct mediation system between the Zionist regime and the Palestinians. Positioning it within 'Arabic' – not out of a collective Palestinian claim to own the symbolic capital 'Arabic', but out of an ambition to create the 'Israeli Arab' – *Al-Mujtama* claimed ownership of the mediatory function. Indeed, from its first publication in September 1954, every issue of *Al-Mujtama* included at least one review of Arabic literature in Israel. These reviews dealt mostly with determining criteria for quality literature and particularly quality Israeli Arabic literature, as defined by Moreh.

One example is Haddad's editorial in the second issue, in October 1954: 'The Relationship of Authors to Their Society'.[73] The article opened with a general indicator for evaluating literature: 'The first indicator for evaluating the literature of a given society is its position toward society, its position with regard to society's chief concerns, hopes and sentiments, because literature is the picture which reflects society, which represents its mind, desires and activity'.[74] In this view, literature is a way of expressing and representing society, which focuses on what we may call 'the concerns of the societal mind'. Describing society in psychological terms is a discursive formation that, in this case, marginalises the central status of the collective compared to the individuals comprising it. After presenting this evaluative standard, Haddad moved on to the Palestinian context: 'If we should like to present the literature of our Israeli Arab society, we must ask ourselves what is the attitude of the writers [. . .] towards their society? What is their role and how do they conduct themselves?'[75] In this way, Haddad stated a clear position *vis-à-vis* the other positions in 'Arabic' relevant to the nature of Palestinian society whose literature he sought to measure and evaluate as well as to determine the nature of 'Israeli Arab society'. He listed the roles of Palestinian writers in Israel and underscored the importance of their social involvement:

> We do not see the writers' responsibility as limited to representing the people's concerns and documenting their imaginings, but in learning the conditions of their society and analysing its various phenomena and selecting the most effective way of dealing with them and providing sound advice and guiding the people to the best of ways and the most appropriate of means, and all that in a fascinating and readable style [. . .] We would like our society to have a loyal, sublime and respectable literature, one that takes into account the interests of most members of society, one that is designed to serve the people, direct their thoughts and improve their minds.[76]

The figure of the writer, as painted by Haddad's indicators for evaluating literature, is one of a social reformer motivated by noble ideals of loyalty, respect and altruism. To propose reform, he must return to society, learn it, examine its problems, find the appropriate solutions and how to achieve them and phrase them in an attractive style. The writer does all that when the interests of most of society are topmost in his mind. Haddad wanted this because Israeli Arab society had suffered from having 'drowned in daydreams, and for a long time our minds have been bogged down by the slumber of sloth and the figments of fancy. Therefore, our writers bear the heavy responsibility of an important mission, the responsibility for the culture of society in new, live, clear, candid and loyal terms'.[77]

Haddad's general reference to the past could seemingly be interpreted in several ways, but in the context of 'Arabic', it had a precise and obvious meaning. The clearly orientalist references to daydreaming, sloth and fancy were borrowed from the Zionist discourse, the local agent of the orientalist discourse, which attributed the Arab defeat to a problem of oriental 'mentality'. The call for constructing a new Palestinian-Arab collectivity was a pipe-dream, a figment of the oriental imagination. Here, Haddad differentiated himself from the contrary position – the one calling to return and reposition oneself as the individual owner of the symbolic capital 'Arabic' – that structured the Palestinians as a collective. In fact, Haddad was implementing the temporal boundary of excessive reading and writing by making a clear distinction between the past, before 1948, and the new present realities and their challenges.

The narrative used by Haddad in this editorial consists of the reformative romantic narrative that characterised Arab public discourse since at least the end of World War I. Therefore, the text could be attributed not only to the Palestinian, but also to the Egyptian or Lebanese contemporary context. This narrative style seems to have developed in the issues published after the early days of *Al-Mujtama*. However, this stylistic development did not affect its contents or thematic-emotional structure, beyond highlighting and illustrating the operational logic of the 'Israeli Arab'.

Thus, for example, in his article 'The Culture of Arab Citizens in Israeli Society', Adnan Abu al-Saud listed the main problems of 'Israeli Arab' society, studied and analysed them, and offered 'fascinating' ways of dealing with them.[78] He did all that with the 'interest' of most members of society uppermost in his mind. A kind of secondary title, probably inserted by the editor, reads: 'A realistic presentation and bold treatment of the issue of culture in our society, the culture capable of producing for us good citizens calling for peace and yearning for stability'.[79] This is a kind of prologue for the article that frames the goal that the reader was expected to achieve by reading it.

This discursive linking of the type of culture and the type of Palestinian was the main pillar in the mission of *Al-Mujtama* as mediator between its readers and the Zionist government mechanisms. Its writers applied the third premise of the structure of feeling that accepts and supports the Zionist regime, calling for peace and yearning for stability. Abu al-Saud went on to describe it as follows:

> What is the duty of this culture and that science? And what is their goal? And what kind of citizens must this culture produce? The duty of this culture is to produce a conscious Israeli Arab citizen [. . .] aware of his past, present and future, cognizant of the development of his society, familiar with the disciplines of science and intellect and the new social sciences, profoundly interested in what goes on around him and what it means, contributive of

> human progress on this planet, working for peace and stability and the building of a life worth living [. . .] The Israeli Arab intellectual is the guarantee for a prosperous Arab future in this country.[80]

The author presented the conscious 'Israeli Arab' man of letters as the agent of Western progress and modernisation in the local context. There are several possible dichotomies here, some explicit, some implicit.

The first dichotomy is between the figure of the pre-1948 revolutionary intellectual and his 'Israeli Arab' counterpart. Social activism for the sake of the collective could be the role of different social figures; the ones most prevalent in Palestinian society at the time were the pre-1948 revolutionary freedom fighter and the post-1948 politician.[81] In this article, it was the intellectual and writer who constituted the role models for progressive social activism and assumed the revolutionary role – but the revolution was different by this time. Abu al-Saud's basic assumption was that whoever dealt with culture was necessarily progressive, human and modern.

The second dichotomy is between the existing Zionist order, whose acceptance the intellectual must mediate in order to lead to progress and modernisation, and the old Arab order with its traditionalism and backwardness, mediated by the revolutionary. Moreover, the 'Israeli Arab' would not settle for his role as mediator but pursue it out of a profound acknowledgement of the cultural ideal that would lead to Arab prosperity. While Khazoom and Moreh were presenting the classification system of the excessive reading and writing mode by applying it to different cases of Palestinians, Abu al-Saud in fact presented the conditions for the Palestinian intellectual in order for him to succeed in passing it. Abu al-Saud's essay is the exemplary mediator in a written form.

One of the main phenomena associated with the modern cultural revival in the Arab world was the diglossia of Arabic. The main question was (and still is) which register would be better suited to the modern and progressive period: the literary register, or the colloquial register with its local dialects?[82] Haddad published an editorial about this issue in *Al-Mujtama*. In 'Literary and Spoken Arabic', he discussed the relationship between the two forms:

> Language is a tool of mutual understanding, and the more cultured a person becomes, the more his spoken language improves and approaches the literary

> form. Whoever has acquired an education uses the simple colloquial form when talking to the ignorant, just as one would use simple words when talking to an infant, and as a teacher speaks to his students [. . .] And the more society advances in science and rises up the ladder of civilization, the more its spoken language will improve [. . .] and approach its literary origins.[83]

This position of the editor reproduced sociopolitical hierarchies through linguistic practices. He stated that literary Arabic was the language of modern progress and claimed that the more society progressed, the more it would use the literary register. This view was typical of the Arab nationalist current, which placed pan-Arab nationalism at the centre of its sociopolitical endeavours. This current saw literary Arabic as a cultural infrastructure able to unify the pan-Arab national identity, but also as a lever for progress and modernity.

When Haddad described the relation between literary and colloquial Arabic, however, he took a rather surprising position that seems to contradict his previous arguments:

> I do not see any cause for conflict between the literary and colloquial [Arabic], nor do I see any reason for one to prevail over the other. This is because language develops positively among the people, and will lean in the right direction as soon as it is used [. . .] Language is a means rather than an end. And as for the dialects, I see no way of changing and unifying them, despite the bickering between the writers and linguists in the Cairo Academy.[84]

The call to preserve the dialects unchanged was high on the agenda of the opponents of pan-Arab nationalism. They argued that each region that had its own dialect had a local nationality (*wataniyya*) unrelated to the other members of the Arab World and their collective nationality (*qawmiyya*). Haddad prepared the reader for a position supportive of a particular Egyptian, Lebanese, or Saudi nationality.

The nationality of the 'Israeli Arab' as a nation with its own dialect coexisted among the other national identities in the region:

> The people of Syria and Lebanon will remain with their dialect and lexicon, which differ from the dialect and lexicon of the people of Saudi Arabia and Yemen. And the people of Iraq and Egypt will remain with their dialect and lexicon, which differ from the dialect and lexicon of the Arabs of Israel

> and Jordan. I see no harm in that so long as the language of writing and broadcasting is uniform, and I see no reason for concern with how people from Syria and Iraq, or from Israel and Egypt, will talk to one another with two different dialects, because if they meet – they will have no trouble understanding each other.[85]

Haddad mapped the Arab nationalities in the region and claimed that each had its own dialect and lexicon, which did not, however, prevent mutual understanding so long as the language of writing and of radio and television broadcasts were uniform. Among the numerous peoples in the region, he mentioned the people of Israel, and within it, a sub-group called 'Israeli Arabs'. The 'people of Israel' were equivalent to the people of Egypt, and both would understand the speech of people from Syria or Iraq.

This discursive move navigated between nations, dialects and peoples and naturalised the nexus between dialect, nationality and 'people', one that at the very least must not be taken for granted. This was the preliminary preparation for breaking the signification chain dominant in the Arab national discourse and to replace the Palestinian people with the Israeli people. In this manner, Haddad applied the second premise of identity, by simply absenting the Palestinians and inserting Israel among the Arab nations, with 'Arabic' as a mediator between the nations of the region.

As in most of his articles, Haddad concluded with a statement not necessarily related to literary or colloquial Arabic. After pointing to the duty to allow everyone access to the right language, without determining what the right language was, he argued that 'the countries that care for their peoples and their wellbeing will spare no effort to provide everyone access to science and work, as well as peace and stability'.[86] Here, as in the discursive formation of Abu al-Saud, the linking of language, science, peace and stability was presented in the contexts of the relations between the members of the Israeli 'people' and those of the Arab peoples in the region – that is, the premise of the structure of feeling that accepts and supports Israel.

The December 1955 issue of *Al-Mujtama* was partly devoted to the identity of Israeli Arab literature. The editorial questioned whether an Israeli Arab literary school existed, what its characteristics were, and how writers should conduct themselves both textually and socially. The issue also featured a review of a literary event held that month, addressing the same issues. Titled 'Towards a Literary School', the editorial opened with a description of the journal's endeavours since it had first appeared in print:

> Ever since the first issues of *Al-Mujtama* were published, it took upon itself to promote literary work and act for the establishment of a local literary entity, thereby creating for the Israeli Arab society its own literary school directly affected by local events and able to accompany the country's development and express the wishes and preferences of its population. The sprouts of the literary movement emerged among a select group of young authors, men and women who converged around *Al-Mujtama* and provided it with their works and presented their opinions in the various [literary] events, discussing their views on literary issues and debating the poem and the story and the writer's mission with regard to both.[87]

It seems that the establishment of a local literary school was designed to enable return and repositioning within 'Arabic' in the distinct position of an Israeli localism, as in Egypt and Lebanon – the two dominant national schools in the Arab world of that time.

Al-Mujtama served as the social institutional infrastructure on which the local school was built by 'young' writers – that is, those who matured as writers after the Israeli year zero. The semi-explicit assumption here is that there existed such an 'Israeli Arab' social entity that was distinct from the level of deserving the title of 'nation' and hence required social products that would articulate its historical narrative. In this manner, Haddad redefined the Palestinian community and its literary product according to the two premises, temporal boundary and identity, of the excessive mode of reading and writing.

Later in the article, Haddad reiterated in almost every paragraph the writers' responsibility: looking for peace and stability, as well as knowing their society and its concerns. But Haddad left the style of writing to the writer's creativity. Note that, in emphasising the importance of the young generation of writers, local society and responsibility, Haddad was engraving the classification criteria of the excessive mode onto his readers. Moreover, by designating them as a sub-group of the Israeli nationality, he was including them as part of the 'people of Israel'.[88]

The speakers in the event, however, were highly sceptical of the very existence of a local literary entity, and even regarding the possibility of describing local literary work in such terms:

Haddad: We read local stories in the Israeli Arab newspapers and journals, and accordingly we ask: Do we have an Arab *qissa* in Israel?[89] I'm raising this question for discussion in a different form as well: How well has the local Arab *qissa* succeeded?

Qaisar: We cannot say that there is a local story, but we have those who try to write one or who imitate [story models]. And the reason for the failure of the local *qissa* is that the journals do not encourage beginners, claiming they want to maintain their [high] literary level.

Taha: The Arab *qissa* is making its first steps. But these steps are cause for optimism.

Arfan: I agree with Taha that there is an [Arabic] *qissa*, but how successful is it? I don't see that there is an Arabic *qissa*, but we do have an Egyptian story and a Lebanese story, etc. And the question now is: Do we have a story that is characterised by the qualities of Israeli Arab reality? My answer is: no. Eight years [since 1948] are not enough to give birth to an Arabic *qissa* with Israeli Arab qualities.[90]

Not all participants who rejected the claim that an Israeli Arab *qissa* existed, one with distinct 'Israeli Arab' qualities, did so for the same reason. Some argued that the literary field did not enable beginners to publish their work. Others claimed that, like Israeli Arab culture in general, Israeli Arab literature was only in its infancy. Still, all rejected being read and written solely by the way in which the Israeli system would define them. They did not deny the influence but read and wrote it differently. These claims displeased Haddad, who probably expected a more optimistic note.

Therefore, in reporting on the event, he summarised the participants' words in a positive tone by turning to the concrete level of settler-colonial reality, one he probably assumed to be undeniable:

> My colleagues have agreed that there is a *qissa* that is not characterised by distinct Israeli Arab qualities, despite some successful attempts. We move directly to the second point: Since we live in an Israeli society that is full of industrial and agricultural activity and progressive social life, does this new life have an impact on our story?[91]

Here Haddad took up the claim of some of the participants that the writers' environment affected their work and rephrased it: the Palestinians were affected by 'progressive' Israeli society. This move, Haddad seems to have believed, would highlight the uniqueness of the 'Arab Israeli' story by underscoring the special context in which it was forged – that is, the impact of general Israeli society on Arab Israeli society. As could be expected, most attendants agreed that there was significant economic and sociocultural influence on the Palestinians living in Israeli society, leading Haddad to conclude that the 'Arab' *qissa* was a product of Israeli Arab society.

At this point, Haddad went on to discuss the influence of Arab culture on Israeli Arab literature. Haddad argued that Arab literature in Israel was affected by factors beyond Israeli society. He said: 'We have different relations with general Arab culture. How does this culture affect our stories?'[92] When presenting the hierarchy of influence, Haddad placed local Arab literature within the framework of Israeli society, and as such it was subject to external influences, such as that of Arab culture. Some of the discussants argued that they were highly influenced by general Arab culture, as they were part of it. Others argued that there existed no such influence, since the contact with it had been cut off since 1948. Haddad, for one, made an intriguing concluding move by arguing that the influence of general Arab culture on the Arabs in Israel was due to its being a sociocultural and religious tradition to which they had been used in the past. He further concluded that the radio broadcasts and smuggled books were also influential.[93] By relegating Arab culture to past traditions, he cut it off from the present of Palestinians in Israel, subordinating them to the present of Israeli society.

In the years it was active, from 1954 to 1959, *Al-Mujtama* functioned as one of the main forces in the arena of 'Arabic'. The articles it published and the range of activities that Haddad initiated around it – such as the Society of Arabic Poets in Israel, the prose and poetry events, and his attempt to establish a publishing house – blazed a trail of return and repositioning in the position of 'the Israeli Arab' within 'Arabic'. Together, these activities and institutions were part of the infrastructure upon which the set of activities of reading and writing were actualised. In that, he used literature and literary criticism, as did the orientalists, to inculcate the three premises of the excessive mode of reading and writing. He marked the external boundaries of space and temporality onto Palestinian readers and derived an internal thematic-emotional boundary. According to the journal's position – that of the 'Israeli Arab' – Israeli Arab literature began with the Israeli year zero, purified of the effects of general Arab literature and planted in local content as result of the Palestinians' concrete subordination to Zionist settler-colonial rule.

The external boundaries here are similar to those constructed by the orientalists. The difference between the positions seems to lie in the internal thematic-emotional boundary, the classification of writers and literature according to the binary of 'good'/'bad' political orientations. The thematic-emotional structure in the position of the 'Israeli Arab', which is a structural variation on minimal loyalty to the State of Israel, has been constituted in several parallel discursive and institutional moves.

According to the narrative of *Al-Mujtama*, there was no mediator between the Palestinian individual and the authorities, but the journal itself was designed to serve as one. Moreover, the figure of the writer and his role as an agent of change replaced the previous social models, that of the freedom fighter and politician. The settler-colonial regime and its orientalist discourse, on the other hand, assumed that, given the nature of culture and intellect, the writers were compliant, gentle and sensitive and, therefore, focused on the writer's internal life, not on his being an agent of change. The thematic-emotional boundary was drawn based on the assumption that progress and modernity depended on the Zionist rule. Yet, according to Haddad, the author who sought to improve his society must be familiar with its problems and act to promote peace and political stability.

The discourse structured by Haddad relies directly on the values of the patriarchal middle class in Arab societies at the time.[94] In order to provide further depth to his position, it is characterised by over-emphasis on that class's patriarchal values, such as respect, loyalty and sublime puritan emotions, exposing the depth of the contradictions in the structure of this position. It requires deconstruction, expropriation and closure of anything that could represent a Palestinian collective independent of the settler-colonial regime, including issues such as Islamic Arab culture and the condition of Palestinian society and its literature before the 1948 war.

This difference between the orientalists and Haddad and his group seems to lay in a deeper set of positions. The former were aiming at building a classification system and teaching their colleagues how to apply it. In contrast, the latter were busy reorganising themselves in such a way that they would succeed in passing it. Haddad and his group applied excessive reading and writing compulsively in order to reclaim a certain 'Arabic' and utilise it in order to be part of the Zionist collective.

The three positions we have seen so far, represented by Emile Tuma, Shmuel Moreh and Michel Haddad, were the central forces constituting the arena of 'Arabic'. Their supporters considered themselves to be players bound by the duty to structure and shape this arena. Now that we have become familiar with the *modi operandi* of each position within 'Arabic', as well as the historical subjects behind them, we can turn to examine the relations between the positions to obtain an overview of the moment of the constitution of 'Arabic'. Outlining the formation of 'Arabic' on the empirical level will allow us to examine the arena's deep structure, placing historical events in relation to the reading and writing patterns of compulsiveness and excessiveness.

'Arabic': A Portrait

Since its very beginning, the Zionist movement was concerned with Arab culture and the Arabic language, and with using their knowledge as an instrument in the struggle for control in Mandatory Palestine. With the establishment of the State of Israel, however, it also began producing an Arab culture – and an Arabic – to serve the mechanisms of the new settler-colonial regime.[95] Arabic was selected as the model for structuring culture, as accepted not only in the Arab tradition, but also in the spirit of the ideology and institutional format of the nation-state, which was the default of every collective at the time.

In the first decade after 1948, the production of language and culture focused on education and mass media, particularly newspapers and journals and, to a lesser extent, radio broadcasts. The education system was dominated and closely monitored by the state's military, intelligence services, political and bureaucratic mechanisms. These mechanisms' control over the printed media focused on political issues. Literature and literary criticism, however, remained a textual space relatively free of the state's iron hand, one where sociopolitical forces operated beside state mechanisms, not under them only.

In this chapter, I have argued that part of the processes of designing 'Arabic' occurred in this institutional, textual arena of literature and its criticism. Undoubtedly, these textual and institutional literay domains were directly concerned with the sociopolitical quotidian, to a degree and in a manner different from what we usually find in non-settler-colonial or Western or post-colonial independence contexts. In order to deal with the production of Arabic, the relevant mechanisms of government had to develop material means of production, on the level of infrastructures and institutes, as well as symbolic means of production on the level of reading/writing and discursive formations.

The previous sections discussed the modes of reading/writing and the discursive formation competing for the definition and production of 'Arabic'. The constitution of 'Arabic' began with the structural changes that occurred with the establishment of the Israeli settler-colonial state. They required a redefinition of the regime's attitude to its Palestinian subjects. The structure of the arena of 'Arabic' at that time was vague, ambivalent and open, and it had to be defined and delineated. However, although the mechanisms of government were able to determine the structural boundaries of Arabic, they could not fully dictate the chain of events that constituted the collective subjectivity of the Palestinians in this arena.

The above review of local Palestinian literature and literary criticism has presented three main positions active within 'Arabic'. The first is Emile Tuma's, demanding the construction of the Palestinian collective in Israel by claiming ownership of the symbolic capital of 'Arabic'. This was an attempt to help the collective regain its ability to lose and, hence, used the compulsive mode of reading and writing. The second position is that of the establishment, represented in different ways by Michael Assaf, Eliyahu Khazzoom and Shmuel Moreh, who all sought to restructure the Palestinians as 'Israeli Arabs'. To do so, they created institutional material and symbolic means of production that structured the 'Israeli Arab' out of discursively resetting the Palestinians' historical existence to zero, with the establishment of the State of Israel. Purifying them of their Palestinian-ness and Arab-ness on the cultural and emotional level, they planted them in the space and temporality of Israeli locality. In this way, they strengthened the premises of the excessive mode of reading and writing. The third position is that of Palestinians who accepted the new, post-*Nakba* situation, with some even identifying with the new Zionist rule and starting to produce the 'Israeli Arab'. They acted as mediators between the sovereign's mechanisms and the Palestinians under their control, if not as agents of the former among the latter.[96] This group presents the criteria that Palestinians should adopt in order to succeed as 'Israeli Arabs' and, hence, accept the dictates of the excessive mode of reading and writing.

The theme arising from these three positions is that of symbolic return to the lost collective of Palestinians, as well as the attitudes and feelings regarding the group of Palestinians under Israeli rule. Each position charts a particular path of return and repositioning that was supposed to structure the group in a certain way. It may be argued that the organising object of 'Arabic' is the group of Palestinians under Israeli rule and the relations of this object to itself, to the Zionist regime and to the Arab world. Thus, 'Arabic' is necessarily an attempt to stitch together part of the irresolvable contradictions in the Israeli settler-colonial state.

The logic of the settler-colonial state's political economy, in respect to the investment in stabilising control, required the structural closure of the inherently unstable relations between the state and the Palestinians under its control. In terms of the political economy of the Palestinian group, however, a social group whose material institutional infrastructure had been destroyed, the structural closure within the settler-colonial rule was not necessarily relevant. In their case, the political economy was one of losing the ability to lose. This led to repetitive recharging – that is, the set of activities of reading and writing that invest new meanings in 'Arabic' in order to re-own it as a cultural property of the Palestinians. Whereas the government mechanisms developed 'Arabic' as a structural stitch, the Palestinians, in both of their positions reviewed above, created a chain of events charging cultural objects within the government structure of 'Arabic'.

This Palestinian trap of charging objects within the space and temporality enabled by the settler-colonial regime is characteristic of most fields of colonial and settler-colonial contradictions in the modern era.[97] What is unique about the context under discussion is the collective desire created in the process and the potential sites of its satisfaction. At this point in the development of the settler-colonial field of contradiction, characterised as it was by total control of the Zionist regime over expropriation and closure on the spatial and temporal material levels, the Palestinian's desire to possess was displaced to a symbolic means of production that could be lost. The symbolic object accessible to the group of Palestinians was themselves as a group, through their culture's mediation. Arabic and its products represented Arab culture. They symbolised it and could be recharged; their materiality enabled a chain of repetitive events. Desire's homing in on Arabic and its products was a structural move not only in the settler-colonial context, but also a historical move involving the characteristics of Islamic-Arab culture. Clearly, these processes made that group of remaining Palestinians unique compared to other groups in Palestinian society, not to mention other settler-colonial contexts.[98]

Unlike other products of Arabic, the field of Palestinian literature has generative potential due to its main characteristic of re-chargeablity via the acts of renewed readings. Within the political economy of the desire to reclaim the ability to lose, the literary event becomes the preferable object of desire for the group of Palestinians in Israel. It is structured as sublimation of a lost collectivity, one that was almost impossible to restore under post-1948 conditions. The act of Palestinian literary criticism may therefore be understood as a path-breaking event towards the realisation of desire in its object. Since the path determines the nature of that realisation and the form of the object, literary criticism attracted both state and Palestinian forces.

The difference between the two Palestinian sub-groups presented above lies in the relation of the Palestinian collective group to the settler-colonial regime, not in the deep structure of the political-economic logic of the desire to possess the ability to lose. Both have displaced the irresolvable contradictions of the settler-colonial regime into their cultural sphere, focusing on Arabic and its products and homing in on the field of literature within 'Arabic' in order to recharge that arena and produce literary events. In the political economy of settler-colonial desire, such events are a displaced representation of the absent collectivity. In the normative model of the nation-state, events of this type should have been derived from the socioeconomic regime and its history; in a certain context, they may have led to a change in the general structure. These normative model dynamics, however, operated differently in the context of the Zionist regime and its interactions with the group of Palestinians under its rule.

I argue that, in the post-1948 regime, there was a structural division of labour, splitting the construction of 'Arabic': whereas the regime operated on the structural level, the group of Palestinians operated on the event level. The monopoly of the former on expropriation and closure created structural, institutional obstacles. These obstacles prevented the Palestinian literary event – because it was a displaced representation of the Palestinian collectivity – from being articulated as a structural change at the regime level. This, in turn, led to the development of Zionist excessive writing with reference to this group of Palestinians. The Palestinian event was deconstructed and rewritten as a Zionist event, starting from imposing the Israeli year zero, the cleansing of its Islamic-Arab history and its charging with a local Zionist spatiality and temporality, built on a thematic-emotional boundary of minimal loyalty to the State of Israel.

These eradicative practices were not limited to a certain social sphere and were not one singular practice, but rather recurring practices operating in that structurally-displaced representation that I call 'Arabic'. Compulsive Palestinian reading, which we have seen here in the form of literary events, was structurally unavoidable because it was a settler-colonial entrapment and because it reproduced the structure due to the obstacles of excessive writing. Compulsive Palestinian reading was performed through the repetitive generation of literary events as the preferable object of the desire to claim the ability to lose. In other words, the generative materiality of the literary event in the modern era became bound up, in that specific settler-colonial context, with the compulsive reading of the colonised native Palestinian. Since this compulsiveness was subordinate to excessive writing, which articulated the Zionist possession, the literary event that was supposed to produce aesthetic structural solutions *à la* Lucien Goldmann was blocked due to having been deconstructed and rewritten over and over again according to the Zionist logic. Thus, 'Arabic' was constructed as a split between the excessiveness and the chain of compulsive events. This split was fuelled by the very fact that it constituted a representative displacement of the irresolvable field of contradictions.

Conclusion

This chapter has addressed the moment of the constitution of 'Arabic' by Israeli mechanisms of settler-colonial governing. These mechanisms structured it as a site designed to control the interactions between the group of Palestinians who remained and the new regime which was established in Palestine after 1948. I have focused on the processes of structuring and designing that site in the first decade after the war and saw three different forces operating in this period, clashing and merging with one another, and sometimes even negating 'Arabic': 1) The orientalist experts who acted as the representatives of the government and its mechanisms. 2) The sub-group of Palestinians who identified with the Israeli Communist Party, as represented by Emil Tuma's corpus, in which he claimed collective Palestinian ownership of 'Arabic'. 3) The sub-group of Palestinians that structured the model for 'Arabic', articulating an 'Israeli Arab-ness'. Through the use of Arabic and its products, all three forces tried to structure a model for the relationship between the regime and its Palestinian subjects.

I have argued that, for structural reasons related to the Zionist settler-colonial regime and for historical reasons having to do with Islamic Arab culture, the field of Palestinian literature acted as a magnet for the irresolvable contradictions of both the regime and the Palestinian groups. Critical essays from that era on Palestinian literature shed light on the reading/writing mechanisms and the discursive formations used by those forces in their struggles to shape 'Arabic', as part of organising the relations between the group of Palestinians in Israel and its new regime. The three forces tried to dictate the nature of 'Arabic' through the literary criticism published in the community of Palestinian readership.

The orientalist experts marked two external boundaries for 'Arabic': one timed the inception of 'Arabic' to the Israeli year zero, and the other determined the national identity of its inhabitants – Arabs, to the exclusion of Arabic-speaking Jews brought up in the Islamic Arab culture. This boundary tied the Gordian knot of national ideology: the language-nationality nexus. From these external boundaries, an internal thematic-emotional boundary of loyalty to the State of Israel was derived. The Palestinians who identified with the Communist Party accepted 'Arabic' as articulating the field of contradictions of the settler-colonial regime, and they claimed collective ownership of 'Arabic' in order to overcome the loss of the ability to lose. The second Palestinian sub-group also accepted 'Arabic', but structured it as 'Israeli Arabic' – that is, an Arabic owned exclusively by the Israeli regime.

The group of Palestinians subject to Israeli rule consists of the community that all three forces wanted to reshape. This made it an object to be controlled. Relations to it constitute the infrastructure on which 'Arabic' had been built. The organising deep structure of 'Arabic' has been shared by the two Palestinian sub-groups, as they have accepted its space and temporality and the object structured through them.

The maintenance of 'Arabic' as an articulation of part of the field of contradictions of the regime over a prolonged period is a task that cannot be taken for granted. In the following chapter, I will argue that, although the fundamental structural coordinates of 'Arabic' were established already in the first decade after 1948, various socioeconomic and political processes led to the development of the Palestinian chain of events in new directions. Following the 1967 war, the type of Palestinian literary event within the Israeli regime became transformed.

One of the most important developments was the acquisition of symbolic capital in the form of academic studies in Israel by Palestinians with Israeli citizenship. For two decades, this group formed a kind of middle class that had an interest in keeping stability in the relationship between the regime and the group of Palestinians under its sovereignty. As part of the constitution of stability and as an expression of the materiality of this class, various sociocultural spheres became academised. These processes transformed the landscape of the literary event within 'Arabic'. While previously it had been the purview of intellectual journalists and politicians, it was now an academic territory. At the same time, critical essays on Palestinian literature, once published mostly in the press, were now published mainly in the form of academic studies, although this was still 'Israeli' academic research. The following chapter will examine the chain of literary events that underlies Israeli academisation.

Notes

1. The extensive research literature on the events of 1948 and the years that followed usually adopts the political-historical approach, with little reference

to the sociocultural history of those pivotal years. See, for example, Mustafa Kabha (ed.), *Al-'Aqaliyya al-Filasṭīniyya fī Isrā'īl fī ẓill al-ḥukm al-ʿaskarī wa-irthuhu* [The Palestinian Minority in Israel in the Shadow of the Military Government and its Legacy] (Haifa: Mada al-Carmel, 2014). For a comparative perspective on how other Palestinian groups' literary production coped with the *Nakba*, see Joseph Farag, *Politics and Palestinian Literature in Exile: Gender, Aesthetics, and Resistance in the Short Story* (London: I. B. Tauris, 2017), 18–74.

2. On isolating the Palestinians from the rest of their society and other Arab countries, see Maha Nassar, *Brothers Apart: Palestinians Citizens of Israel and the Arab World* (Palo Alto: Stanford University Press), 49–52.
3. On 21 October 1948, Israel officially established the Military Government to administer the Palestinian population under its rule. Relying on the 1945 British Defense (Emergency) Regulations, this military body was in charge of every aspect of the Palestinians' life, including food, education, employment, movement and housing. It was terminated on 9 November 1966, but its regulations continued to be enforced by various police and para-military organs for several more years. See Hillel Cohen, *The Good Arabs: The Israeli Security Agencies and the Israeli Arabs, 1948–1967* (Berkeley: University of California Press, 2010), 39–64.
4. See Saʿdi, *Thorough Surveillance.*
5. For a comparative perspective on how other Palestinian groups' literary production coped with the *Nakba*, see Jabra I. Jabra, 'The Palestinian Exile as Writer', *Journal of Palestine Studies* 8, no. 2 (Winter 1979), 77–87.
6. On processes of losing an object of desire and recharging an alternative one, see Sigmund Freud, 'Mourning and Melancholia', in *The Standard Edition of the Complete Psychological Works of Sigmund Freud*, vol. 14, transl. J. Strachey (London: The Hogarth Press and the Institute of Psychoanalysis, 1955), 237–58.
7. See the writings of one of the prominent promoters of the idea of pan-Arab national revival, for example: Sattiʿ Al-Huṣri, *Fī l-lugha wa-l-adab wa-ʿalāqathum bi-l-qawmiyya* [On Language and Literature and their Relation to Nationalism] (Beirut: Dar Al-Taliah, 1966).
8. For more on the historical development of Arabic and its status in Islamic Arab culture, see, for example, Ramzi Baalbaki (ed.), *Al-Lugha wa-l-huwiyya fī l-waṭan al-ʿArabī: Ishkāliyyāt Tā'rīkhiyya wa-thaqāfiyya wa-siyāsiyya* [Language and Identity in the Arab Homeland: Historical, Cultural and Political Issues] (Doha: Arab Center for Research and Policy Studies, 2013).
9. See, for example, Abu Hanna, *Ṭalā'iʿ al-nahḍa.*
10. For a detailed discussion of these Palestinian intellectuals and writers' activities before 1948, see Nassar, *Brothers Apart*, 15–45.

11. See, for example, Mendel, *The Creation of Israeli Arabic.*
12. On the Arab education system, see, for example, Ismael Abu-Saad, 'Palestinian Education in Israel: The Legacy of the Military Government', *Holy Land Studies* 5, no. 1 (2006), 21–56. On teacher training colleges, see Ayman Agbaria (ed.), *Hakhsharat Morim baḤevrah haFalasṭinit biIsrael: Praḳṭiḳot Mosadiyot uMediniyut Ḥinukhit* [Teacher Training in the Palestinian Society in Israel: Institutional Practices and Educational Policy] (Tel Aviv: Resling, 2013). On newspapers and journals, see Mustafa Kabha, 'Al-Ṣaḥāfa al-'Arabiyya fī ẓill al-ḥukm al-ʿaskari, 1948–1966' [The Arab Press under the Military Government, 1948–1966], in *Al-'Aqaliyya al-Filasṭīniyya fī Isrā'īl fī ẓill al-ḥukm al-'askarī wa-irthuhu* [The Palestinian Minority in Israel in the Shadow of the Military Government and its Legacy], ed. Mustafa Kabha (Haifa: Mada al-Carmel, 2014), 123–70.
13. For comparison with North Africa under the French rule, especially the case of Tunisia, see Mohamed-Salah Omri, 'History, Literature, and Settler Colonialism in North Africa', *Modern Language Quarterly* 66, no. 3 (September 2005), 273–98.
14. As seen in the introduction, the terms 'sign' and 'arena' are the products of analyses by Voloshinov, Williams and Bourdieu.
15. On the structure of feeling, see Williams, *Marxism*, 128–35; on orientalist experts, see Eyal, *Hasarat*, 70–117.
16. For a discussion of the role of literature in Third World contexts, see Aijaz Ahmad, 'Jameson's Rhetoric of Otherness and the "National Allegory",' *Social Text* 17 (Autumn 1987), 3–25; Fredric Jameson, 'Third World Literature in the Era of Multinational Capitalism', *Social Text* 15 (Autumn 1986), 65–88.
17. On the Israel Communist Party, see Habib Dunia Nahas, *The Israeli Communist Party* (London: Croom Helm, 1976); Asʿad Ghanem, *The Palestinian-Arab Minority in Israel, 1948–2000* (New York: State University of New York Press, 2001); Musa Budeiri, *The Palestine Communist Party 1919–1948: Arabs and Jews in the Struggle for Internationalism* (Chicago: Haymarket Books, 2010).
18. On the institutional, material infrastructure of the Israeli Communist Party in the Palestinian literary context, see Abu Saleh, *Al-Ḥaraka al-'adabiyya.*
19. Emile Tuma's biography has never been written as such, but his writings have been collected and published by the Emile Tuma Institute for Palestinian and Israeli Studies in Haifa. See Emile Tuma, *Al-A'māl al-kāmila* [Collected Writings], 5 vols (Haifa: Emile Tuma Institute of Social and Political Studies, 1995–97). For partial presentation of Emil Tuma's intellectual and political biography in the context of the Israeli Communist Party, see Musa Budeiri, 'Iqrār bi-l-dhanb: 'Īmīl Tūma wa-l-taqsīm alladhī lam yaḥduth' [Acknowledging Guilt: Emil Tuma and the Division That Did Not Happen], *Bidayyat*, 18–19 (2017–18), 201–25.

20. For more on the group of orientalist experts and their writings in the Arabic press in Israel, see Mustafa Kabha and Dan Caspi, 'MiYerushalayim haḲedoshah ʿad haMaʿayan: Megamot baʿItonut haʿAravit beIsrael' [From Jerusalem to the HaMaayan: Trends in the Arabic Press in Israel], *Panim* 16 (2001), 44–55.
21. Most of the literature on this sub-group of Palestinians addresses their political conduct *in relation to* the authorities, but few studies have attempted to look into its motives. Particularly noteworthy in this context is Azmi Bishara's argument that this position is not limited to a certain group within 'Arabic'. It is a position among the Palestinians in Israel of the twenty-first century. See Azmi Bishara, 'Al-'Arabī al-Isrā'īlī: Al-Khiṭāb al-siyāsī al-mabtūr' [The Israeli Arab: The Disjointed Political Discourse], *Majallat al-Dirasat al-Filastiniyya* 24 (1995), 26–54.
22. This pattern in which literature takes the role of expressing and treating the oppressed of the colonial regimes is also salient in Ngugi w Thiong'o's discussion of African literatures. See Thiong'o, *Decolonising the Mind*, 4–33.
23. For an initial mapping of these forces, see Sarah Ozacky-Lazar, 'Hitgabshut Yaḥase haGomlin ben Yehudim ṿe'Aravim beMedinat Israel: ha'Aśor haRishon, 1948–1958' [The Crystallisation of Mutual Relations between Jews and Arabs in the State of Israel: The First Decade, 1948–1958] (PhD diss., Haifa University, 1996), 124–45.
24. In his last study, *Thorough Surveillance*, Ahmad Saʿdi has analysed archival documents of committees charged with managing, supervising and controlling the Palestinians at that time.
25. Michael Assaf (Osofsky) (1896–1984; immigrated to Palestine from Poland in 1920) was a journalist and orientalist, co-founder and co-editor of *Ḥaqīqat al-Amr*, chief editor of *Al-Yawm* and editor of the Arabic section of the leading Hebrew daily newspaper *Davar*. See Kabha and Caspi, 'MiYerushalayim'.
26. The requirement of minimal loyalty, in contrast to full loyalty, is due mainly to the Zionist binary classification system: Jews vs Non-Jews. While the former should have full loyalty, the latter could not, hence the 'minimal' loyalty. See Michael Assaf, 'Hishtalvut haʿAravim beIsrael' [The Integration of Arabs in Israel], *HaMizraḥ HaḤadash* 1 (1949), 2.
27. Assaf, 'Hishtalvut', 6.
28. Assaf, 'Hishtalvut', 6.
29. Assaf, 'Hishtalvut', 6.
30. *Al-Yawm*, 24 May 1950. See Kabha, 'Al-Ṣaḥāfa al-'Arabiyya', 133.
31. Comparing the Palestinian case with Egypt and India, in this regard, highlights the distinctive settler-colonial dynamics in contrast to the colonial one. See

Ahmed, *Women and Gender in Islam*, 144–68; Cohen, *Colonialism and its Forms of Knowledge*, 16–56.

32. On the history of Arabic and its relationship to Hebrew under the Israeli regime, see Suleiman, *War of Words*, 137–217.
33. For a detailed historical account of these Palestinian intellectuals, see Nassar, *Brothers Apart*, 15–77.
34. On *Al-Jadid* and its positioning in the literary field, see Nabih Al-Qasim, *Al-Ḥaraka al-Shi'riyya al-Filasṭīniyya fī bilādinā min khilāl majallat Al-Jadīd, 1953–1985* [Palestinian Poetry in Our Country through *Al-Jadid*, 1953–1985] (Kufr Qaraʿ, Israel: Dar al-Huda, 2003).
35. On Emile Tuma's biography, see Nassar, *Brothers Apart*, 38. For his literary criticism, see Ahmad Sa'di (ed.), *Nadwa ḥawl kitāb al-duktūr Imīl Tūma 'Mukhtārāt fī l-naqd al-adabī'* [A Workshop on Dr Emil Tuma's Book 'Selected Essays in Literary Criticism'] (Haifa: Emil Tuma Institute for Social and Political Research, 1993).
36. Emile Tuma, *Mukhtārāt fī al-naqd al-adabī* [Selected Writings in Literary Criticism] (Haifa: Emile Tuma Institute of Social and Political Studies, 1993), 14.
37. Tuma, *Mukhtārāt*, 15.
38. On the *unheimlich* or *uncanny*, see Sigmund Freud, 'The Uncanny', in *The Standard Edition of the Complete Psychological Works of Sigmund Freud*, vol. 17, transl. J. Strachey (London: The Hogarth Press and the Institute of Psychoanalysis, 1958), 217–52. On this Freudian conceptualisation in literature, see David Ellison, *Ethics and Aesthetics in European Modernist Literature: From the Sublime to the Uncanny* (Cambridge: Cambridge University Press, 2001). On the use of this term in Palestinian literary criticism, see Ismail Nashef, 'Mawt al-Naṣṣ' [The Death of the Text], *Majallat al-Dirasat al-Falastiniyya* 96 (Autumn 2013), 96–117.
39. The two articles were published in a collection of essays: Tuma, *Mukhtārāt*, 30–35. For more on Qawar-Farah's writing, see Mahmud Ghanayim, *Al-Madār al-ṣa'b: Riḥlat al-qiṣṣa al-Filasṭīniyya fī Isrā'īl* [The Difficult Path: The Journey of the Palestinian Story in Israel] (Haifa: Haifa University, 1995), 61–105.
40. Najwa Qawar-Farah, *'Abirū sabīl* [Passers-By] (Beirut: Dar al-Rihani, 1956).
41. Tuma, *Mukhtārāt*, 30.
42. Tuma, *Mukhtārāt*, 30.
43. Tuma, *Mukhtārāt*, 30.
44. Tuma, *Mukhtārāt*, 31.
45. Tuma, *Mukhtārāt*, 31.
46. Tuma, *Mukhtārāt*, 31.

47. Najwa Qawar-Farah, *Durūb wa-maṣābīḥ* [Lanes and Lanterns] (Nazareth: Al-Hakim, 1956).
48. Tuma, *Mukhtārāt*, 33.
49. Tuma, *Mukhtārāt*, 33.
50. Tuma, *Mukhtārāt*, 34.
51. Tuma, *Mukhtārāt*, 35.
52. Michel Haddad (ed.), *Alwān min shi'r al-'Arabiyya fī Isrā'īl* [Colours of Arabic Poetry in Israel] (Nazareth: Al-Hakim, 1955); Jamal Qawar, *Salmā: Majmū'at aqāṣīṣ shi'riyya* [Salma, a Collection of Poetic Stories] (Nazareth: Al-Hakim, 1956).
53. Eliyahu Khazzoom, 'Shirah 'Aravit BiIsrael' [Arabic Poetry in Israel], *HaMizraḥ HaḤadash* 7, no. 3 (1956), 232.
54. Khazzoom, 'Shirah 'Aravit', 232.
55. On the poets of the *Mahjar* / diaspora, see Ihsan 'Abbas and Mohamad Yousuf Nijim, *Al-Shi'r al-'Arabī fī l-mahjar* [Arabic Poetry in the Diaspora] (Beirut: Dar Sadir, 1967).
56. Khazzoom, 'Shirah 'Aravit', 232.
57. Khazzoom, 'Shirah 'Aravit', 232.
58. Khazzoom is referring to the Lebanese-American poet Jubran Khalil Jubran, author of *The Prophet*.
59. Khazzoom, 'Shirah 'Aravit', 232.
60. Shmuel Moreh, 'HaSifrut baŚafah ha'Aravit beMedinat Israel' [Arabic Literature in the State of Israel], *HaMizraḥ HaḤadash* 9, no. 1–2 (1958), 26–39.
61. Moreh, 'HaSifrut', 26.
62. Moreh, 'HaSifrut', 26.
63. Moreh, 'HaSifrut', 27.
64. Moreh, 'HaSifrut', 27.
65. Moreh, 'HaSifrut', 33.
66. Moreh, 'HaSifrut', 33.
67. Moreh, 'HaSifrut', 33.
68. Moreh, 'HaSifrut', 33.
69. Moreh, 'HaSifrut', 34.
70. Michel Haddad, 'Ḥikāyat al-Mujtama'' [The Story of Society], *Al-Mujtama'* 3 (November 1954), 1.
71. On the journal's status in the contemporary local press, see Mahmoud Abassi, *Taṭawwur al-riwāya wa-l-qiṣṣa al-qaṣīra fī l-adab al-'Arabī fī Isrā'īl* [The Development of the Novel and the Short Story in Arabic Literature in Israel] (Haifa: Kull Shay', 1998), 36–47.

72. Haddad, 'Ḥikāyāt al-mujtama'', 1.
73. Michel Haddad, "Alāqat al-udabā' bi-Mujtamaʿlhim' [The Relationship of Authors to their Society], *Al-Mujtamaʿ* 2 (October 1954), 1–3.
74. Haddad, 'Alāqat al-udabā'', 1.
75. Haddad, 'Alāqat al-udabā'', 1.
76. Haddad, 'Alāqat al-udabā'', 1.
77. Haddad, 'Alāqat al-udabā'', 3.
78. 'Adnān Abu al-Sa'ūd, 'Thaqāfat al-Muwāṭinīn al-'Arab fī l-mujtama' al-Isrā'īlī' [The Culture of Arab Citizens in Israeli Society], *Al-Mujtamaʿ* 2, no. 1 (January 1955), 6–10.
79. Abu al-Sa'ūd, 'Thaqāfat al-muwāṭinīn', 6.
80. Abu al-Sa'ūd, 'Thaqāfat al-muwāṭinīn', 6–7.
81. On these cultural figures in Palestinian literature, see Shimon Ballas, *HaSifrut ha'Aravit beTsel haMilḥamah* [Arabic Literature under the Shadow of War] (Tel Aviv: Am Oved, 1978).
82. On the diglossia of Arabic, the social structure and their relationship, see Haeri, 'Form and Ideology'.
83. Michel Haddad, 'Al-Fuṣḥā wa-l-ʿāmiyya' [Literary and Spoken Arabic], *Al-Mujtamaʿ* 2, no. 9 (September 1955), 3.
84. Haddad, 'Al-Fuṣḥā wa-l-ʿāmiyya', 3.
85. Haddad, 'Al-Fuṣḥā wa-l-ʿāmiyya', 3–4.
86. Haddad, 'Al-Fuṣḥā wa-l-ʿāmiyya', 4.
87. Michel Haddad, 'Naḥwa madrasa 'adabiyya' [Towards a Literary School], *Al-Mujtamaʿ* 2, no. 12 (December 1955), 3.
88. Michel Haddad, 'Ḥawla l-qiṣṣa' [On the Story], *Al-Mujtamaʿ* 2, no. 12 (December 1955), 9–11.
89. Haddad and the participants in the event used the term *qiṣṣa* without specifying it as a 'short story' or a 'novel'. It seems that they meant both.
90. Haddad, 'Ḥawla l-qiṣṣa', 8–9.
91. Haddad, 'Ḥawla l-qiṣṣa', 9.
92. Haddad, 'Ḥawla l-qiṣṣa', 10.
93. Haddad, 'Ḥawla l-qiṣṣa', 9.
94. On the values of this class and their positioning in modern Arab society, see Hisham Sharabi, *Neopatriachy: A Theory of Distorted Change in Arab Society* (Oxford: Oxford University Press, 1993).
95. For similar settler-colonial linguistic and ideological practices in the Native American context in the USA, see J. Bayley Marquez and Juliet Rose Kunkel,

'The Domestication Genocide of Settler-Colonial Language Ideologies', *American Quarterly* 73, no. 3 (2021), 461–82, https://doi.org/10.1353/aq.2021.0046

96. On the cultural identification processes of the occupied with the occupier, see Frantz Fanon, *Black Skin, White Masks*, transl. Charles Lam Markmann (New York: Pluto, [1952] 1991). In *The Location of Culture*, Homi Bhabha further elaborates on this matter and proposes a boundary-transgressing conceptualisation of the two identities. In the case of the 'Israeli Arab', it may be argued that, while the identity is hybrid, structurally it is liminal. Its fluid edges are quite narrow, since it is built on a void resulting from the loss and the erasure and purification that followed it.
97. Beck presents a comparative analysis of South Africa and Tanzania, in which the language, the land and the nation are such spaces and temporalities. See Marie Rose Beck, 'Language as Apparatus: Entanglements of Language, Culture and Territory and the Invention of Nation and Ethnicity', *Postcolonial Studies* 21, no. 2 (2018), 231–53, https://doi.org/10.1080/13688790.2018.1462085
98. As for the other Palestinian groups, Jabra Ibrahim Jabra has argued that the Palestinian exiles became 'knowledge peddlers', a reference to the successful integration of the Palestinian intelligentsia in the labour market in Arab and non-Arab regions. This indicates a certain similarity between the symbolic means of production possessed by the various Palestinian groups, but the uniqueness of the group under Israeli rule lies in its desire for the symbolic capital of Arabic and its products specifically. See Jabra, 'The Palestinian Exile'. As for other Palestinian groups' literary practices in the post-*Nakba* era, see Farag, *Politics and Palestinian Literature in Exile*, 18–33. For a comparative perspective on other settler-colonial cases, see Amal Eqeiq, 'Writing the Indigenous: Contemporary Mayan Literature in Chiapa, Mexico and the Palestinian Literature in Israel' (PhD diss., University of Washington, 2013), 34–73.

3

The Mediation Position in 'Arabic': The Mimetic Mask

The genre of literary criticism is not static. Its structures and the functions that it plays vary in time and space. In the first and formative phase of the arena of 'Arabic', literary criticism was mainly limited to daily newspapers and literary journals. Over the next phase, it underwent profound institutional changes that displaced the critical practice to new spheres. This displacement took place on different levels – in the institutional space where it was created, in the types of criticism and knowledge required, and within the reading public. This chapter argues that the literary criticism in 'Arabic' became academised, tracing the structure of this academisation process.[1]

There is consensus in the research literature on the Palestinians in Israel that the 1967 war was a turning point in the relationship between them and the Zionist regime.[2] Most researchers argue that, at this juncture, a temporary relationship became permanent. Prior to the war, many Palestinians perceived the Israeli regime as a temporary system of control, and their attitude towards it was therefore characterised by suspended delay. After the 1967 war, however, most of the Palestinians in Israel came to view the regime as a permanent power system which demanded their integration. However, without downplaying the importance of that war, it appears from a close reading of Palestinian literature that deeper processes took place in the settler-colonial field of contradictions, with the war being only one of their manifestations.[3] Atallah Mansour's novel *In a New Light*, for example, addressed the issue of waiting versus integrating, despite having been published before the war.[4] War is the culmination of sociohistorical processes and interferes in the operation of the processes that led to it in the first place. I argue that the 1967 war was a structural turning point, as it imposed the narrowing of the range of options hitherto available to the Palestinians and created new fields of collective practices. Specifically, the war catalysed the construction of a certain literarity that operated as a mechanism for the structuring of the subjective internality of the 'Israeli Arab'.[5]

Tawfiq Fayad's novel *The Deformed* was one of the first articulations of the transition from describing the external reality of Palestinians' lives to examining their internal reality, thereby attempting to constitute the Palestinian subject.[6] Its publication evoked an extensive public discussion among the Palestinians in Israel and attracted more critical reviews and opinion articles than any novel or anthology to this day.[7] The structuring of the subject also occurred in the institutional sphere of 'Arabic'; its distinct manifestation after 1967 was the academisation of literary criticism. This chapter focuses on processes of the early 1970s, when the institutional formalisation of the processes from the earlier period of 'Arabic' began. This, so I argue, was the result of the constitution of a new site in 'Arabic' – academic literary criticism written by Palestinians in Arabic and directed mostly at the Palestinian readership in Israel and, sometimes, also at readers throughout the Arab world.[8]

Until the early 1970s, most academic texts on Palestinians and their literature were written by Israeli scholars in Hebrew and English. The main target audience was Israeli and Western academics, not Palestinians in Israel. During the 1970s, however, a new type of literary criticism began to appear as part of the dynamics of 'Arabic'. This academic corpus of knowledge was written in Arabic by Palestinians studying at Israeli universities. These Palestinian scholars acquired their knowledge and modern views on literature and literary criticism in Israeli academia from the previous generation of orientalist experts. Most of these Palestinians scholars studied in Arabic language and literature departments – only very few studied general or comparative literature at the time. It is my argument that this group of Palestinian academics constituted a new position within 'Arabic', formed from a combination of new and already existing structural elements.

Studies have indicated two seemingly contradictory processes that occurred simultaneously among the Palestinians in Israel following the 1967 war. On the one hand, the Palestinians developed strategies and tactics of integration in the structural space allowed by the state and its mechanisms. On the other hand, they began to express their national Palestinian and Arab identities publicly to themselves, as well as in the state's public space, and to institutionalise that identity through organised collective action.[9]

Palestinian academics who specialised in Arabic language and literature took part, as a group, in constituting the new position in 'Arabic'. They represent a complex example for this ostensibly enigmatic contradiction: they integrated in the Israeli academic world, and the knowledge they acquired in it – as well as its symbolic means of production – was Zionist *par excellence*.[10] At the same time, however, they studied their own language and culture, albeit through the mediation of the Zionist orientalist knowledge establishment. They repositioned themselves within 'Arabic' in a new position that did not seek to reclaim any existing symbolic capital and did recognise the state's ownership of the symbolic capital – Arabic. These Palestinian scholars possessed academic knowledge of Arabic, but they were not the owners of Arabic in the Israeli settler-colonial context. The question then is: What is the nature of Palestinian scholars' ownership of symbolic means of academic knowledge production formalised as literary language in Arabic, given that these symbolic means of production have been reproduced from the hubs of knowledge production controlled by the orientalist, Zionist settler-colonial establishment?

The Palestinian academics who started producing knowledge in Arabic on Arabic literature in Israel for the Palestinian and Arab readership were graduates of the Israeli education system. Their typical educational track included elementary and secondary studies in the Arab education system. For their post-secondary education, some studied in seminars for Arab teachers and then went on to study in Israeli universities, while others moved directly from high school to one of the departments of Arabic language and literature.[11] Many began working as teachers in the Arab education system and were promoted to principals and superintendents. At the same time, they pursued studies for a second and third degree. Their typical professional careers were threefold. Some worked in the Israeli education system in senior roles of superintendence and writing Arabic language and literature curricula. Others held administrative offices in the education system, in addition to teaching in seminars for Arab teachers or as external university lecturers. The third path was an academic career at an Israeli university, usually in Tel Aviv or Haifa, and less so in the Hebrew University of Jerusalem. I will focus on the latter track, because these academics were the ones directly involved in constituting the new site in 'Arabic' through academic literary criticism.

The educational and professional tracks of this group of academics shaped its structural position *vis-à-vis* the government mechanisms in charge of education and knowledge/power. Its institutional material infrastructure is a direct derivative of 'Arabic'. Yet, the group integrating into Israeli academia belongs to two systems that have clear hierarchic knowledge/power relations. I argue that this group led a new return and a repositioning path within 'Arabic'. This new position mediated between the Palestinians and their language and culture, after these had been reorganised to suit the Israeli academic discourse. These mediators specialised in modern scientific knowledge, the study of Arabic as an academic discipline with 'objective' tools of analyses. They served as a secondary owner of this mediation system. Their ownership of the symbolic means of production of the science of Arabic literature in Israel was not exclusive. In addition to the dependency on the state's institutional material infrastructure, their ownership was a by-product of their position as mediators between different layers in the settler-colonial regime.

In the structure of the colonial mode of production, the mediatory position plays a key role in the conduct and maintenance of the regime. Ownership, of both the material means of production and symbolic/discursive tools to produce scientific knowledge, derive from conflicts that have taken place outside the sociohistorical context of the occupied nation. In the case of Palestine, these conflicts occurred in the context of nineteenth-century Europe.[12] In order for this mode of production to operate in its settler-colonial version, however, it had to rely on the colonised native group for workforce and various raw materials. The colonised natives were required to perceive themselves as part of this mode of production, despite being external to it. Therefore, the native group needed to reorganise according to the structure of the mode of production following the violent act of colonisation. The settler group thus initiated a structural intermediate position to mediate between itself and the native group.[13] The action of the mediation position was divided into two kinds of mediation modes: those related to the material means of production, and those related to symbolic means, which were in charge of reproducing ideological legitimacy for the new settler-colonial regime. In the Israeli context, multiple roles were attributed to the mediation of symbolic means of production. Compared to other settler-colonial regimes, the over-investment by the Israeli regime in this mediatory position derived mainly from the mechanisms of transforming the representation of the historical act of settler-colonisation into perceiving it as part of the 'nature' of its modern history.

Historically, the Palestinian mediators originated in the Arab education field, which was founded by the regime's mechanisms in order to inculcate an emotional structure of minimal loyalty to the State of Israel.[14] The members of the first group formed in the mediatory class were Palestinian teachers working in the Arab-Israeli education system. This core of educators dominated the mediatory class in quantitative terms until the mid-1980s. Their control of this position and its structure led to mediation strategies that spanned behaviours, thoughts and feelings of mimetic characteristics.[15] The teachers, responsible for the educational mediation system, were situated between the Israeli knowledge/power production mechanism and the group of students. They were supposed to mimic the knowledge/power of the owners of this mechanism and pass it on to their students. The latter would then follow an emotional grammar of minimal submission, accepting the emotional structural threshold of minimal loyalty to the State of Israel.[16]

Here, the field hierarchy is divided into three levels. The mediating level, that of the teachers, is supposed to mimic the level of the establishment, while that of the students is supposed to mimic the level of the mediating teacher. I argue that this mimetic strategy controlled the body of knowledge produced by Palestinian academics on the Palestinians in Israel, particularly the knowledge that they produced on the Arabic language and literature of the Palestinians in Israel. This political economy of mediation is an organising principle of knowledge about Arabic and its products. It structures the path of return and repositioning in 'Arabic' on the mimetic exchange level. In the course of this mimetic practice, Arabic and its products are reproduced by generating knowledge about, and hence controlling its use by, the Palestinians.

In the dynamics charted by the political economy of mediation, Palestinian scholars have come to know themselves through knowledge of their language and culture, as produced by Israel. Moreover, they must internalise this knowledge in order to use it to produce literary criticism on Arabic Palestinian literature in Israel and to communicate it to their Palestinian and broader Arab readership. The mediation process requires Palestinian academics to forget what they know about the Arabic they acquired as their native tongue and cultural language, as well as the knowledge acquired after 1967 from studies on Arabic published in the Arab world. This erasure organises the Palestinian's internality as a raw material, which thus cannot be considered as modern subjectivity.

This subjectivity is the result of structuring through the mediating knowledge/power, which Palestinians received from Israeli scholars. These two levels of the mediation process – identity erasure and the acquisition of new knowledge – were framed by the mediating group as part of the modernisation process that they experienced in Israeli academia. At the same time, there occurred a different dynamic of recharging the object itself with intense desire, with almost erotic passion for literary Arabic and its products. Nevertheless, although this phenomenon was prevalent among Palestinian academics studying Arabic, only few studies seem to have addressed it.[17]

The issue of an all-consuming desire for Arabic requires an analytic approach different from the mediation system. The erasure process recharges libidinal energy onto the body of the collective 'mother', Arabic. First, this desire is directed at literary Arabic and the so-called 'treasures' inherent and unique to it, with Arabic as a pure and self-contained object. This type of object is the opposite of the hybrid mediatory position, which draws on the two positions that it mediates. A second level of manifestations of desire for literary Arabic is that which recharges the object with procreative passion, a kind of heterosexuality displaced into the body of the language-woman. Here, the recharging is a connection with the generative structure of language, allowing the conception of its products, which are a kind of extension of its body, or even its children. Modern Arabic literature researcher Youmna Al-Eid has argued that, unlike Western processing of sexuality on the textual level, it is addressed in Arabic literature by way of displacement of the political oppression in Arab societies.[18] The sexual discourse substitutes for the lack of collective political freedom. This is opposed to modern Western literature, where political freedom substitutes for the oppression of sexual desire. Although the manifestations of desire for literary Arabic among Palestinian academics were mainly verbal, Al-Eid's insights represent an analytic point of departure for analysing this desire.

The foregoing demarcation of the mediatory position has identified a distinct institutional-material group: Palestinian scholars involved in the study of Arabic language and literature who were employed in tenure-track positions at Israeli universities. Some of them were engaged in academic criticism of Palestinian literature in Israel. Published in English and Hebrew, their findings in the form of Arabic-language literary criticism were aimed at a Palestinian readership. Beginning in the late 1960s, this group was active in Israel's three leading academic institutions; in each, its members were grouped together around an Israeli researcher. At the Hebrew University of Jerusalem, it was Shmuel Moreh; at Tel Aviv University (TAU), it was Sasson Somekh; and the coordinator of the Haifa University group was David Semah. The TAU group was particularly prominent, since many of its members were appointed to tenured positions in the Department of Arabic Language and Literature. Their studies displayed a high quality and complex relationships with Somekh's research corpus. Note also that, over the course of their academic careers, the Palestinian members of this group published their scientific studies on modern Arab and Palestinian literature as Arabic literary criticism intended for the Palestinian public. Accordingly, in what follows I will focus on this case as a kind of prototype in the process of structuring the new mediatory position within 'Arabic'.

Three of Somekh's many Palestinian students meet the criteria relevant for this chapter, which include a background in the Israeli education system followed by a tenure-track position in Israeli academia: Mahmoud Kayal, Suleiman Jubran and Mahmud Ghanayim. Kayal began his doctoral studies with Somekh in the mid-1990s and graduated in 2001; therefore, he took no part in the processes of structuring the mediatory position in 'Arabic'. Jubran began his doctoral studies in the late 1970s and graduated in 1985. He studied modern Arabic poetry, autobiographies, Palestinian and *Mahjar* literature. Although his academic publications are relevant here, he published only few critical reviews on Arabic Palestinian literature. Ghanayim received his MA in

1982 and his PhD in 1990, both supervised by Somekh. He studied modern Arab and particularly Palestinian literature. Most of his studies on the latter were published as Arabic literary critical essays and as books in local literary journals and publishing houses directed at the Palestinian readership; therefore, they are central to the structuring of the mediatory position in 'Arabic'. Accordingly, his critical essays and books will be the focus of this chapter.

The following pages will present a new position that developed in the arena of 'Arabic' during the 1970s: academic literary criticism written in Arabic by Palestinian academics. Engaged with Palestinian literature in Israel, it was directed at the Palestinian readership in Israel. I will describe the operational modes of this position through a genealogical analysis of the knowledge/power structure that produced this literary criticism. Our initial mapping of the group of Palestinian scholars publishing such literary criticism texts indicates an academic genealogy centred on the three major Israeli universities of that time. I chose to focus on the research corpus created in the TAU Department of Arabic Language and Literature. First, I will concentrate on the complex relationship between Somekh's writings on modern Arabic literature and those of his Palestinian student Mahmud Ghanayim, who later became a researcher and lecturer in the same department. I will then discuss how the latter's literary criticism corpus, together with texts by other scholars, structured the mediatory position in 'Arabic'.

Sasson Somekh: Russian Formalism Travels to the Holy Land

Sasson Somekh's lineage in the body of knowledge about Arab and Palestinian literature includes three generations: himself; Mahmud Ghanayim; and Dorit Gottesfeld, Mahmud Ghanayim's student.[19] Somekh viewed his own lineage as emblematic of the success of the Zionist lineage. In other words, his project was not academic alone. For him, the academic sphere served as a tool for reweaving the complex ties between Arab Jews and the cultures and societies of the Arab world, mainly in Iraq and Egypt. Somekh, however, did not consider Arab Jews as integral to the Arab world. Their reweaving into the Arabic context was part of the Zionist project.[20] His activities involved: integration into the Zionist project, producing knowledge on Arab and Palestinian literature, intensive and prolonged activities in 'Arabic', interpersonal relations with writers and intellectuals in the Arab world appropriated by the establishment as part of the Zionist regime's normalisation process with the Arab states, and holding various official positions designed to promote this normalisation through academic and literary endeavours.[21]

In this sub-section, I argue that Somekh's extensive activities were part of the literacy mechanisms of the Zionist mode of excessiveness, which required the Palestinian mode of compulsive reading among his Palestinian students and which was formalised as academic literary criticism in 'Arabic'. In what follows, I will examine the knowledge/power framework embodied in the mechanism of the Zionist excessive mode of writing on literature and literary criticism. Somekh and others established this mechanism through their studies on Arab and Palestinian literature. He bequeathed this framework to his students and readers, many of them belonging to the Palestinian readership in Israel. In adopting this framework, these readers developed the Palestinian mode of compulsive reading. Moreover, it was this knowledge/power framework, with its materiality, substance and style, which enabled the mediatory position in 'Arabic' and structured it in the post-1967 period.

Somekh gained academic prominence upon publishing his book on Naguib Mahfouz, based on his doctoral dissertation written under the supervision of Oxford's Mohammad Mustafa Badawi.[22] Somekh initially had no intention to study Arabic literature; he had travelled to England to study general linguistics and specialise in Hebrew linguistics. It was the establishment's intervention that changed the course of his life, as he described in his autobiography:

> After two or three months [in London], I received an offer from Tel Aviv University. [. . .] It was a highly tempting offer, albeit one that involved multilateral shocks: to abandon London for Oxford University, [. . .] abandon Hebrew and general linguistics for a study of modern Arabic literature. [. . .] Tel Aviv University offered to cover my living and tuition costs in Oxford until I completed my PhD studies. Upon returning to Israel with the coveted degree, I would be appointed to a tenure-track position at the university.[23]

Thus, Somekh's specialisation in Arabic literature was dictated by the establishment's needs. TAU sought to create a department of Arabic language and literature, which required lecturers and researchers. This was a major milestone in the development of the academic establishment regarding the production of knowledge on Arabic language and literature and its impact on the forces – and persons – active in 'Arabic'. Somekh's entrance into this field and the location he chose for himself – or that was chosen for him – largely shaped his subsequent activities in that field. His activities were translated into mediatory mechanisms within 'Arabic' and the interfaces between it and the other spheres of activity of the Zionist excessive literacy mode. Somekh was continuously active in contributing to journals on Arabic literature intended for the Palestinian readership in Israel. A prominent example is the journal *Al-Sharq*, established in 1970. *Al-Sharq* was the offspring of the newspaper *Al-Anba*, in turn the establishment successor of *Al-Yawm*, which had stopped being published in 1968.[24] In an article published by Somekh in *Al-Sharq* in 1972, he described the movement between Arabic literature and the Hebrew readership in a language that waxes poetic in describing the interest shown by Hebrew readers:

> The reputation of the Shiloah Institute at Tel Aviv University has extended to the furthest ends of the globe.[25] Moreover, books by Israeli scholars on social, political, literary and economic aspects of Arab countries have been translated into various European languages, as well as Arabic. The truth is that Israeli interest in the Arab world, whether academic or general, is far from new. This interest has a relatively long history in this country; it began long before the establishment of the State of Israel.[26]

Even in the context of 1972, in which this article was published in Arabic, it is difficult for the reader not to be taken aback by the naïve tone in which the Israeli interest in the Arab world is presented. The question is, what was Somekh's goal in highlighting the supposedly genuine interest of the Zionist regime (across its different periods) in the Arab world? Later in the article, Somekh described Israeli academic institutes, their translators and the types of texts translated. He provided a sort of inventory shining a positive light on translation projects as bringing together societies, cultures and countries. However, Somekh distinguished between different types of literature: the humane type, which supported the Zionist Movement, and that which opposed Zionism and the State of Israel as an occupying entity. In the second type, which in fact the author did not consider 'literature', certain Palestinian writers were quite predictably conspicuous. The article suggested that Somekh sought to separate Palestinian culture from the rest of Arab culture, arguing that, had it not been for the Palestinians, there would have been no conflict between the Arab world and Zionism and Israel. After reviewing most of the Arabic literature translated into Hebrew, he wrote:

> And finally, Jordanian and Palestinian prose found its Hebrew translators. Author Shimon Ballas translated an anthology called *Palestinian Stories*, published in 1970. The Palestinian problem is at the centre of this anthology, to such an extent that sometimes the sound of hostility and hatred becomes particularly shrill. Nevertheless, the anthology does include stories addressing the problems of Arab society on both banks of the Jordan River, including stories by the late author Samira Azzam (1924–1967), which are full of nostalgia and sincere poetic longing. And as for the stories by Ghassan Kanafani, they are full of that same angry spirit against the Zionist Movement [like] several other Arab writers who have taken advantage of the tragedy of the Palestinian refugee as a toy to play with and exploit for their own enrichment. Despite the translator's effort to offer the Hebrew reader stories at an appropriate artistic level, the sociopolitical tone drowns these efforts and the stories' artistic quality is inferior (apart from that of Samira 'Azzam and Ghassan Kanafani) to that of mediocre Egyptian or Iraqi authors . . .[27]

Here, Somekh concocted a causal link between his judgement of Palestinian literature as inferior in quality and its hostility, rancour and rage at the Zionist Movement and the State of Israel. The Palestinians did not know how to write appropriately artistic literature, which led them to write inferior texts full of hatred. If only they could write properly, even at a mediocre level, they would certainly have changed their collective feelings toward the regime.

Somekh's attitude toward the Palestinians, and their culture and literature, resembles that of the orientalist experts discussed in the previous chapter. His implicit assumption was that they were not a truly national group; and this was attested by the fact that they lacked a real literature. This discursive formation, which measures literary quality by the yardstick of the writers' attitude toward Zionism, is a variation on the Zionist mode of excessive literacy. Somekh considered Azzam's literature as high quality, as it dealt with 'nostalgia and poetic longings' and avoided dealing with the Palestinian tragedy in a manner hostile to Zionism. Particularly interesting is the reference to Kanafani, who was assassinated by the Israeli Secret Service in Beirut that same year.[28] Here, too, Somekh chose to dissemble and present an ambivalent position regarding Kanafani – he is hostile, yet remarkably talented. Perhaps it is in this category, or rather blurring of categories, represented by Kanafani that the discursive boundaries of literary criticism in 'Arabic' end and a different establishment practice begins.

Somekh's establishment positionality was not only expressed institutionally, but also manifested by the knowledge/power that he imposed over Arab and Palestinian literature. Once he entered a privileged position in the Israeli academic sphere, Somekh had a clear position: literature was to be measured by the standards of Russian formalism. I argue that, in the settler-colonial context of the Palestinians in Israel, Somekh's position served to maintain the settler-colonial regime.[29]

In his book on Naguib Mahfouz, Somekh used the relations between the Egyptian writer's novels and Egyptian society and its historical processes as a spatio-temporal analytic axis. The book's main argument is that the modernisation processes of Egyptian society are articulated in the dynamic internal rhythm of Mahfouz's novels. Those written in the early stages of his career are slow-paced, while the novels written some two decades later are faster-paced. Somekh's main units of analysis consist of characters, design, structure and language. These are structural units, and diachronic social history and its impacts on the literary field are not reflected in Somekh's units of analysis. Yet, they determine a fundamental part of Somekh's research on Mahfouz. Once Somekh started working in his permanent academic position at TAU, his historical and structural analytic framework became radically transformed. He referred to this in passing in his autobiography when he mentioned the people who were in contact with him in his early days there, influencing his ideas.[30]

Somekh's new analytic framework ignored, in an apparently selective manner, the role of history in the complex relations leading to the literary event, whether novel, play, or short story. Nevertheless, as we shall see below, Somekh did assign history an important role. History, and the fields of contradictions relevant to the formalisation of the literary event, were silenced. They became a kind of stain in the structure of the literary critical essays intended for the Palestinian readership. Cross-referencing Somekh's studies in a certain period with those passages in his autobiography that refer to the same period can clarify the processes of change that denied history its role as an analytic element. In describing Somekh's academic work, his autobiography inventoried his relationships with various senior public officials and prominent professors. His positioning within the formal academic field, his relation to knowledge/power as grounded in his position in the dominant current and the intensity of his contacts with the mechanisms of power all contributed to the exclusion of history as an analytic element in the theoretical framework of his work. The following passage is revealing in this regard:

> And what about my studies? [. . .] Placing particular emphasis on the distinct literary aspects of works [by Mahfouz and Yusuf Idris] (language, structure, design, characters), with adherence to the principle set by the Russian literary researchers of the formalist school – 'concentrating on the literarity of literature' – i. e., the literary scholar should focus on those aspects that the literary work alone can express and avoid as much as possible using the literary text *per se* in order to study social and political issues.[31]

Here, Russian formalism is not a theoretical tool or analytical framework used by Somekh together with other tools. It is part of the ideological structure of the knowledge/power regime, which dominated the Zionist academic sub-field in which Somekh was active at that time. This regime ascribed to the Islamic Arab Orient an ahistorical essence that did not change along the diachronic time axis. Paradoxically, however, Somekh is to a certain extent a scion of the Arab-Islamic and Jewish Orient. And although my focus here is on the change in the analytic framework of power/knowledge, which he bequeathed to his Palestinian students who occupied the mediatory position in 'Arabic', it appears that, as a member of the secular middle class, Somekh sought – almost obsessively – to shed any remnant of the Islamic and Jewish Arab traditionalism with which (Ashkenazi) Zionism had stigmatised the Arab Jews.[32] He adopted a secular identity in order to pass the Zionist screening on the personal level; in doing so, he positioned himself as an outsider to Islamic Arab culture and could therefore accept, albeit partially, the orientalist view of the supposedly ahistorical essence of that culture. This is partially because the displacement of the contradiction is always partial and insufficient to capture the structure and content of the contradiction. Therefore, the outlet located by Somekh in Russian formalism was a fairly effective compromise that resolved some persistent contradictions in the fields in which he was active – both as an Arab Jew *vis-à-vis* White Zionism, and as a modern scientific researcher and Zionist *vis-à-vis* the Palestinians.

In order to examine these transformation processes, I will utilise a textual corpus consisting of the literary critical essays and books published by Somekh in Arabic, intended for Palestinian readers in Israel. These texts appeared in *Al-Sharq* and *Al-Carmel*, the latter published by Haifa University, as well as books published by the Arab Book Foundation, which was founded by the Histadrut, the TAU publishing house and local Palestinian publishers.[33]

I will focus on the founding period of the mediatory position, its rise and the beginning of its decline as a historical option for the Palestinians in Israel – from the early 1970s to the early 1990s. During those years, Somekh published dozens of essays and literary reviews, as well as three books intended for the Palestinian readership in Israel. Apart from one article in 1986, most refer to specific literary texts rather than theoretical issues *per se*; these are discussed only inasmuch as they are applicable to literary texts. I will extract his theoretical framework by following Somekh's analytic moves in these publications and tracing the genealogy of his theoretical and judgemental comments on literature.

The Knowledge Framework: The Settler-Colonial Mediation

The framework used by Somekh to produce knowledge on Arabic literature generally, and particularly Palestinian literature, is derived from the position he selected, or that was selected for him, within the Israeli academic field. This position commits to a theoretical worldview, as is proper for a scholar, but displaces its power relations to ostensibly objective spheres. According to this position, the study and criticism of literature is a 'scientific discipline', with tools of analysis and knowledge production that are 'essentially objective'. Somekh's position dissolved the brutality of settler-colonialism and recast oppression as a process of modernisation imposed by the settler on the native. Literature served as a platform for the modernisation process. Literary criticism in Palestinian settler-colonial contexts charted the way to ascend to the elevated platform of modernisation, detaching literature from sombre settler-colonial realities. In what follows, I will present the pillars of this theoretical framework and see how Somekh applied it to Arabic texts.

Disconnecting Literature from Reality

In a 1986 article, Somekh referred directly to the relationship between literature and reality.[34] He opened by reviewing the development of literary criticism in Europe since the early twentieth century. What is fascinating in this review is not the currents and scholars it mentions, but rather those it omits. Its narrative is linear: only those included in it belong to the history of literary criticism in Europe. In Somekh's words, . . .

> In the first decades of the twentieth century, important changes took place in the methods of literary research and its various currents. During this period, critical schools emerged in European and American cities, most of which directed most of their attention to the literary text itself. In France, there was growing emphasis on 'textual interpretation' [. . .]; in England and the United States, the school of 'new critics' appeared [. . .]; and in the first decades of this century an important critical school emerged – the Russian 'formalist school', which took interest in studying the language of poetry and encouraged critics and literary researchers to focus on what some of its members called 'the literarity of literature'.[35]

Somekh was accurate in suggesting that these three currents appeared at the same time. However, presenting them as the only major developments in literary research and criticism is problematic, if not outright tendentious. Somekh ignored rival schools whose dialectics shaped the currents that considered the literary text as an exclusive research object beyond which the researcher must not venture lest he stumble across reality. Russian formalism, for one, was careful to consciously steer clear of representatives of the communist regime, but also of scholars and intellectuals such as Bakhtin and Lukacs.[36] The problem was due to what Somekh tried to achieve in this biased presentation of the field of literary research. He argued:

> Together, these schools and currents freed academic research, and to a certain extent literary criticism, from the need to expend energies on 'secondary' matters and engagement with issues that are related to literature, but are not

> inherent thereto (such as philosophical, psychological, intellectual issues and so forth). The call for 'the literarity of literature' and for focusing on the text does not mean that the author and critic need to keep a distance from intellectual and sociopolitical issues, but that the literary researcher's mission is fundamentally different from that of the sociologist, the psychologist, or others.[37]

Somekh's stated aim was to establish the study and criticism of literature as scientific disciplines. He built a scale of relevance in literary research, separating what is inherent to the discipline from what is not. Not only were political power relations considered secondary here, but also psychology and philosophy: everything that is not in the literary text is secondary to it. However, Somekh did not elaborate on the nature of this secondariness, nor did he close the hermeneutical circle. When he concluded his study of the literary text, he did not point to its position with regard to the reality that had produced it, but he remained within the literary system itself. In this article, for example, he demonstrated his argument by creating different types of intertextuality and claiming that these were textual relations within that same literary system. In that, he reduced the literary event to the level of language.

The Critical Journey: From Language and Back

According to Somekh's knowledge framework, language is the raw material of literature. Therefore, his main scholarly interest was in examining various aspects of the use of language in literary texts. Almost all of his Arabic texts dealt with elements of Arabic, the ways in which they are put into use by the writer and the ways in which they interact. He used this to construct a literary system. Somekh tended to delve into endless comparisons between the complexity of Arabic and the literary modes of its use in an attempt to support the argument that the literary text is independent of sociohistorical reality.

One of the best examples of this approach may be found in Somekh's 1984 study of language in the literary corpus of Yusuf Idris.[38] This book marked the culmination of a series of publications on Idris, begun by Somekh in the early 1970s. The book opens with a chapter titled 'Sensitivity to Language'. Somekh presented Idris as a writer whose high sensitivity to language was central to his literary practice, arguing that this characteristic was the cornerstone of his texts. Based on this argument, Somekh examined the elements of language in the subsequent chapters. From the lexical to the narrative level, the interrelations of these elements structured the literary event. For example, this is how Somekh described the elements of language in dialogues:

> [T]he basic law in intellectual language is that grammatical or functional words are in Spoken Arabic, as are interjections; and as for dictionary words [as opposed to Spoken Arabic words], we find that these are mostly in Literary or Semi-Literary Arabic. And it happens that the compositions in Literary Arabic are more frequent in this text than in that analysed above, given that the theme of the dialogue and its characters are closer to the pure intellectual sphere.[39]

Here, Somekh presented a verbal analysis, on the level of the word and sentence, and examined the register – Spoken as opposed to Literary Arabic. This analysis presented a stage in the examination of the structure of the literary system and was designed to assess the artistic aspects of use of these language elements. According to Somekh, these were the literary material and its systemic functions, and this was also the boundary of the scholarly engagement with literature.

The Literary System

Somekh assumed that the literary work was a system that existed in its own right and interacted with other literary works. In his studies, he did not mention whether there was a systemic or other relationship between the literary work and social systems. When he analysed the systemic structure of literary works, he suggested that the literary system processed materials from social systems, but he did not refer to this analytically. The basic issue here is the presence of sociohistorical conditions that enable the supposedly independent existence of the literary system, separately from others. However, what is the meaning of this theoretical knowledge framework, through which Somekh produced knowledge/power on the other systems of which he himself was a structural part? This question gains particular relevance when this knowledge is published in Arabic and directed at the Palestinian readership in the Israeli settler-colonial context.

In a series of short essays published in the first issues of *Al-Sharq*, Somekh presented his systemic analysis by applying it to several short stories by Yusuf Idris. In a short essay from 1972, 'Movement and Pace in Sunset March', Somekh analysed two elements or sub-systems and argued that the relations between them formed the story's systemic skeleton.[40] He discussed a scene in one of the stories where the seller of licorice juice (*irq al-sus*) stands on a bridge. Somekh argued that this description placed the seller at the centre of the scene, with the passers-by and bridge in the background. He went on to argue that this picture was not static, but dynamic, with its development structured through the changes in the voices that Idris raised from within the fabric of the narrative. The relations between the two sub-systems – the picture and sounds – constructed the story. At this stage, Somekh moved on to discussing the language used by Idris, arguing that it embodied these relations, by virtue of the author's artistic sensitivity to language.[41] Somekh's systemic analysis stopped at the mention of the artistic quality of the story and its writer's unique talent.

Artistry as a Supreme Value

According to Somekh, the added value did not lie within the literary system, its elements and its infrastructure by themselves. Rather, it is the author's task to structure them into an artistic form that stands out as a trademark, a style that distinguishes the author and his work from others. Somekh did not refer directly to his view, with regard to the essential nature of artistic form. He tended to reveal his view in the context of the writer's level of modernity, when he examined whether the writer adopted what seemed modern to Somekh. Somekh's modernity was contrasted with traditionalism. Traditionalism, in the Arab-Islamic context, was for Somekh a factor that inhibited the development of Arab culture in the present period.[42] This issue was particularly prominent in Somekh's studies focusing on the relationship between literary and spoken Arabic. To him, the first was representative of the traditionalist current, whereas the second represented the modern current, which had broken free of the shackles of the Arab-Islamic past.[43]

Somekh wrote few studies about Palestinian writers living in Israel; most of his literary critical works were about modern Egyptian literature. Two articles about Michel Haddad and his poetry were an exception to this rule. The first, 'Toward a Complex Meaning', was published in *Al-Sharq* in 1980. This article was the Arabic translation of Somekh's introduction to

Haddad's 1979 anthology, edited and translated into Hebrew by Somekh.[44] The second, 'Modernist Form in Michel Haddad's Poetry', was published in *Al-Carmel* in 1983.[45] In both, Somekh argued that Haddad was the father of Arab modernism in Israel. He attributed this directly to the fact that Haddad had grown up in Nazareth, an 'Israeli' tourist attraction open to the world, and to the Christian origins of Haddad's text, whose integration in the text produced *bona fide* modernity. In the introduction to the anthology, Somekh described Haddad's development as a poet and located him along the continuum between traditionalism and modernism, in contradistinction to other Arab and Palestinian poets:

> It's hard to say that, in the early stages of his writing, Haddad was characterised by distinct originality. And there he appears, in the late 1960s, boasting completely new poetry, modern poetry with barely a trace of shabby romanticism, poetry that opposes naïve statements that have but one meaning. And he attempts to penetrate the depth of experience not necessarily by way of 'generalisation', but through linguistic expressions and associations that arise simultaneously. He does all that with a style and art not known to traditional Arabic poetry, [. . .] a style that avoids the Palestinian national theme. And we must recall that all this happens at a time when the value of the poets of resistance is growing higher throughout and even beyond the Arab world.[46]

The compliments that Somekh showered on Haddad, and particularly on his modern revolutionary approach in the context of 'Arabic', are not surprising. Indeed, the shabby 'romantic' and the unidimensional 'naïve' are discursive formations that Somekh borrowed from the establishment orientalist discourse on Palestinian national culture. What is interesting here is the construction of modernity as a bidirectional activity. On the one hand, it relies on intra-linguistic activity that forms by way of free associations, with the psyche being at the centre of literary practice. On the other hand, one must become purified of Arab-Islamic tradition and Palestinian national collectivity. This modernism is not divorced from reality, but what appears to be supreme artistic value is reduced in the context of 'Arabic' to a certain position, that which is accepting of the Zionist settler-colonial regime in Palestine.

Here I have enumerated four elements of the knowledge framework that Somekh developed and applied in his work. These are the cornerstones of the mediatory position in 'Arabic'. Together they form the foundation of the Zionist excessive literacy mode in the moment in which it is applied to a certain literary event. The knowledge framework rewrites the literary event with reference to the Zionist regime and formalises it as Zionist, whether using the term 'modern' or 'scientific'. In order for the excessive act of reading/writing to be completed at the structural level of the Zionist settler-colonial regime, it requires the compulsive literacy mode, applying the framework in literary criticism and academic research. As we have seen, Somekh was one of the concrete carriers connecting the modes of excessiveness and compulsiveness. The two main connecting points through which Somekh was active were the foundation of literary and academic journals and their maintenance over a period of two decades, as well as the formation of a group of Palestinian students whom he supervised as a university professor.

On Settler-Colonial Mimesis: The Mediatory Position as an Allegory

Beginning in the early 1970s, a complex relationship developed between Sasson Somekh and Mahmud Ghanayim. One of the first textual encounters between Somekh and Ghanayim took place in the early 1970s, when both published short essays in *Al-Sharq* about the first collection of poems by Faruq Muwasi.[47] Somekh's short article was his introduction to the collection itself, but Ghanayim's was a poetry review essay first published in the journal. The two suggest a basic difference between the writers' worldviews at the time.

Somekh began by examining the emotional charge in Muwasi's poetry:

> What is the secret of this sadness? What is the reason for the elegies and the intricate series of lamentations that fill the first collection by our poet? 'Pain', 'impatience', 'gloomy nostalgia', 'sadness', 'grief', 'misery', 'anguished longing'. These words and others like them are almost the backbone on which Faruq Muwasi's poetry leans. Is it because our poet is made of masochism and sheer love of pain? But wait a minute, [. . .] he has not shut the door of hope and has not shut his eyes from seeing the light and dawn. Most of his poems end in a manner contradictory to their beginning, which is full of a painful and desperate tone. [. . .] Hope and pain live together in the depths of our soul.[48]

Somekh tried to argue that Muwasi's preoccupation with the themes of pain and despair was derived from the relation between despair and hope, and that the poet was not truly desperate or melancholy, nor was he a masochist. But this begs the question, what is it about those contents that daunted Somekh as a reader? Is one not free to choose the contents of one's poetry? Or perhaps Somekh was daunted because these themes were deemed problematic in the context of the Palestinians in Israel? As usual in his literary criticism, Somekh went on to attribute these themes to the experimental nature of Muwasi's poetry. Muwasi was not sad or despaired, and his emotional charge was not negative – he structured the contents of his poetry according to the formal language he used.[49] It was the textual reality that required engagement with the negative emotions, and not the reality that lay beyond the poetic act.

Unlike Somekh, Ghanayim approached Muwasi's poetry from a different and almost contradictory point of view. He examined the classical metres that Muwasi used to determine the extent to which the poet managed to structure his poems according to the traditional formula of classical Arabic poetry, and he even asked whether that structure dialogued with the structures in the poems of the classical poets. Ghanayim opened his article by examining the status of classical metres in modern Arabic poetry:

> The doctrine of classical metres [*al-arud*] is of eternal significance, despite the fact that some try to belittle its value and mock the critic approaching this aspect of our tradition [. . .] The doctrine of classical metres lives and dies in the bed of time, and as I have shown, this is clearly evident in rhyming poetry and all the more so in free verse [. . .] Before me lies the poetry collection of poet Faruq Muwasi – his debut. The poet has been writing poetry for some ten years now and has recently published the collection *Waiting for the Train*. This collection evinces a successful attempt at applying the classical metres.[50]

Ghanayim's main argument is that there is no good or bad in the very use of Arab-Islamic tradition in poetry, only that part of that tradition does not pass the test of time. Ghanayim referred to poetic and metric structures common in various periods in Arab-Islamic history, noting which of them survived in the neoclassical eras and which made it to the current modern period. He argued that Muwasi had been successful in absorbing and applying this tradition, based on his comparison with classical poets, and that Muwasi even innovated and added to the tradition, based on his comparison with neoclassical poets.

In many ways, Ghanayim's article belongs to the textual genre that characterises renaissance periods and their attempt to read the present by enlivening the 'glorious' past. In his arguments, Ghanayim relied mainly on modern Arab sources from Egypt and Iraq, thereby locating himself in the modern Arab body of knowledge. This essay by Ghanayim, which enlivened the Arab tradition, held multiple meanings in the Palestinian context of the early 1970s. It clearly did not articulate a mediatory position but was situated within 'Arabic' without a clear position. Whereas Somekh's point of departure was the Israeli reality and the Palestinians' position towards it, Ghanayim's was the enlivening of Arab-Islamic tradition in modern Egypt and Iraq, and throughout the Arab world. However, Ghanayim's approach would undergo conceptual development and transformation, and apparently the decisive factor in this development was his integration in Israeli academia, first as student and later as researcher.

Ghanayim first demonstrated his acceptance of the dominance of the Zionist academic narrative over Palestinian literature in Israel in an article published in *Al-Sharq* in 1977 on the Palestinian short story in Israel.[51] He adopted almost verbatim Shmuel Moreh's constitutive 1958 article on Palestinian literature, using his ideas as a historical and theoretical framework for analysing the phenomenon of the Palestinian short story.[52] As we have seen in the previous chapter, the framework laid down by Moreh claimed that the year zero of the Palestinians and their literature was 1948, that the only inhabitants of 'Arabic' were the Palestinians, and that they were required to declare minimal loyalty to the State of Israel.

After Ghanayim had accepted this framework early in the article, he used it to analyse various social themes from Palestinian lives in Israel, as presented in the short stories. He presented, for example, the themes of land, village, sex and love as having been unsettled by modernism in the wake of the establishment of the State of Israel.[53] Note that, at this stage, Ghanayim's main arguments did not disconnect Palestinian literature and treat it as a separate system, as did Somekh's. It appears that this was an intermediate stage in Ghanayim's intellectual development, where he parted with his Arab-Islamic origins and accepted the assumptions of the Zionist framework of excessive writing, but he did not yet formalise or displace this framework into the academic sphere.

In a follow-up article published in 1979, 'Studies on the Local Short Story', Ghanayim dealt with three other themes: refugeehood, the relationship between the two nations and a theme he called 'towards a good universal story'.[54] At the end of that article, in a sub-section called 'Artistic Form: Structure and Style', Ghanayim emphasised that only a few Palestinian writers had managed to structure a short story at an appropriate artistic level. He offered two examples for such success: Zaki Darwish and Muhammad Ali Taha. Both were presented as belonging to the second post-1948 generation – that is, born and bred under the Zionist regime. Although Ghanayim's criterion for success is not clear enough, he relied on the assumption that the story is a system in itself, made up of parts that have to maintain a reasonable relationship between themselves. Like Somekh, Ghanayim pointed to the relationship between the literary character and the dialect it would use: a peasant would use spoken Arabic, whereas an intellectual would use a form of Arabic closer to the literary register. His presentation was rather practical and technical but, as we shall see, this analytic line would run as a scarlet thread through Ghanayim's studies, having been indoctrinated by Somekh himself. I will now move on to describe the characteristics of the mediatory position in 'Arabic', as embodied in the literary critical corpus published by Ghanayim from 1980 to 1995.

The Substance and Form of Mediation: The Academisation of 'Arabic'

Beginning in the early 1980s, Mahmud Ghanayim published four books, edited one collection of literary critical articles and compiled an extended bibliography of the journal *Al-Jadid*. He has published dozens of academic literary articles and essays in Arabic, Hebrew and English journals. Recently, he has also published a book in English about Palestinian literature in Israel. He worked at TAU, from the mid-1980s, for more than four decades, while holding a teaching position at Beit Berl College. He received his tenure position at TAU after completing his doctoral dissertation in 1990. Ghanayim clearly has been a major figure in the field of criticism and research of Palestinian literature in Israel, and by virtue of the structural settler-colonial context, he has situated himself within 'Arabic' in a mediatory position derived from the symbolic capital of the knowledge/power that he had accumulated as Somekh's student. I will examine the substance and form of this mediatory position according to the analytic framework established by Somekh. In doing so, I will explore the use that Ghanayim made of this framework in his Arabic texts on Palestinian literature, intended for the Palestinian readership in Israel.

Divorcing Literature from Reality

In his writings, Ghanayim accepted, in principle, Somekh's assumption that literature is disconnected from reality. The fact that this matter is not theoretically formalised in his corpus is relevant for our purposes. He approached the analysis of literary texts as though these were independent units unrelated to reality. When he delved into their contents, their themes, their form and characters, however, he suddenly referred directly to the reality that supposedly was disconnected from the literary text. Hence, his disconnection differs from Somekh's, and we need to look into its nature and how it differs from the model dictated by the latter.

One of the symbols of the Palestinian national movement across generations is the poet Abdelrahim Mahmoud. He fought in the 1948 war and died in combat near the village of Al-Shajara in the Nazareth area. The ideal of the poet-warrior was built around him, an ideal that came to be one of the main axes of the post-1948 Palestinian resistance culture, particularly after the ascendancy of the Palestinian Liberation Organisation (PLO) in the early 1970s.[55] Ghanayim's first book, published in 1980, addressed Mahmoud's poetry and was probably based on his academic work from the time he studied for a graduate degree in the Department of Arabic Language and Literature and Islamic Studies at TAU.[56] In other words, Ghanayim's choice of studying Mahmoud's poetry was not divorced from the daily issues of Palestinian lives at the time. Ghanayim chose to examine the Palestinian national model of the relationship between poetry and colonisation, and the resistance to it. He claimed that, when he began his research, he found a chaotic situation with regard to Mahmoud's poems, their interpretations and related studies. Ghanayim claimed that, in itself, Mahmoud's poetry had not been studied, and he took it upon himself to do so, outside the context of Mahmoud's legacy and activity in resisting the Zionist colonisation project.

According to Ghanayim, the substance of Mahmoud's poems is refusal – he was an objector even in his love poems. Their form relied on the traditional Arab style, and according to Ghanayim, it did so inappropriately. Ghanayim compared Mahmoud to Ibrahim Tuqan, another Palestinian poet from the same period, and highlighted the latter's intellectual aesthetic finesse, which he argued is lacking in the former's poetry. Ghanayim presented Mahmoud as an insistent objector, who believed that using brutal, crude force was the path to liberation. He further argued that the halo around Mahmoud was empty, without any aesthetic poetic project of any added value to substantiate it. Implicitly, he tried to untie the semiotic and symbolic links between poetry and resistance to colonisation – a major link in the Palestinian dominant semiotic chain. He adopted the claim of the orientalist experts of the former generation, to the effect that pre-1948 prose and poetry could not be regarded as a starting point. He adopted and applied Somekh's argument that poetry could be divorced from reality, at least on the declarative textual level. Nevertheless, Ghanayim's judgement of Mahmoud's poetic text carried with it direct implications for the reality supposedly divorced from poetry. His first analytic move, arguing that literature must be disconnected from reality, actually misleads the reader.

In 1982, Ghanayim completed his thesis under Somekh's supervision. Titled 'The Textual Structure in Emile Habibi's *The Pessoptimist*', it was published in book form five years later under the same name.[57] In what follows, I will refer to the book rather than the thesis, since the former was published by a Palestinian publication house and intended mainly for the Palestinian readership in Israel. In the introduction to the book, Ghanayim stated his methodical and theoretical intentions and placed them in the context of the criticism and study of Palestinian literature:

> Perhaps due to my negative approach to the reality [of current literary criticism], I would like to publish a study on a Palestinian novel and rely on a stylistic-structural perspective, at a time when studies on sociopolitical contents and their problems are so common. And although I do not reject some of these currents that steer the critical research of our new literature, in this study I chose to rely on the stylistic-structural perspective in order to understand the literary text in Emile Habibi's *The Pessoptimist*.[58]

The ambivalent tone with which Ghanayim opened his book suggests his accurate reading of 'Arabic'. Here, the ambivalence was a rhetorical move through which he sought to clarify the boundaries and limitations of the existing literary critical discourse. He situated his research within a theoretical current – the stylistic-structural current – arguing that it enables an understanding of the literary text in a manner required by its literary nature. Ghanayim went on to elaborate on his methodical and theoretical framework and the type of analysis it affords:

> The approach adopted by this study relies on an analysis of the language and structure of the literary text. However, in no way does it do this in order to present a purely linguistic analysis, but in order to reveal the semiotic function or meaning borne by language and supported by this structure. Understanding the linguistic dimensions and structural elements is very helpful in understanding the contents evoked by the literary work, through the complex linguistic relations and structural conflicts weaved into it. These, undoubtedly, create the work itself.[59]

Here, Ghanayim presented the characteristics of his analytic framework in order to explain to the reader that the contents of a literary work were derived from its structure, rather than *vice versa*. Moreover, he was emphatic in comparing his framework with other common frameworks. But disconnecting literature from reality using the stylistic-structural analytic framework was not without purpose. The focus on literature and the marginalisation of reality, whether as an analytic element or as a background from which the work grows and in which it intervenes, are part of a broader project, that of constituting the modern subject. Namely, in order to rise up the ladder of modernity, literature must be divorced from reality. This is how Ghanayim structured it in his introduction:

> My choice of the great author Emile Habibi and his magnificent work *The Pessoptimist* was not random. It was not my intention to apply modern theories to any work. The opposite was true – I was attracted to this novel because I considered it a unique literary work that moved the local story from its locality and managed to bring it across the thick fences that accompanied its process of developing into modernity. The question that motivated the study was: How did *The Pessoptimist* succeed in embracing modernity despite

> its adherence to traditional sources? The [study's] moment of birth lay in understanding the linguistic components and structural elements operating in a complex and intricate manner in the text of this novel.[60]

Excluding reality and glorifying the literary work as independent in itself were both modern moves to extract Palestinian literature from local traditionalism. Moreover, it appears that these moves were not dependent on any deliberate choice made by the critic and researcher, but derived from the modern literary material itself, as in Habibi's novel. Ghanayim argued that not only was the stylistic-structural framework preferable to others in its ability to explicate literary works; it also paved the way to a deep understanding of modern literature. Naturally, understanding the literarity of modern literature and making it accessible to the Palestinian readership in Israel would enable its extraction from the traditional locality into modern universalism. These insights, so concluded Ghanayim, led him to focus on the internal components of the work and what he did not declare, but carried out – the exclusion of reality.

Until the late 1980s, the mediatory position in 'Arabic' was only partly established – there had been no organised and comprehensive discourse on the history of 'Arabic' since 1948, directed in advance at the Palestinian readership in Israel. It was Ghanayim who, in 1995, wrote the first monograph that presented the history of 'Arabic' through a literary criticism that divorces literature from reality, thereby cutting 'Arabic' off from its settler-colonial context.[61] The rewriting of the history of the Palestinian literary field in Arabic by Palestinians in Israel preoccupied both Palestinian and Israeli Jewish researchers.

Three major research projects are relevant in this regard. The first is Mahmoud Abassi's doctoral dissertation, which deals with the years between 1948 and 1976. Abassi was Shmuel Moreh's student, and although he completed his study in 1982, the book based on it – *The Novel and Short Story in Arabic Literature in Israel* – was published in 1998. The second project is that of Shimon Ballas. His book on war literature from 1948 to 1973 – *Arab Literature under the Shadow of War* – was published in 1984, based on his doctoral dissertation, which he had written in French. The third study is by Ami Elad-Buskila, whose book *Dreamt-of Homeland, Lost Country* was published in Hebrew in 2001, six years after Ghanayim's book, intended for an Israeli academic readership.[62] Therefore, Ghanayim's book is clearly foundational in the two fields relevant for our purposes here – the Israeli academic field and 'Arabic' – and in their overlapping space.

The Difficult Path: The Journey of the Palestinian Story in Israel attempts a narrative framing of the history of Palestinian literature in Israel since 1948.[63] It includes most of the materials published by the author, over more than two decades, about the Arabic literature of Palestinian writers in Israel. The manner in which this material is organised into a complete historical narrative is interesting. This narrative tells the reader the story of the Palestinian journey from the point of view of the mediatory position in 'Arabic'. The main axis is the gradual process of literature's detachment from reality, a kind of maturing into modernity of the literary material. Ghanayim structured the narrative of literature's divorce from reality along two mutually supportive paths. The first is the disconnection of the group of Palestinians in Israel from the Palestinian collective and its integration into the Zionist settler-colonial regime. The second is the disconnection of literature from sociohistorical reality. Ghanayim's narrative presents Palestinians who view themselves as 'Israeli Arab' and detach themselves from the Palestinian collective, as writers who can create modern literature unrelated to their settler-colonial reality.

To reinforce such an understanding of the history of literature, Ghanayim presented Palestinian literature in Israel as a special phenomenon, separate from other types of Palestinian literature. He relied on Abdel-Muhsen Taha Badr's classic study on the development of the Egyptian novel.[64] Badr argued that the history of the Egyptian novel may be divided into three major stages: entertainment, moral didactics and aesthetic art. He assumed that the transition across the stages involved a distancing from reality and the formation of a self-sustaining literary system, whose main aspect is the artistic structure it achieves. In *The Difficult Path*, Ghanayim demonstrated this through Najwa Qawar-Farah and Tawfiq Fayad. Qawar-Farah's literary work is described as an initial stage, influenced by the romantic current led by Jubran Khalil Jubran and others, involving a preoccupation with the morality of supreme virtues.[65] Conversely, in *The Deformed*, Fayad presents a literature that attempts to develop in aesthetic-artistic directions, but due to extra-literary causes, this project is cut short.[66] According to Ghanayim, it took years for the artistic literary text to appear in the form of Habibi's novel.[67]

Somekh focused, as we have seen, on the Egyptian literary field, on the writings of Mahfouz, Idris and others; therefore, his analyses lack the urgency of the charged realities of the settler-colonial regime. Ghanayim, on the other hand, was situated in a settler-colonial context that required a different approach to the divorcing of literature from reality. In Ghanayim's book, the overall narrative is that of a modernisation process, while Somekh assumed the modernisation to have been completed. The Palestinian writer must acquire the modern tools of producing an artistic, read modern, literary text. Somekh's writers have already done so and are modern in the literary sense and in others. As a mediator, Ghanayim presented a model he had borrowed from the Israeli system of academic knowledge that has not only divorced literature entirely from reality, but where literature is privileged over reality (of the natives in the settler-colonial one, of course). Literature is a displaced site of settler-colonial reality – it has a reality of its own and is made of language.

The Critical Journey: From Language and Back

The mediatory position in 'Arabic' presents the analysis of the literary text's language as essential for understanding it and as a self-sufficient basis for proper – that is, scientific – literary criticism. Published in 1987, Ghanayim's *The Textual Structure in Emile Habibi's The Pessoptimist* presents literary criticism as a journey that begins in language, only to return to it, and it does so in the most mature and well-developed form in Ghanayim's corpus, directed at the Palestinian readership in Israel. Informed by the tradition of the study of Arabic, Ghanayim analysed the various aspects of language – grammatical, rhetorical, semantic, morphological and so on – seeking to highlight Habibi's virtuosic irony as a modern literary style.

In the first chapter, titled 'The Conflict between Structure and Content', he referred to *The Pessoptimist*'s words and sentences that rely on old-fashioned Arabic language and literature:

> The reader of a text of this kind vacillates between two worlds: the world of meaning, or content, and the world of form. As for the world of content, it is realistic and borrowed from daily life. Saeed Abu al-Nahs is a living personality that may live among us – we may find him on the street or in the office

> or anywhere else. [. . .] What remains is the burden of form, and in Emile Habibi's form, we find a stylistic elevation that returns the reader to a period different from that of the content. It does not match the realistic content and does not flow with it, but is rather reminiscent of the language of old sources such as al-Jahiz, al-Hamadhani, al-Hariri and others.[68] Thus, the reader finds himself swinging between new content and old form.[69]

The reader's experience described by Ghanayim is the result of an ironic tension that is due to the gap between content and the language register used to express it. In Ghanayim's view, the act of reading and the associated experience place the reader on a pendulum, as it were, swinging between two dichotomies. Ghanayim pointed to the formalisation of Arabic's materiality, both semantically and morphologically. Habibi's intervention consisted of his redefining of the relation between the meaning and the form that carries it. However, at no point along this analysis did Ghanayim turn our attention to the fact that, in order for this swinging motion to occur, at least as a semiotic-structural chain, the reader must be familiar with the history of the possible registers of content and form available in Arabic.

The second chapter, 'The Conflict of Dimensions', addressed another linguistic intervention by Habibi. Here, the focus was not on the relation between form and content, but on the transformations of the sentence itself – as in the deconstruction of an expression usually made in spoken Arabic and its reconstruction in literary Arabic or vice versa; the invention of neologisms according to the rules of Arabic in a manner that surprises the reader; the use of the structure of a journalistic article in a prose text; the use of a folktale structure; and so on. In reference to the journalistic style in *The Pessoptimist*, Ghanayim wrote:

> Another characteristic of *The Pessoptimist* is the use of the unique style of the journalistic article. [. . .] Our purpose here is to point to the elements that *The Pessoptimist* borrows from it, in which we identify divergence from the novel style, or more generally, from prose style. Journalistic language is different from that of prose literature. The journalistic essay uses a standard and patterned language. Conversely, the language of prose is not standard, whether using a high or low register. This also applies to the essay's inner structure. [. . .] Emile Habibi took advantage of this possibility in

> *The Pessoptimist* in an exceptional way, aligning the styles of the novel and the essay, thereby forming a style that is at once high and low brow.[70]

The emphasis here is on language in various genres of writing. What is interesting is not the journalistic genre itself, but its standard format. By comparing it to the language of literature, we can understand the latter, and we can comprehend how Habibi constructed his text. Ghanayim argued that Habibi used several languages. The important point is not the use of languages in itself, but the claim that this use is subordinate to the language of prose or literature, whose non-standard structure allows it to contain several languages and reorganise them in the literary semiotic structure. Beyond Habibi's irony and virtuosity, the following question arises: What conditions enabled the development of various types of language in modern Arabic culture, and what sociohistorical conditions enabled, or rather required, the transgression of the boundaries between the languages of different genres?

The book's last chapter focused on the language of dialogue and its characteristics in *The Pessoptimist.* Ghanayim tried to reconstruct the type of language used in Habibi's dialogues based on the characters' traits, the context and the ironic structure. He argued that Habibi used these characteristics in order to recreate the stylistic structure of his virtuosic irony. Thus is the case, for example, with reference to characters of different ages, such as elderly persons and children, or people of different educational or national backgrounds (mainly Jews):

> The question that arises here has to do with the nature of the factors that determine the language of the dialogue. Are they related to the character itself – its education, social status, age, or nationality? In order to formulate the question in a manner applicable to *The Pessoptimist*, we will examine how the dialogue varies with the character's educational level, a matter forced upon us due to the tradition that has developed in some Arabic novels, whereby literary Arabic is the one used by intellectuals or persons of higher social standing, whereas spoken Arabic is used by the partly or completely uneducated and people of low social standing. It is easy to examine this matter in *The Pessoptimist*, since its range of characters is broad.[71]

The varying use of language in the dialogues is not derived from a referent located outside language, but rather from other language structures. When

Ghanayim talked about the character's traits, he referred only to the character as composed of literary material, which is language. Therefore, it is the alignment of two language structures that is in the focus of analysis here. The linguistic variability is central to the intra-textual literary activity. The relations in the structure of the text and the changes that they undergo are mainly changes that the language undergoes at the different junctions of the novel.

As opposed to the axis of divorcing literature from reality, which carries some of the charged references to the settler-colonial reality, it appears that the axis of language in the mediatory position in 'Arabic' is significantly overlapping with Somekh's model. Ghanayim adopted the principle that the material of literature was language, and his analysis therefore focused on language and its various structures. Word, sentence, format and dialogue are examined along the axis ranging between spoken and literary Arabic, and on that stretching between modernity and traditionalism. The problematic issue in mediation of this kind is that the literary essay is not aware of itself beyond the level of establishment-academic reflection. Namely, the text claims to truly understand the phenomenon, but is unaware that it must also understand its own understanding. This is where the systemic element enters the mediatory position.

The Literary System

In his studies on Palestinian literature in Israel, written in Arabic for the local Palestinian readership, Ghanayim failed time after time to develop a systemic analysis of the literary works he discussed. The pattern of this 'failure' may be analysed as symptomatic of a more profound problem in the analytic framework itself, or in the empirical literary material that Ghanayim presented, but it appears that the problem lay in the nature of their linkage. In what follows, I will chart the pattern of this 'failure' and then move on to analyse and interpret it.[72]

Ghanayim usually began his book-length studies of literary works by deconstructing them into elements of the Arabic language. He devoted a chapter to each, analysing the way in which the author used it. The moment in which these elements were to be joined together into a literary system was either rudimentary or completely lacking. Thus, for example, in his book on Abd al-Rahim Mahmoud's poetry, he characterised it according to the forms of various content areas.[73] Ghanayim did not tie the content areas and their formal relations together into a single system with a systemic organising logic. This is particularly evident in *Structure of the Text*.[74] In the introduction, he argued that his study was stylistic-structural. The added systemic step is implicit from the text, but not referred to directly. In a chapter that could be expected to tie the various structural elements together and present a kind of literary system, he summarised the characteristics of each element separately and then moved on to discuss the general level of literary genres, arguing that . . .

> The study of *The Pessoptimist*'s style raises several aspects of the literary genre issue. The first is that the modern novel can use styles from the ancient Arab tradition after modernising it. [. . .] The second aspect has to do with the answer to the question, To which literary genre does *The Pessoptimist* belong? Clearly, this is a novel of a new genre that is still evolving in Arabic literature – it relies on the author's approach to the ancient Arab tradition, his perspective on it, and his ability to play with it. [. . .] Thus, the present 'realistic' processed content requires a special style in modern Arabic literature.[75]

The problem with the emphasis on style and the analytical delving into its characteristics is twofold. On the one hand, Ghanayim did not clarify the logic of the stylistic work as systemic, but settled with describing its elements and the *modus operandi* of each, separately. On the other hand, according to his statement in the introduction, the style is part of the literary system and refers to other elements of that system. If we accept the argument that style is a mediatory factor between the elements and the literary system as a whole, then we require an analytical argument clarifying why this level of analysis is self-sufficient. Since this issue arises repeatedly in Ghanayim's research corpus, we may conclude that this is a structural matter within the framework of the mediatory position, from which he made his statements.

This issue of the literary system is even more critical in Ghanayim's *The Difficult Path*, since this study attempted a history of the Palestinian field of literature from 1948 until its publication in 1995. In this book, there exist at least two literary-systemic levels: that of each literary work and that of the field. Ghanayim analysed each work in terms of its content, structure and style. He assumed, without any explicit theoretical formalisation, that style was the most important in terms of the work's literarity. However, he did not examine how the three factors operated together as a system. As in his analysis of *The Pessoptimist*, here too it stopped at style. The problem is created when this stopping is examined against the background of literature's divorce from reality. This is because style must exist in its own right – something that would become possible only if it were framed as a separate systemic unit.

The systemic level of the field of Palestinian literature in *The Difficult Path* is presented as though it has undergone a process of development since 1948. Ghanayim divided this process into three main periods: the initial period characterised by confusion and searching, when the dominant current among the writers was the romantic or moral current; the second period, when the artistic-literary text crystallised, to use Badr's terminology, and the field was dominated by the realistic current; and the third period, that of the mature artistic-literary text, when experimental modernism became dominant among writers.[76] Ghanayim presented the field of Palestinian literature in Israel by analysing and discussing specific literary works, which he analysed as self-contained units rather than as part of a broad literary system. His analysis describes a developmental process of the entire field, one that relies on the concept of modernisation, but it is applied at the level of the specific literary work, separately of others operating in the very same field. In this picture of the history of Palestinian literature in Israel, as drawn by Ghanayim, different works have no inherent literary relation to each other's structure and the systemic relations in which they operate.

How can we explain this pattern of 'failure'? First, in terms of knowledge/power relations, the mediatory position in 'Arabic' is dual. Apart from mediating between the academic establishment and the Palestinian readership in Israel, this mediatory position is located in the field of 'Arabic', which in itself is a mediatory field between the settler-colonial establishment and the Palestinians. This position does not enable a systemic view because it is blind to the entirety of elements and their interrelation; it lacks systemic language.

Second, as a mediatory position, the systemic event of creating knowledge and power – in our case, establishment-academic knowledge – is not part of its working mechanism. The mediatory mechanism is little more than a knowledge transmission channel. For example, Ghanayim relied almost directly on Somekh whenever he referred to a major knowledge issue that involved stating a position; he needed the authority of Somekh to articulate his positions. The mediatory position would allow events of transmission but no connections that are not derived from the existing power structure. This characterises the relationship between Zionist excessive literacy and Palestinian compulsive literacy modes. Mediation allows the transfer of knowledge between the Israeli academic establishment and the Palestinian reading public, without the risk of disturbing the power relations between them; indeed, it reinforces them.

The Artistic as a Supreme Value

The category of 'artistic story' appeared for the first time in Ghanayim's *The Difficult Path*. In the first chapters, when Ghanayim analysed the first two periods in the history of the field of literature, he paused, as we have seen, in the style-structure unit of analysis. However, the fourth chapter, where he characterised the field's 'mature' period, is titled 'Towards an Artistic Story'. To glean the meanings that Ghanayim ascribed to the term 'artistic', I will follow his analysis of Emile Habibi's *Saraya, the Ogre's Daughter*, considered by Ghanayim to be the most successful Palestinian artistic story.[77]

Having analysed *The Pessoptimist*, also by Habibi, Ghanayim presented *Saraya* as a model for the modern novel because it breaks down the separation between different literary genres and presents a development in Habibi's writing. As the first characteristic, Ghanayim introduced Habibi's deceptive play with the genres of biography and novel. The narrator in *Saraya* speaks in several voices, the transitions between them creating a textual tension that confuses the reader.[78]

The second characteristic is the use of symbols, which according to Ghanayim serves Habibi's journey toward modernism.[79] Ghanayim provided examples from *Saraya* where the symbol consists of several levels, referencing historical events, folktales, anecdotes from the Arab-Islamic tradition, elder wise men's tales, myths and so on. He interpreted these symbols to reinforce his argument that the main characteristic of the modern text was its ability to contain ironic intertextuality:

> One of the characteristics of modernism in literature is ironic intertextuality. Intertextuality manipulates the literary text, whether ancient or contemporary. Through this manipulation, the writer conducts an intelligent, indirect dialogue, forming new relations with the absent text [. . .] Intertextuality occurs in modernism in several ways, some of which are the following:
>
> 1. Distancing from direct references and direct quotes in favour of symbolic and mythical language.
> 2. Forming a deep relationship to the absent text to deepen the content communicated by the text that manages this association.
> 3. Dialoguing with reality through a dialogue with literature, based on the laws of literature rather than the laws of reality. This approach meets the revolution against the classical theory of literature that has emphasised literature's mimetic aspect. Conversely, intertextuality mimics literature rather than mimicking reality directly.[80]

Undoubtedly, Habibi made extensive use of these modern techniques, and they became a significant part of his style in some of his later works. Our question, however, concerns whether we should value the literary work according to the criterion that artistic value is supreme. When trying to examine what lies behind this statement, we will find writing techniques that Ghanayim listed in a kind of inventory of what he called 'modernism'. Two of them refer to the divorcing of literature from reality. Yet, Ghanayim in this study did not refer at all to the other half of the modernism coin: literature's intervention in reality, following that divorce. This raises the following questions: Does artistic value exist from the moment literature breaks with reality? How is the dialogue conducted according to the laws of literature? And, most importantly, what is the meaning of these literary laws in the Palestinian settler-colonial context?

The structural reasons for the mediatory position that lead to over-valuing the artistic aspect of the literary text aim at redefining the modernism that Ghanayim's readers are supposed to consume. As many reseachers have argued, however, modernism's artistic value lies in a movement that brings together several levels and stages in the relations between literature and reality. The arguments claim that these relations do not include literature's independence of the laws of reality and reliance on its 'autonomous' laws. The relations between literature and reality require the intervention of the literary event in the reality from which it has been separated.[81] Regardless of one's position towards modernism, it is safe to argue today that the mere distancing from reality is insufficient to produce modernism's artistic value. In our case, however, and in order to play its basic role in maintaining the mediatory position, modernism must be subjected to hegemonic knowledge and power relations – that is, it must be used as an ideological discursive tool. In this usage of modernism, literature must abide by its own 'independent' laws, blind to the possibility that these laws redefine reality, or at least the attitude of the Palestinian reader towards it.

The formalisation of this complexity is embodied in a type of declarative act. The iron cage of the mediatory position enables a single form of communication – transmitting the knowledge conveyed to it. This form of communication is basically a declarative one, relying on what the mediator does *not* have, for the mediator is just a transmitter. This declarative act relies on the lack of authentic modernism, due to social and other contradictions. All the mediator has is an empty position in the settler-colonial hierarchy: once it has been filled, it must become empty again in order to fulfil the mediatory function. This void is the basis for the declarative of what modernism, or for that matter any other aspect of the literary text, is.

This sub-section has made it clear that Ghanayim adopted Somekh's analytic framework, processed to a certain degree within his mediatory position. Ghanayim adapted and applied the axis of literature's divorce from reality, and he even addressed language as literature's sole building material. Nevertheless, due to the structure of settler-colonial knowledge and power, the mediatory position could not allow the axis of the literary system and that of artistic value to be applied beyond the declarative level. This type of communication, the declaration, is an essential formalisation derived from the nature of the mediatory position. This position's *raison d'être* is a process of constant emptying in order to be refilled. In the following sub-section, I will position these framework axes as a single unit structuring the mediatory position. This will allow us to examine the mediatory position in reference to other positions in 'Arabic', as well as the literary modes of excessiveness and compulsiveness.

The Outlines of the Palestinian Mimetic Mask

Settler-colonial mimesis is not imitation, but processing. It is a set of operations applied to different aspects of the lived and imagined realities that occur within the structural space and time of the settler and the colonised native. This processing maintains the knowledge/power relations of the system of domination and control. However, the processed materiality has a powerful impact on its formalisation of the mimetic mask as a social product exchangeable among the settlers as well as the natives. For our purposes, the materiality is determined by the Arabic language and its products as socio-historical matter. Specifically, I will explore its instantiation as the literary criticism of Palestinian literature in Israel.

In the previous sub-section, I have argued that the processing proceeded along the four axes of Somekh's theoretical framework. Ghanayim adapted this framework, applying it to Palestinian literature in literary critical texts intended for the Palestinian readership in Israel. The following questions remain: When the four axes are connected, what are the outlines of the mediatory position as a processing site? What are the outlines of the theoretical framework, in its operation as a single and complete processing unit? And can it serve as an analytic example for the compulsive literacy mode?

Prior to charting those outlines, I will describe what lies beyond them, outside the mediatory position. I am referring to what does not arise in literary critical texts, due to the processing carried out through the stylistic-structural theoretical framework discussed above. The main absentee, so to speak, is the passion for Arabic – language as an object of desire for those dealing with it as professional scholars. In many senses, the status of Arabic and its products in the cultural history of the Arab nations is symbolically approximate to that of the mother.[82] It is language that conceives meaning; it structures the bosom of Arab culture that protects its offspring and keeps them safe. The Arabic language is an object re-cathected at any juncture of profound change in Arab culture.

In the case of the Zionist settler-colonial regime, the structure of the mediatory position is equivalent to the mother's abandonment of her children, albeit unconsciously. This is because the settler knows Arabic better than her own kin. Moreover, once constituted as such, it is that settler who determines the nature of the relations between Arabic and those brought up in her bosom. Such a dynamic cannot be articulated consciously by the Palestinians occupying the mediatory position, Mahmoud Ghanayim included. Therefore, intense desire for Arabic and its products can only be expressed in sites excluded from 'Arabic', such as interpersonal conversations in daily life. This is a desire designed to recharge the body of the mother who has abandoned her children. The mediatory position is the structural closure of this abandonment. Therefore, the first outline of the mediatory position is affective aridity, translated into respect and awe for the settlers. Desire cannot be an analytical category within the knowledge/power framework of mediation.

The second outline, related to the exclusion of desire from the mediatory position, is the absence of the anxiety of influence, in Harold Bloom's term.[83] Among most of Somekh's students reviewed for the purpose of this study, including Ghanayim, we witness a consistent attempt to resemble the 'father' Somekh, at least on the textual level. The more similar to Somekh they became, the more valuable their success. This relationship pattern is reminiscent of the master-disciple pattern that Abdellah Hammoudi has identified in the knowledge/power relations of Moroccan society. It is also reminiscent of Faisal Darraj's description of politician-intellectual relationships in the context of Palestinian political culture, particularly in the PLO administration.[84] In both cases, the structural relationship does not enable the disciple and intellectual originating in a rural area to achieve the position of producing critical knowledge/power frameworks that transform the structural relations between them and their superiors in the hierarchy of the power system within which they operate. These relations structure the fixation in the relations between the Palestinian mode of compulsive literacy and the Zionist mode of excessive literacy.

The third outline of the mediatory position consists of the theoretical framework used by Ghanayim for processing within the mediatory position in the field of 'Arabic'. This framework operates as a unit, cleansed of emotional, historical and literary instances. The divorcing of literature from reality is a basic step in this cleansing process. It is reinforced and reproduced, following displacement: from engagement with emotional and historical material to engagement with the materiality of language in its guise as an independent system. Not only is the material of language pure – so are the laws of the literary system. The artistic model of modernism is presented through ironic intertextuality. The basic idea is that, in their creative voyage, the writers should attempt to detach from sociohistorical reality. The writer must disengage from reality by dialoguing with other texts, and only other texts. The processing unit is a logical-mathematical mechanism bordering on the natural, an objective mechanism devoid of any emotional or ideological biases. In Ghanayim's application of that processing unit, the first two axes – that of disengagement and that of language – have operated according to the desirable model, while those of the literary system and artistic value have not.

The mediatory position is characterised by an ambivalent structural tension, related to the relationship between the settler, the native and their history. This is one of the causes of Ghanayim's failure to apply the axes of the literary system and artistic value. The mediatory position is of a second order in the Zionist settler-colonial regime: for it to exist, the regime must allow it. It is therefore unable to operate as an independent mechanism and would never become an autonomous system. Whenever it tries to operate independently, control and oversight mechanisms will block it and relocate it as a mediatory position within 'Arabic'. At the same time, the symbolic capital of knowledge/power accumulated by the Palestinian operators of the mediatory position may enable them to break free of the iron cage of mediation, thanks to the mobility and other characteristics of symbolic capital (see, for example, Darwish and Shammas).[85] In this context, the control and surveillance mechanisms operate on two levels. They create an emotional structure of loyalty and identification with the mediatory position, while at the same time limiting the ownership of the symbolic capital of the knowledge/power framework, to prevent any accumulation that could lead to creative work independent of the mechanism. The failure in the twin axes of literary system and artistic value is symptomatic of this ambivalent dynamic. Both axes, at least on a symbolic level, evince the mobility of the creative work's symbolic capital and, thus, the symbolism of the knowledge/power of the critic of that work.

The fourth outline of the processing unit of the mediatory position is the logic of disengagement that disconnects its operation from the content it processes. Every literary work must be divorced from reality; every work is made up of the materials of Arabic; every work is a literary system; every modern literary work has artistic value. Accordingly, every piece of content is relocated in reference to the mediatory position, 'Arabic' and the settler-colonial regime. The totality of the re-inscription of each literary event within the framework of the mediatory position, as well as the broad systems out of which it operates, is reminiscent of the nature of the Zionist mode of excessive literacy. As a bridge spanning the structures of excessiveness and compulsiveness, the mediatory position operates partly according to the logic of compulsiveness, in reference to the excessive mode that lies above it. In our case, the excessive mode operators are Somekh and the Zionist academic establishment. The mediatory position also operates according to the logic of excessiveness, with reference to the literary events produced by Palestinians in Israel.

The fifth outline concerns the value produced and distributed by the processing unit among Palestinians who read/write, by virtue of their location in the mediatory position. I begin by dividing this value into its material and symbolic aspects, despite the problematic nature of this distinction. Undoubtedly, there is a material economic value to the mediatory position, as it provides a safety net of belonging to a false middle class. This middle class is false because it lacks collective ownership of symbolic means of production. Its materiality is divorced from reality, reminiscent of the petit bourgeoisie of developing countries.[86] In other words, the collective group of mediators acts like a variation on the character of the junior public official. This material-class insecurity is reproduced in the processing unit through the fetishisation of academic ranks and honours. For example, this group of Palestinian academics demonstrates ritualistic behaviours and feelings, reminiscent of Palestinian patriarchal society's rites of passage of wedlock and death, when it comes to declaring an academic rank on the public level of the mediatory position.

Based on these outlines, I will now address the question of what type of return to and repositioning in 'Arabic' is demanded by the mediatory position. On the one hand, it does not appear that this position involves the discursive articulation of the loss of the ability to lose. The desire for re-cathexis is displaced onto the mother's body – Arabic and its products – that has been denied to or has abandoned the son. This dynamic is accompanied by the structural disappearance of the anxiety of influence and the establishment of traditional master-disciple relations in modern academic guise. On the other hand, the mediatory position has secondary ownership of symbolic capital of knowledge/power that may be activated socially only in reliance on the regime's material infrastructure. Hence, the mediatory position does not demand return and repositioning as owners of the symbolic means of production in order to redefine the Palestinian collective as able to lose. It is also not a Zionist establishment position in the traditional form, as encountered in the previous chapter. Although the mediatory position accepts the existing condition of 'Arabic' as part of the mechanisms of the Zionist regime, this acceptance also must include the acceptance of the regime as its exclusive owner. This is because the mediatory position, with its symbolic capital of knowledge/power, can only exist on the material-institutional basis of the regime itself.

The demand of ownership in literary criticism was an accelerated process of modernisation that occurred within the field of 'Arabic'. Implicit here is the assumption that Palestinians may not demand ownership of means of production for which they are not yet prepared. But the desirable modernism is partial: it cannot lead to true ownership of the means of production and to the structuring of some kind of collective, national or otherwise. This is similar to the status of Palestinian sub-contractors in the Israeli construction market. They are not the entrepreneurs or the builders, nor can they be the landlords. They only carry out tasks that the latter do not want to perform themselves. This comparison sheds light on the issue of ownership of the symbolic means of production in the mediatory position. Like Palestinian sub-contractors on the Israeli construction market, Palestinian academics are artisans working within 'Arabic' and its products. In their position, they can certainly not become the engineers or architects of symbolic means of production, and they certainly cannot be their entrepreneurs or owners.

The mediatory position is not one of literacy in its own right, not even in the standard sense of the compulsive mode of literacy, since it, too, follows the logic of the Zionist mode of excessiveness. It utilises the logic of the compulsive mode of literacy, by applying the model of modernisation to Palestinian literature, but it does not demand return and repositioning as owners of symbolic means of production. Like the petite bourgeoisie, it serves in a series of roles that belong to the sector of services provided to the owners of the means of production, operating as a class-marker that distinguishes between the middle and working classes, lest they intermix. Therefore, the mediatory position is critical for activating the modes of excessiveness and compulsiveness. Yet, it remains external to them. Neither excessive nor compulsive, it acts as a bridge that spans them both, within the Zionist settler-colonial regime.

Conclusion

This chapter has discussed the processes of the constitution of the mediatory position in 'Arabic', extracting the type of return and repositioning that this position demands of the Palestinians in Israel. The main argument is that the mediatory position has been made possible thanks to the maturation of structural processes in the relationship between the Palestinians and the Zionist regime related to the 1967 war. Following these processes, literary criticism in 'Arabic' underwent an accelerated process of academisation involving state and professional agents and institutions. The field of Israeli academia took an active part in reconstituting literary criticism as a form of academic knowledge/power imparted to Palestinian academics who were involved in establishing the mediatory position in 'Arabic' and who read and wrote from that position.

Among several Zionist scholars in Israeli academia who have supervised Palestinian academics, I have focused on Sasson Somekh, given the central role that he played in the processes of constituting 'Arabic' in the post-1967 period and in particular the mediatory position within it. Mahmud Ghanayim is one of the most prominent Palestinian scholars among Somekh's students. Both Somekh and Ghanayim wrote in Arabic for the Palestinian readership. This chapter has reviewed Somekh's publications on modern Arab, and particularly Egyptian, literature, as well as Ghanayim's publications on Palestinian literature. I have extracted the theoretical framework used by Somekh in writing to the Palestinian readership, which he imparted to his student Ghanayim. This framework consists of four axes: literature divorced from reality, language as the raw material of literature, the literary system and the artistic as the supreme value. The analysis of Somekh and Ghanayim's literary critical corpus has suggested that the first two axes were applied successfully by Ghanayim, in comparison with Somekh's model, while failing time after time when it came to applying the latter two – the literary system and artistic value. I have argued that this failure is emblematic of the structural relations that constitute the mediatory position in the hierarchy of knowledge/power relations within 'Arabic', as well as the relations between the mediatory position and the field of Israeli academia on the institutional-material level.

This theoretical framework operates as the processing unit of the knowledge/power transmitted through the mediatory position to the Palestinian readership in Israel. The outlines of this unit are complex: suppression and exclusion of the desire to recharge Arabic as a mother who structures the collective identity; the exclusion of the anxiety of influence and the constitution of traditional master-disciple relations in modern academic guise; a pseudo-mathematical logic; disengagement between the unit's working mechanism and the content of the processed material; and the contradiction between a middle-class image, reflected in the value that the unit produces and distributes among its occupants, and their conduct, which is reminiscent of a petite bourgeoisie. These characteristics chart a certain type of return and repositioning within 'Arabic': the mediatory position accepts the regime's ownership of the symbolic means of production in 'Arabic'. It thereby also loses the ability to lose, as a permanent condition grounding its conduct. The mediatory position demands modernisation through Zionist mechanisms, allegedly in order for its occupants to be the owners of symbolic means of production in 'Arabic'. An examination of the type of modernism that it processes indicates, however, that this modernism is only partial, as it does not allow ownership of the symbolic means of productions itself. Therefore, the Palestinian mask of settler-colonial mimesis, the processing unit in the mediatory position, constitutes an iron cage of these knowledge/power relations. It does not enable the resolution of the fundamental contradiction of the settler-colonial regime: the settler-native relationship.

For some Palestinians at least, the mediatory position has not met the test of the socioeconomic changes that have washed over the relations of the Zionist regime's material and symbolic production since the early 1990s. The completion of Israel's integration in the new division of roles of late capitalism, embodied in its relation to the Palestinians as neo-settler-colonialism, transformed the coordinates of the knowledge/power relations within settler-native relations. These changes led to the emergence of new positions in 'Arabic' and transformed the nature of its work, involving a reduction in the status of the mediatory position towards the end of the 1990s. The following chapter will review the new positions within 'Arabic', analyse their construction processes and extract their operational logic.

Notes

1. On the academisation of the Palestinian issue and on the Palestinians in Israeli academia, see Baruch Kimmerling, 'Ideology and Nation-Building: The Palestinians and their Meaning in Israeli Sociology', *American Sociological Review* 57, no. 4 (1992), 446–60.
2. See, for example, Bishara, *Al-'Arab fī Isrā'īl.*
3. On the relation between wars and the cultural field in the Palestinian-Israeli field, see Ismail Nashef, *On Palestinian Abstraction: Zohdy Qadry and the Geometrical Melody of Late Modernism* (Haifa: Raya Publications, 2014), 22–34. On the effects of the 1967 war on other Palestinian literary fields, see Hanan Ashrawi, 'The Contemporary Palestinian Poetry of Occupation', *Journal of Palestine Studies* 7, no. 3 (Spring 1978), 75–96.
4. This is the first novel written in Hebrew by a Palestinian writer: Atallah Mansour, *BeOr Ḥadash* [In a New Light] (Tel Aviv: Karni, 1966). For the English translation, see Atallah Mansour, *In a New Light*, transl. Abraham Birman (Elstree, Herts.: Vallentine Mitchell Publications, 1969). For the settler's point of view on Mansour's novel, see Rachel Feldhay-Brenner, *Inextricably Bonded: Israeli Arab and Jewish Writers Re-Visioning Culture* (Madison: University of Wisconsin Press, 2003), 173–205.
5. On the concept of literarity, see Jacques Rancière, *The Politics of Aesthetics*, transl. Gabriel Rockhill (New York: Continuum, 2004), 9–46.
6. Tawfiq Fayad, *Al-Mushawwahūn* [The Deformed] (Haifa: Kull Shay, [1963] 2008).
7. See, for example, 'Isa Lubani, 'Al-Mushawwahūn li-Tawfīq Fayāḍ' [Al-Mushawwahun by Tawfiq Fayad], in *Dirāsāt fī l-'adab al-Filasṭīnī al-maḥalī* [Studies in Local Palestinian Literature], ed. Nabih al-Qassim (Acre: Dar al-Aswar, [1964] 1984), 34–37.
8. On the Palestinian readership, see Ami Elad-Buskila, *Moledet Niḥlemet, 'Erets 'Avudah: Shishah Praḳim baSifrut haFalasṭinit haḥadashah* [Dreamt-of Homeland,

Lost Country: Six Chapters in Modern Palestinian Literature] (Or Yehuda, Israel: Maariv, 2001), 42–48.

9. See, for example, Ian Lustick, *Arabs in the Jewish State: Israel's Control of a National Minority* (Austin: University of Texas Press, 1980).
10. For a detailed sociological account of the Palestinian academics, see Andre Mazawi, 'University Education, Credentialism, and Social Stratification among Palestinian Arabs in Israel', *Higher Education* 29 (1995), 351–68.
11. On seminars for Arab teachers, see Agbaria, *Hakhsharat Morim.*
12. For more on the colonial mode of production, see Mahdi 'Amel, *Muqaddimāt naẓariyya* [Theoretical Introductions] (Beirut: Dar Al-Farabi, 1990), 329–68.
13. On the relation between labour and collective consciousness in the context of the Palestinians in Israel, see Ismail Nashef, 'A Deconstruction of Collusion', *Jadal* 12 (2012), 1–7.
14. Much has been written about the Arab education system in Israel. This literature examines how the system may be 'improved' without examining its structural roles in the settler-colonial Zionist regime. See, for example, Majid Al-Haj, *Education, Empowerment, and Control: The Case of the Arabs in Israel* (Albany: State University of New York Press, 1995).
15. On the history of mimesis as a site of particular kinds of relationships, see Gunter Gebauer and Christoph Wulf, *Mimesis: Culture, Art, Society*, transl. Don Reneau (Berkeley: University of California Press, 1995).
16. For more detail on the teacher-pupil relationship in the Palestinian context in Israel, see Ayman Agbaria and Hellali Pinson, 'Navigating Israeli Citizenship: How Do Arab-Palestinian Teachers Civicize Their Pupils?' *Race, Ethnicity, and Education* 22, no. 3 (2019), 391–409, https://doi.org/10.1080/13613324.2018.1511527
17. On desire in colonial contexts, see Robert Young, *Colonial Desire: Hybridity in Theory, Culture, and Race* (London: Routledge, 1995). For the Arab colonial context, see Joseph Massad, *Desiring Arabs* (Chicago: University of Chicago Press, 2007).
18. See Youmna Al-Eid, *Fī maʿrifat al-naṣṣ* [On Knowledge of the Text] (Beirut: Dar Al-Adab, 1983). For a different approach to the interface of sexuality, language and literature in the Arab context, see Abdallah Al-Ghadhami, *Al-Mar'a wa-l-lugha* [Woman and Language] (Casablanca: Al-Markaz Al-Thaqafi Al-Arabi, 1997).
19. Dr Gottesfeld, currently a lecturer at Bar-Ilan University, wrote her dissertation under Ghanayim's supervision. It was subsequently published as follows:

Dorit Gottesfeld, *HaEtsba'ot haNistarot: Siporet Nashim Falasṭiniot* [The Hidden Fingers: The Prose of Palestinian Women] (Tel Aviv: Resling, 2013).

20. For a different critical view of the the positionalities of the Arab Jews, see Ella Shohat, *On the Arab-Jew, Palestine, and Other Displacements: Selected Writings* (New York: Pluto Press, 2017).
21. For example, Somekh headed the Israeli Academic Center in Cairo from 1996 to 1998.
22. See Sasson Somekh, *The Changing Rhythm: A Study of Najib Mahfuz's Novels* (Leiden: Brill, 1973). Badawi is one of the leading researchers of modern Arabic literature in both the Arab and Anglophone worlds; see M. M. Badawi, *A Critical Introduction to Modern Arabic Poetry* (Cambridge: Cambridge University Press, 1975).
23. Sasson Somekh, *Yamim Hazuyim: Ḳorot Ḥayim 1951–2000* [Call it Dreaming: Memoirs, 1951–2000] (Tel-Aviv: Hakibbutz Hameuchad, 2008), 97–98.
24. On *Al-'Anbā'*, see Wang Yu and Hillel Cohen, 'Marketing Israel to the Arabs: The Rise and Fall of *al-Anbaa* Newspaper', *Israel Affairs* 15, no. 2 (2009), 190–210.
25. Shiloah Institute was established in 1959 under the auspices of the Israeli Oriental Society and in 1965 was integrated into TAU. It was named after Reuven Shiloah (Zaslani), who died that same year. He was one of the major founding figures of the Israeli intelligence services. See Haggai Eshed, *Reuven Shiloah, the Man Behind the Mossad: Secret Diplomacy in the Creation of Israel*, transl. David and Leah Zinder (London: Frank Cass, 1997).
26. Sasson Somekh, 'Al-'Adab al-'Arabī wa-l-qāri' al-'Ibrī" [Arabic Literature and the Hebrew Reader], *Al-Sharq* 3, no. 1–2 (1972), 49.
27. Somekh, 'Al-'Adab al-'Arabī', 56.
28. Kanafani was assassinated in Beirut on 8 July 1972, and the issue of *Al-Sharq* featuring Somekh's article was the June-July issue.
29. For a history of the Israeli literary criticism and its relation to the Zionist project, see, for example, Hannan Hever, *HaSipur vehaLe'om: Kri'ot Biḳortiot beḲanon haSiporet ha'Ivrit* [The Story and the Nation: Critical Readings in the Canon of Hebrew Prose] (Tel Aviv: Resling, 2007); Yitzhak Laor, *Anu Kotvim Otakh Moledet: Massot 'al Sifrut Israelit* [We Write You, Homeland: Essays on Israeli Literature] (Tel Aviv: Hakibbutz Hameuchad, 1995).
30. Somekh, *Yamim Hazuyim*, 132.
31. Somekh, *Yamim Hazuyim*, 136.
32. Sasson Somekh, *Bagdad Etmol* [Bagdad Yesterday] (Tel-Aviv: Hakibbutz Hameuchad, 2004), 12–13.

33. On publishing houses and journals in the Palestinian literary field in Israel of that time, see, for example, Elad-Buskila, *Moledet Niḥlemet*, 42–48.
34. Sasson Somekh, 'Al-'Alāqāt al-naṣṣiyya fī l-niẓām al-'adabī al-wāḥid' [The Textual Relations in One Literary System], *Al-Karmel* 7 (1986), 109–29.
35. Somekh, 'Al-'Alāqāt al-naṣṣiyya', 109–10.
36. On the history of these currents and the problems with their theoretical arguments, see Terence Hawkes, *Structuralism and Semiotics* (Berkeley: University of California Press, 1977).
37. Somekh, 'Al-'Alāqāt al-naṣṣiyya', 110.
38. Sasson Somekh, *Lughat al-qiṣṣa fī 'adab Yūsuf Idrīs* [The Language of the Story in Yusuf Idris's Literature] (Tel-Aviv, Acre: Tel-Aviv University, Srouji Publications, 1984).
39. Somekh, *Lughat al-qiṣṣa*, 47.
40. Sasson Somekh, 'Al-Ḥaraka wa-l-iyqā' fī Mārsh al-ghurūb' [Movement and Pace in Sunset March], *Al-Sharq* 2, no. 8 (1972), 5–9.
41. Somekh, 'Al-Ḥaraka wa-l-iyqā'', 8–9.
42. See, for example, Sasson Somekh, 'Masraḥ Mahmūd Taymūr: Lughat al-ḥiwār fī ṣiyāghatayn' [Mahmoud Taymour's Theatre: A Dialogue in Two Versions], in *Abḥāth fī l-lugha wa-l-uslūb* [Studies in Language and Style], ed. Sasson Somekh (Tel-Aviv: Tel-Aviv University, The Arab Publishing House, 1980), 24–27.
43. Somekh, *Lughat al-qiṣṣa*, 11–16.
44. Sasson Somekh, 'Naḥwā l-ma'nā l-murakkab' [Toward A Complex Meaning], *Al-Sharq* 10, no. 1 (1980), 26–29.
45. Sasson Somekh, 'Ṣīghat al-ḥadātha fī shi'r Michel Haddad' [Modernist Form in Michel Haddad's Poetry], *Al-Karmel* 4 (1983), 49–66.
46. Somekh, 'Naḥwā l-ma'nā', 26–27.
47. Faruq Muwasi, *Fī intiẓār al-qiṭār* [Waiting for the Train] (Nablus: The Association of Print Houses Cooperative, 1971). For the articles about it, see Sasson Somekh, 'Fī intiẓār al-qiṭār' [Waiting for the Train], *Al-Sharq* 1, no. 2 (1971), 8; Mahmud Ghanayim, 'Al-Tajārib al-ʿarūḍiyya fī shiʿrnā l-ḥurr: Dīwān fī Intiẓār al-qiṭār li-Fārūq Mawāsī' [Experiments in Classical Metres in Our Free Verse Poetry: 'Waiting for the Train' by Farouq Mawasi], *Al-Sharq* 2, no. 3 (1971), 15–20.
48. Somekh, 'Fī intiẓār al-qiṭār', 8.
49. Somekh, 'Fī intiẓār al-qiṭār', 8.
50. Ghanayim, 'Al-Tajārib al-'arūḍiyya', 15–16.
51. Mahmud Ghanayim, 'Al-Mawḍūʿāt al-ijtimāʿiyya fī l-qiṣṣa l-qaṣīra l-maḥaliyya' [Social Themes in Local Short Stories], *Al-Sharq* 7, no. 5–7 (1977), 9–23.

52. Ghanayim, 'Al Mawḍū'āt al-ijtimā'iyya', 9–10. See Moreh, 'HaSifrut.'
53. Ghanayim, 'Al Mawḍū'āt al-ijtimā'iyya', 12–18.
54. Mahmud Ghanayim, 'Dirāsāt fī l-qiṣṣa l-qaṣīra l-maḥaliyya' [Studies on the Local Short Story], *Al-Sharq* 9, no. 4 (1979), 17–41.
55. Ballas, *HaSifrut ha'Aravit.*
56. Mahmud Ghanayim, *Bayn al-rafḍ wa-l-iltizām: Dirāsa fī shi'r 'Abd al-Raḥīm Maḥmūd* [Between Refusal and Commitment: A Study of Abd al-Rahim Mahmoud's Poetry] (Jerusalem: Abu-Arafa, 1980), 5.
57. Mahmud Ghanayim, *Fī mabnā al-naṣṣ: Dirāsa fī riwāyat Imīl Ḥabībī 'Al-waqā'i' al-gharība fī ikhtifā' Sa'īd Abī al-Naḥs al-Mutashā'il'* [Structure of the Text: A Study of Emile Habibi's Novel 'The Extraordinary Chronicle of the Disappearance of Said Abu al-Nahas the Pessoptimist'] (Jat, Israel: Al-Yasār, 1987). For an introduction on Emile Habibi's literary corpus and *The Pessoptimist* see, Abu-Manneh, *The Palestinian Novel*, 96–115; Refqa Abu Remaileh, 'The Afterlives of *Iltizam*: Emile Habibi through a Kanfanisque Lens of Resistance Literature', in *Commitment and Beyond: Reflection on/of the Political in Arabic Literature since 1940s*, ed. Friedrike Pannewick and George Khalil (Wiesbaden: Reichert Verlag, 2015), 171–84.
58. Ghanayim, *Fī mabnā l-naṣṣ*, 11.
59. Ghanayim, *Fī mabnā l-naṣṣ*, 11.
60. Ghanayim, *Fī mabnā l-naṣṣ*, 11.
61. Ghanayim, *Al-Madār al-ṣa'b.*
62. Abassi, *Taṭawwur al-riwāya*; Ballas, *HaSifrut h'aAravit*; Elad-Buskila, *Moledet Niḥlemet.*
63. Ghanayim, *Al-Madār al-ṣa'b.*
64. Badr is one of the pioneering researchers of modern Arabic literature using modern scientific tools. His book *The Development of the Modern Arabic Novel in Egypt* became a recognised classic in the study of literature from Egypt and other Arab countries. He had many students from different Arab societies, who applied his model to modern Arab literatures; see 'Abd al-Muhsin Taha Badr, *Taṭawwur al-riwāya al-'Arabiyya al-ḥadītha fī Miṣr, 1870–1938* [The Development of the Modern Arabic Novel in Egypt, 1870–1938] (Cairo: Dar al Ma'arif, 1963). For a critical exposition of the Egyptian literary field, see Richard Jacquemond, *The Conscience of the Nation: Writers, State, and Society in Modern Egypt*, transl. David Tresilian (Cairo: The American University in Cairo Press, 2008).
65. Ghanayim, *Al-Maḍār al-ṣa'b*, 61–105.

66. Ghanayim, *Al-Maḍār al-ṣa'b*, 109–47.
67. Ghanayim, *Al-Maḍār al-ṣa'b*, 151–83.
68. Prominent scholars and authors from various periods in Arab-Islamic history.
69. Ghanayim, *Fī mabnā l-naṣṣ*, 28.
70. Ghanayim, *Fī mabnā l-naṣṣ*, 81.
71. Ghanayim, *Fī mabnā l-naṣṣ*, 110.
72. The word 'failure' here is not used in a judgmental-normative sense, but in reference to a discursive juncture in Ghanayim's corpus. In his book on modern Arab, non-Palestinian literature, which is based on his doctoral dissertation, systemic analysis is successfully applied. See Mahmud Ghanayim, *Tayār al-wa'ī fi l-riwāya al-'Arabiyya al-ḥadītha: Dirāsa 'uslūbiyya* [Stream of Consciousness in the Modern Arabic Novel: A Stylistic Study] (Beirut: Dar al-Jil, 1992).
73. Ghanayim, *Bayn al-rafḍ wa-l-iltizām.*
74. Ghanayim, *Fī mabnā l-naṣṣ.*
75. Ghanayim, *Fī mabnā l-naṣṣ*, 139–40.
76. Badr, *Taṭawwur al-riwāya.*
77. Emile Habibi, *Sarāya bint al-ghūl: Khurāfiyyah* [Saraya, the Ogre's Daughter: A Fairytale] (London: Riyad al-Rayyis, 1992).
78. Ghanayim, *Al-Madār al-ṣa'b*, 249–57.
79. Ghanayim, *Al-Madār al-ṣa'b*, 257.
80. Ghanayim, *Al-Madār al-ṣa'b*, 271–72.
81. See, for example, Rancière, *The Politics of Aesthetics,* 7–46.
82. The Arabic language is the object of many literary works, both ancient and modern. It is often presented as a beloved or, interchangeably, as a mother.
83. Bloom has discussed the relations between generations of poets and the way in which they shape the formalisation process of the poetic work. Although he has focused on poets, his theoretical framework may be applied to other creative endeavours, including literary criticism and academic work. See Harold Bloom, *The Anxiety of Influence: A Theory of Poetry* (Oxford: Oxford University Press, 1973).
84. Abdellah Hammoudi, *Master and Disciple: The Cultural Foundation of Moroccan Authoritarianism* (Princeton: Princeton University Press, 1997); Faisal Darraj, *Bu's al-thaqāfa fi l-mu'assasa l-Filasṭīniyya* [The Wretchedness of Culture in the Palestinian Establishment] (Beirut: Dar al-Adab, 1996).
85. Mahmoud Darwish and Anton Shammas left the settler-colonial regime in similar stages of their respective careers, as their creative projects began to mature. Despite their divergent styles and ideological affiliations, they clearly share a

position in terms of the relationship that they managed to establish between their work and the mediatory position in which the Zionist colonial regime sought to confine them.

86. On the petite bourgeoisie in Egypt, see, for example, Mahmoud Hussein, *Class Conflict in Egypt, 1945–1970*, transl. Alfred Ehrenfeld and Michel Chirman (New York: Monthly Review Press, 1973).

4

The Procedure Liberated: 'Arabic' in the Hands of Palestinian Experts

Since the early 1990s, the relations between the Zionist regime and the Palestinian citizens of Israel have seen profound changes. Some of these changes were related to the new socioeconomic processes in the Zionist regime, which consisted of local manifestations of global processes.[1] Other changes were directly related to the relations between the Zionist regime and the Palestinians, particularly the Palestinian citizens of Israel.[2] These two spheres influenced each other in a way that strengthened certain aspects of the changes and weakened others. One of the strengthened aspects has been the formation of a Palestinian civil society and its institutionalisation within the Israeli public sphere.[3] Undoubtedly, a Palestinian civil society had existed previously. However, starting from the early 1990s, it gained unprecedented momentum and became institutionalised, on the basis of new socioeconomic conditions that had not been in place previously. One of the major issues within Palestinian civil society in Israel is the state's intervention in the structure and boundaries of the public sphere. Consequently, most civil society organisations have been preoccupied with the status of Arabic and its products in the Israeli public sphere, thus intervening directly in 'Arabic'.

One of the most obvious manifestations of the relationship between globalisation in Israel and local changes experienced by the Palestinians in Israel has been the rise of those civil society organisations in the Israeli public sphere. The civil sphere had predated that process and had multiple manifestations, but it was arranged around two foci – partisan and government politics – and it relied on the infrastructure of Christian and Muslim religious institutions. Partisan affiliation, the relations with the government and religious affiliation set the boundaries of the civil sphere where Palestinians were active, as well as the nature of their activities. Moreover, these sites were directly subordinated to the party, the government, or religious institutions, both materially and ideologically.

The traditional positions in 'Arabic', such as the mediatory position and the positions of orientalist experts and members of *Al-Jadid*, were partly expressive of the civil sphere. The most significant change occurred when these positions in 'Arabic' broke free of the direct control of the ruling parties and religious institutions and began negotiating with them on a new basis. The socioeconomic foundation for that negotiation was constituted by processes of privatisation and decentralisation that took place in Israel, as well as the takeover of increasing areas of social, material and symbolic production by market forces.

These global forces, operating already in the 1970s, have been called by different names. To describe them here, I will employ the terminology of late capitalism, and to refer to the relations between the Zionist regime and the Palestinian citizens of Israel, I will use the parallel term of 'late settler-colonialism'.[4] These processes affected the Palestinian civil sphere in two ways. First, the global movement of capital defeated the nation-state model, transgressing its boundaries and defying its regulations.[5] Second, a neoliberal professional discourse developed, re-organising the civil sphere and its range of possible practices.[6]

Among the Palestinians in Israel, these developments coincided with the decline of Palestinian national ideology and old patterns of collective action that had been used to dominate the previous period, mainly party politics. At the same time, as result of the academisation process of the Palestinian labour force in Israel, a broad class of academic professionals began to establish itself, their body of knowledge allowing them to internalise the new professional neoliberal discourses. At this junction, Palestinian civil society organisations began to grow and to connect to the global capital movement dedicated to organisations of this type. The professionalisation of the public sphere organisations dealing with the Palestinian collective in Israel led to fundamental changes in the collective's self-image and to the construction of a new type of Palestinian subjectivity among the Palestinian citizens of

Israel. These collective and subjective forms redefined the status of Arabic and its products. They intervened in the structure of 'Arabic' and the nature of positions at work within it, trying to break through the arena's structural boundaries, mainly the financial dependence on Israeli governmental funds. In order to thoroughly clarify the processes undergone by 'Arabic', I will first present and analyse the new Palestinian collective and subject.

Most of the socioeconomic basis of Palestinians active in the new civil sphere consists of the mobile symbolic capital of an academic education devoid of ownership of the material means of production. This symbolic capital, however, can be easily translated into the terms of a global professional neoliberal discourse. Consider, for example, Palestinian lawyers who studied at Israeli universities before working in international human rights organisations. Their mobility, in reference to symbolic means of production and their ownership, led to two moves among civil society activists. First, they developed a discourse critical of the Zionist regime that was not limited to the strictly national/settler-colonial aspect but expanded to universal values of individual and collective rights.[7] Second, a critical discourse developed also toward the perceptions, practices and attitudes of Palestinian institutions in Israel. These institutions remained active on the foundation of the previous period, whether through Palestinian nationalism in its local version, or through the position of mediation between the regime and its Palestinian subjects. Palestinian national heritage was invoked as part of an attempt to redesign the collective memory, as in literary and poetic corpuses and symbols of struggle. Conversely, practices and events derived from the mediatory position between the coloniser-settler and the colonised native were purged from the reshaped memory of this group, recast in a negative frame.

These collective memory dynamics – namely, dynamics of purging and empowerment – were enabled by the institutionalisation of a certain procedural process unique to civil society organisations. The logic of this procedure is legal-professional: the subject activating and being activated by the discourse is recognised as such based on the subject's profession and legal status.[8] Accordingly, the civil discourse of Palestinians in Israel constructed the (Palestinian) collective as an indigenous minority, an entity that could be presented as a group with recognised legal status in the human rights discourse, without violating the late settler-colonial order.[9] In order to translate both collective and individual Palestinian national identity into the terms of legal-professional discourse, its aspects of belonging and their *modus operandi*, including collective memory, had to be redefined. The collective and individual subject here has a right to a language of his or her own. In the previous, national period, the collective had no legal-professional right to a language: the language was 'organic' to the collective and embodied in the individual subject.

After the collective became a legal status and the individual a professional specialising in the legality of that status, the definition of the collective and individual became a strictly procedural affair. This procedure can receive various names – rights, status, law, ethics – but its *modus operandi* will remain the same.[10] In general, the following came to operate on the basis of legal procedures: paths of return, re-owning the lost collective self, repositioning and reframing the current relations of the community in terms of its Others from within 'Arabic', whether by accepting it as the main collective arena, or by attempting to break its boundaries. Therefore, these operations came to require a professional expert, such as a psychologist, lawyer, researcher, or linguist, to activate it at bureaucratic levels. For example, public signs in Israel are often misspelled in Arabic. Such misspellings are corrected procedurally by a committee authorised to determine the content of the signs and must therefore include a professional expert of Arabic. This chapter will examine the working logic of the path of return and the repositioning of the procedural position in 'Arabic' and its various manifestations.

It may seem that legal procedures and their bureaucratic actualisations governed civil society organisations among the Palestinians in Israel. Yet, the realities of 'Arabic' suggest a more complex situation. Later in this chapter, I will argue that the emergence of this procedural logic transformed the Zionist mode of excessive literacy. It developed from reading/writing about events, or series of events, occurring within the Zionist regime to encompass excessive reading and writing about entire social domains. In the period under consideration, new practices of excessive literacy came to define a whole domain, such as the field of education, and not only teachers and texts. This was carried out based on the field's connection to the settler-colonial state of Israel, as opposed to previous practices that had defined a singular event only, similar to a novel in contrast to the whole literary field.

A fascinating example is the 2007 law titled *Supreme Institute of the Arabic Language*, to be discussed further below. As mandated by this law, the Academy of the Arabic Language in Israel is responsible for a given domain – that of Arabic and its products as a field. It functions apart from any single event in Arabic and its products that require excessive reading/writing. The procedural logic of the academy is one of compulsive reading/writing of the whole domain of Arabic. It reads and writes the field of Arabic as a shadow image of the field of Hebrew.

A preliminary review of the implications of these developments for 'Arabic' indicates that the positions within it during the period under study came to represent a spectrum ranging between two poles. The first pole represents mediatory positions, which mediate between whole fields, and not merely between events. The second pole represents a declarative, national position that tries to break free of the dialectic cage of coloniser-settler and colonised native. These positions are based on a legal-professional foundation consisting of two premises: 1) the Palestinian community is a legal entity; 2) therefore, mainly professionals with legal expertise should manage it. Its procedural logic is as follows: the community is re-built through activating bureaucratic processes.

The newly-developed mediatory position translated academic knowledge about Arabic into professional knowledge that could be disseminated by a legal body claiming a professional monopoly over Arabic and its products as a field. The claim for a professional monopoly on a legal basis does not merely apply to the material and institutional basis, such as the Academy of Arabic Language in Israel. It also organises the type of intervention in the body of Arabic and its products – for example, the published lists of new terms in Arabic translated from Hebrew by the academy.

At the opposite pole of the range of positions, the declarative national position argues for a monopoly over the essence of the Palestinian collectivity. Arabic is part of this essence and must be purified of Hebrew and liberated from the 'Arabic' arena. For example, representatives of this position published the Arabic terms that should replace the widespread Hebrew terms used by Palestinians in Israel.

The range of positions between these two poles, the developed mediatory and the declarative national positions, includes the positions of previous periods. They are organised within it, subject to the legal-professional discourse and its procedural logic. Some of the officials who held key positions in 'Arabic', such as Mahmud Ghanayim and Sasson Somekh, continued to play central roles within it in this period as well. The textual and public actions of the representatives of the positions to be discussed below will usually include layers from earlier periods, but their social manifestation will follow the later zeitgeist.

In order to represent this range in its full breadth and depth, I will focus on three central positions within 'Arabic'. The first is that of NGOs active among Palestinians in Israel. I will examine the relation of these NGOs to 'Arabic', based on an analysis of two vision statements published in an attempt to reorganise the relations of Palestinians with the State of Israel.[11] The second is that of the academy, founded in 2007 by Israeli law. I will look at its corpus to explore the nature of its action within 'Arabic', deriving from its structural mediatory position. The third position is that of the Arab Culture Association, which combines the legal-professional logic with a basic claim to represent the Palestinian collective. It makes this claim by virtue of its professionalism, which lends it an in-depth understanding of the essence of the Palestinian collective. I will discuss the association's activities relating to Arabic and its products. I will conclude that these activities constitute an attempt to redefine 'Arabic' and thereby reclaim it.

This chapter will chart the developments in the arena of 'Arabic' over the past three decades.[12] I will argue that significant global processes occurred during this period, including the institutionalisation of the *modus operandi* of late capitalism/settler-colonialism. In addition, developments in the complex relations between Palestinians and the Zionist regime in Israel transformed the *modus operandi* of 'Arabic' and the structure of this arena. The legal-professional basis, with its procedural expertise and logic, became the organising principle of the textual and public activities within 'Arabic'. This produced a new range of positions within 'Arabic' that will be examined here through three specific positions. It appears that they all share the common denominator of moving from working on isolated events to working on an entire domain – that is, 'Arabic'. The question remains: How are we to understand excessive Zionist reading/writing, and its compulsive Palestinian counterpart, as overarching principles that organise the Zionist regime, and in particular the arena of 'Arabic', in its recent incarnation?

The Vision Statements: Language as a Right

In the early 2000s, several Palestinian NGOs separately published vision statements regarding the future of the relations between the Palestinian community in Israel and the State of Israel. These vision statements consider the Palestinians in Israel a national minority with legal status, mainly in its relationship to the State of Israel. Its legal status grants the 'indigenous' group universal rights, one of which is the right to Arabic and its products. However, the vision statements do not elaborate on the meaning of this right. I will attempt to assess its nature, based on an analysis of the vision statements and of interpretations published by some of those who participated in writing them.

The vision statements were published following the changes in the relations between the Zionist regime and the Palestinians in Israel, which resulted from events in October 2000 and the Second Intifada, a period characterised by severe and violent clashes.[13] The statements were formulated as part of attempts to reroute direct and violent conflicts to other channels, whether on behalf of the state apparatus or on behalf of the Palestinians citizens. These attempts managed to prevent escalations that could lead to direct confrontations, but the change in the nature of the relations with the state was inevitable. The four vision statements were: the Haifa Declaration published in 2007 by Mada al-Carmel: Arab Centre for Applied Social Research; the Democratic Constitution published that same year by Adalah: Legal Centre for Arab Minority Rights in Israel; the Equal Constitution for All published in 2006 by the Musawa Centre for the Rights of Arab Citizens in Israel; and the Future Vision of the Arabs in Israel, published that same year by the High Follow-Up Committee for Arab Citizens of Israel, at the behest of its Chair, Shawqi Khatib.

This sub-section focuses on the Haifa Declaration and the Democratic Constitution. The Equal Constitution for All was written by a single individual (Yousef Jabareen), while the Future Vision was a collection of summaries of studies on various life areas conducted by Palestinian researchers at the request of the Chair of the Follow-Up Committee. Conversely, the

Haifa Declaration and Democratic Constitution are collective texts that took several years to develop prior to reaching their final version, hence their particular importance for Arabic and its products among Palestinians in Israel.

The Haifa Declaration

The Haifa Declaration aims at redefining the relations between the Palestinian community in Israel and its various interlocutors, most particularly the Israeli establishment. It was initiated in 2002 by a group of Palestinian academics who developed their careers in the Israeli academic sphere; most of them had held a permanent academic position in it at some point.[14] In addition to their academic work, since the early 1990s members of this group established NGOs dealing with applied sociopolitical research. They attempted to create an alternative body of knowledge about the Palestinians, in contrast to the knowledge created by Israeli academia.[15]

These NGOs formulated strategies to raise funds from non-Israeli sources as well as to acquire global discursive formations of civil society organisations concerning individual and collective rights. These would be partly literal translations from European languages into Arabic and Hebrew, as well as interpretations of knowledge acquired in Israeli academia – for example, on how to apply universal rights to the Palestinian community in Israel. The adoption of global discourses facilitated contacts with bodies of knowledge/power inaccessible to this group in Israeli academia, such as the discourse on the rights of native people in Africa and the Americas. Particularly noteworthy in this regard were discourses on colonialism, post-colonialism, indigeneity, settler-colonialism and Global South-based solidarity.

This generation of Palestinian academics tried to integrate local knowledge/power from within Israel with knowledge/power from global bodies to create a Palestinian indigenous discourse applicable within the boundaries of the group of Palestinians in Israel.[16] However, despite their collective emotional structure, most of these academics did not acquire discursive formations of knowledge/power that had developed in the Palestinian national movement in the diaspora, among the intellectuals of the Palestinian Liberation Organisation, or in modern Arab thought, at least not during the period under study.[17] This blend of Israeli and global knowledge/power, as well as the absence of the other Palestinian and Arab components, is clearly evident in the textual and narrative structure of the Haifa Declaration, as well as in articles written by its formulators.[18]

The Haifa Declaration tries to define the boundaries of the group of Palestinians in Israel in reference to themselves and to other social and national groups. It refers to four main areas.[19] The first area consists of internal social issues, such as the patriarchal structure, religious affiliations and women's status. The second is the relation between Palestinian citizens and the State of Israel, as articulated in the status of the national minority, in the state's Jewish character and in the history of the relations between the two. The third concerns the relationship between this group of Palestinians and other parts of the Palestinian people and the Arab nation, articulated in relations of belonging, common culture, economic contacts and so on. Finally, the fourth area is the national identity of Palestinians in Israel: their being part of Arab and Palestinian nationality, the reinforcement of this identity and the rewriting of national identity under Israeli rule.

The text of the Haifa Declaration directly refers to Arabic on three occasions, but its relation to it is indirectly woven throughout the entire document.

The first direct reference to Arabic is as follows:

> *Our national identity* is grounded in universal values and culture, in the *Arabic language* and Arab culture, and in collective memory, which draws on both our Palestinian and Arab history and on Arab and Islamic culture. It grows and gains strength through the live and combined relation with these elements and is continually nourished by our ongoing relations with our land and homeland.[20]

Here, Arabic is an element of national identity, referred to directly after universal values and culture. It belongs to Arab culture yet is distinct from it. It is emphasised here as almost equivalent to the entire Arab culture. In the dynamics of constructing a national identity arising from this quote, one finds several circles of identity: Palestinian, Arab, Islamic and universal. These circles all refer to the past and to collective memory and interact in a way that facilitates growth. It appears that this identity model is structured on Arabic, which retains the past and present and enables future growth.[21] Language is not only an identity element, but also the model according to which national identity is constructed. Hence, it is even more important than the circles of Palestinian, Arab and Islamic identity.

Here, the declaration builds bridges that span the gap of being isolated from the rest of Arab people, after the mechanisms of the Zionist regime cut off the relations of the group of Palestinians with Arab-Islamic history and culture. At the same time, it accepts the nation-state model and the status of the national language within it as a constitutive space-time of identity. Moreover, it appears that the authors of the declaration refer to literary Arabic, denying the Palestinian dialects any status in structuring the national identity. To a significant extent, they substitute – albeit partially – the Zionist national model with the secular Arab national model of the status of Arabic.

The second reference to Arabic in the Haifa Declaration occurs when it discusses the effect of the Zionist occupation/colonisation on Palestinians in Israel and suggests ways of dealing with it. Here, Arabic is an asset to which one may return as the group deals with the Zionist settler-colonial regime, in order to remain in and to safeguard the Palestinian homeland:

> Despite the failure in realising our national project and despite the partial separation caused by the *Nakba* between us and the rest of the Palestinian people and the Arab nation; despite attempts to instil ignorance among us with regard to Palestinian and Arab history, to split us into religious groups and reduce our identity to a distorted 'Israeli Arab' one, we have never spared efforts in maintaining and strengthening our Palestinian identity and our national dignity. We hereby affirm our adherence to our belonging to our homeland and to our Palestinian people and the Arab nation, in terms of culture, *language* and history, and reiterate our right to remain in and safeguard our homeland.[22]

The 'Israeli Arab' identity is the result of settler-colonialist oppressive forces operating to isolate this group of Palestinians from the rest of Palestinian society and from the Arab nation as a whole. This identity includes – or rather enforces top-down – a certain history, language and culture. From the point of view of the Haifa Declaration, these distort the collective identity of the Palestinians in Israel. Despite the failure of realising a Palestinian national project, Palestinians in Israel have opposed those oppressive forces and adhered to belonging to the homeland and to the Arab nation. This adherence relies on Arab history, language and culture. The basic assumption is that these are inalienable elements of identity. Therefore, they use them to oppose the processes initiated by the regime in order to manipulate Palestinians in Israel to suit the regime's interests.[23]

The Haifa Declaration proposes a solution for the existing situation, one that is directly derived from the present stage in the history of the relations between the group of Palestinians and the Zionist regime: changing the status of the Palestinians from a group of individuals who demand civil equality to an institutional recognition of a national minority group with collective national and civil rights. The declaration enumerates these rights. One of its demands is for Arabic to be of equal status to Hebrew in the reformed state:

> The solution of a democratic state based on equality between the two national groups – the Israeli Jews and the Palestinian Arabs in Israel – is the only one that will ensure the rights of both groups in a just and equal manner. This requires changing Israel's constitutional structure and changing its definition from a Jewish to a democratic state based on national and civil equality between the two national groups and grounding the principles of justice and equality between its citizens and inhabitants. The practical implications of this change include the revoking of all laws that discriminate directly or indirectly on a national, ethnic or religious basis, primarily the immigration and civil status laws; the promulgation of laws grounded in the principles of equality and non-discrimination; *implementing the equality between Arabic and Hebrew as two official languages with equal status in the state*; applying the principle of multiculturalism to all groups; effective participation of the Palestinian minority in government and decision-making; veto rights in all matters related to the status and rights of Palestinian citizens in Israel and ensuring their right to cultural autonomy that will enable them to exercise their right to determine policies in matters pertaining to their culture and education, to manage them and formulate their contents. [. . .] These principles all ensure our right to self-determination as an indigenous minority.[24]

The proposed solution to the intrinsic conflict is founded on a legal-procedural logic conceived and formulated by professional academics who have studied the two national groups. Since what we have before us are two unequal national groups – Israeli Jews and Palestinians – the solution is nationality-based equality. Nationality is a legal entity that grants its members certain rights that have to be written into law. According to the authors, by definition every national group has a language and is entitled to anchor its right to and use of it in law and to ensure its public visibility.

The question is, what does a law stating that Arabic is equal in status to Hebrew mean exactly? What is interesting in this declaration is the rejection of discriminatory laws and the support for equality laws. The implementation begins by ensuring the status of Arabic as an official state language. The authors enumerate additional areas, beyond Arabic, where equality needs to be secured: multiculturalism, a share in power and decision-making, and cultural autonomy. This is a list of sovereignty-markers. The authors state that these are the principles that will ensure the self-determination of the group of Palestinians in Israel.

If we set aside for a moment the problematic issue of splitting the right to self-determination of a nation among the various groups that comprise it, Arabic is seen here as a marker of political sovereignty.[25] This approach may be examined from several perspectives. Based on the classic nation-state ideology, one may argue that Arabic is an element like all other elements in the Palestinian national identity; therefore, enhancing its status is metonymically akin to establishing the collective itself as a political sovereign. Conversely, it may be argued that Arabic has a special status in the context of national identity and that it is more important than other identity elements. This is because Arabic is not only related to Palestinian nationality but has been bequeathed to this nationality as part of the pan-Arab nationality, as an embodiment of an even broader Islamic tradition. The pan-Arab and Islamic significance of Arabic situates it as a marker of political sovereignty. However, it may be argued that this emphasis on Arabic and its sovereign status is actually due to a void, rather than to its role as a cornerstone in the structure of Arab and Palestinian identities. This void is the result of the historical disconnection, forced by the Zionist regime upon this group of Palestinians, from modern Arab culture and the rest of Palestinian society. Therefore, enhancing the status of Arabic, the ultimate signifier of imagined Arabness, bridges the void that results from the ongoing disconnection due to various practices of the Zionist regime.

The path of return and repositioning charted by the Haifa Declaration enables the Palestinians and the Israeli establishment to maintain the existing nation-state format in the dominant settler-colonial order. The internal division of its institutions and their organising principles are built on the participation of the two national groups in power. Under the Haifa Declaration, Arabic and its products would be a constitutive structural site of the Palestinian national identity and play the same function as played by 'Arabic' in the previous 'national' era. However, the outcome would not be an 'Israeli Arab', but a Palestinian – a citizen with rights equal to those of a Jewish citizen in Israel. This undoubtedly involves a change in the contents of 'Arabic', but not in the relations between Arabic and the Palestinian nation, on the one hand, and the state, on the other. As in the structure of 'Arabic', here, too, Arabic would constitute national identity, albeit ostensibly independent of the Zionist regime, and the state would provide the structural site of these processes of constituting identity on the infrastructure of language.

The Haifa Declaration represents a change in the profile of the Palestinian community and its relations with the State of Israel. It is noteworthy that Arabic was central in demanding that change on legal and professional ground, while retaining a reminiscence of national standing. Arabic is here portrayed as both the expression of national identity and a legal right in itself. Other Palestinian NGOs took Arabic as a legal right, divorcing it from its national colouring. Adalah and its Democratic Constitution provide such an example.

The Democratic Constitution

Adalah: Legal Centre for Arab Minority Rights in Israel is an NGO founded in 1996, with the aim of promoting the legal status of Palestinian citizens of Israel and protecting their individual and collective rights. It also serves to represent Palestinians in the Occupied Territories against the Israeli occupation apparatuses. As such, it addresses the legal public status of Arabic in Israel, including the filing of several class-action lawsuits demanding that state and local authorities as well as private sector organisations include Arabic in their publications. Adalah views Arabic as a signifier of the presence of Palestinians in Israel as a national minority in its homeland. In 1999, Adalah petitioned the High Court of Justice against municipalities with a mixed population, demanding that they post street signs in Arabic, in addition to Hebrew.[26] If the municipalities in Israel posted bilingual signs with an equal presence of Arabic and Hebrew, so they argued, most Palestinians would feel equal in the public space. This action indicates that Adalah accepts the existing structure of the regime and tries to redefine it by making the markers of the collective identity of the Palestinians in Israel equally visible.

What is interesting in Adalah's legal arguments is the combination of the Israeli legal discourse and the global discourse – one that relies on international conventions and on other cases of national, cultural and linguistic conflicts.[27] This combination is designed to encourage equality in the Israeli legal discourse and to enrich it with legal achievements from similar cases. Adalah's vision statement, its democratic constitution, is constituted along those lines.[28]

In March 2007, following two years of group work, Adalah published its democratic constitution as a proposal for a constitution for the State of Israel. The proposal retains the principles and institutions of the nation-state format– the parliament, the government and the legal system – in their present shape and does not seek to revolutionise them. Attention is devoted mainly to the division of power between Jewish Israelis and those whom the proposal calls 'Arabs' in Israel. These 'Arabs' are not presented as a nation in the imagined federal arrangement, but as a cultural and linguistic minority. This is made explicit in the foreword by the Chair of Adalah's Board of Trustees, Marwan Dwairy:

> Upon its tenth anniversary, Adalah published the Democratic Constitution as a proposed constitution for the State of Israel, based on a bilingual and multicultural democratic state. This constitution is informed by universal principles, international human rights conventions, the experience of other nations and the constitutions of various democratic countries.[29]

The words 'bilingual and multicultural democratic state' are central to the proposal and serve as an organising discursive formation for what is included in and excluded from it. What is surprising here is the use of the term 'bilingual' instead of 'binational', the term commonly used at the time in Palestinian academic and intellectual circles where Adalah members played a major and active role (such as Adalah Director Hassan Jabareen). The avoidance of the term 'binational' is thus deliberate, and we must consider the reasons for it, at least on the textual levels. After presenting the constitution itself, I will address the question of charging language with meanings of sovereignty, whether as momentary or as permanent substitute for nationality.

The proposed constitution is divided into four sections, each devoted to a different content area. The introduction presents a statement of purpose, anchored in a historical and legal context, and a vision for resolving the conflict. The second section presents the principles of government; the third lists basic rights and liberties; and the fourth presents various limitations on revisions to the constitution. Every section explains the legal rationale of its wording and refers to the national and international principles and conventions upon which the authors have relied. In the introduction, Arabic is presented as a characteristic that defines the state as democratic, whereas in the other chapters Arabic and Hebrew are the benchmarks for the acceptability and reasonability of the state's actions. Both languages are used to protect their users' rights, but at the same time they are assigned the power of a sovereign that enables intervention in the basic rights and liberties of both 'Arab' and Jewish citizens. These two qualities, being a defining characteristic versus being a procedural criterion, require us to apply a different analytic approach than that applied heretofore.

Let us begin with the introduction and examine the role of language as a defining characteristic of the state. At the start of this section, the authors provide a rationale for their position by grounding it in the 1948 Universal Declaration of Human Rights and other international principles.[30] They compare the situation of the Palestinian Arabs in Israel to those principles in order to highlight their history of oppression and dispossession since 1948, thus arriving at the conclusion that this group of Palestinians is an 'indigenous minority'.

> This proposed constitution states that the basic rights of the Arab minority include, among other things: the restitution of its lands and properties based on the principle of restorative justice, effective sharing in decision-making, realising its right to cultural autonomy and *recognising its Arabic language as an official language in the State of Israel.* [. . .] Realising these rights, however, is contingent on the existence of an egalitarian society. Therefore, this proposed constitution states that it is essential to ensure the economic and social rights of all inhabitants and citizens.[31]

In their review of the basic rights of the Arab minority in Israel, the authors refer to the right to have their language, Arabic, recognised as an official language. The idea that recognition of the Arab minority's language is a basic right relies on the 1992 UN Declaration on the Rights of Persons Belonging to National or Ethnic, Religious and Linguistic Minorities.[32] In the national Palestinian discourse that evolved in the PLO and political parties in Israel, as well as in the pan-Arab discourse, Arabic is one of several identity elements, and its recognition is not seen as a basic right because it is pre-existent. The emphasis on recognition as a right is a byproduct of the existing power system in the Zionist regime. Making the exercise of these basic rights contingent on an egalitarian society forms a kind of preamble to the introduction's concluding paragraph, which suggests the obvious and direct solution for the relations of Palestinians and the State of Israel:

> In a country that does not rule and occupy another nation and which is constituted on full equality between all its inhabitants and between the various groups in it, Jewish and Arab citizens will respect each other's rights to live in peace, dignity and equality and will be united in their recognition and respect both for the differences between them and to the diversity of all groups in a bilingual and multicultural state.[33]

This definition is couched in negative terms: the end of the conflict will lead to mutual respect of the basic differences between Arabs and Jews. The state is the guarantor of this vision and must be a democratic one that treats all its citizens equally, represented as they are by their language and culture. The state and its mechanisms operate according to a sovereign logic that is realised on the legal-procedural level, and language and culture must be translated into practices informed by this logic. Adalah proposes a practical approach to such a translation in the second section, titled 'The Foundations of Government and Regime'. Article 17, 'A Bilingual State', enumerates the practicalities of bilingualism, as follows:

A Bilingual State

17. A. Hebrew and Arabic are the official languages of the State of Israel and have equal status in all functions and activities of the legislative and executive branches of government.

B. All official notices, including laws, orders and regulations, will be considered valid after having been published, printed and distributed simultaneously in both official languages.
C. The verdicts of the Supreme Court, district courts and appellant courts will be published, printed and publicised in both official languages immediately after having been given.
D. Every litigant may use either of the official languages in legal proceedings, according to his [or her] choice.
E. Mixed local authorities will use both official languages equally in all their functions and activities.
F. Two types of educational institutions, including higher education institutions, will be established, in Hebrew and Arabic each; and every person will be entitled to choose an educational institution in which either of the two official languages is being used for instruction.
G. Legal arrangements will be made for providing an appropriate and equal status to the two official languages in national electronic media.[34]

This article refers mainly to the three branches of government – legislative, executive and judicial. The areas of education and, to a certain extent, electronic media are also relevant to the government as they instil the establishment ideology and ensure the basic reproduction of the orders of government.

This mapping of the constitutional-procedural aspects of language onto the authorities that embody state authority gives language a sovereign status, and at the same time it gives the sovereign a democratic character. Note that the phrasing in demanding equal, bilingual presence refers only to the presence of languages. This conceptualisation of bilingualism does not refer to the grammar of language and to the meanings ascribed to it or to its visibility as a signifier of sovereignty in the State of Israel, beyond what seems equal between the two languages by virtue of their very presence – that is, seeing Arabic words in the public sphere. Once language is subordinated to the constitutional-procedural sovereign logic, it ceases to be a language in the sense we have used hitherto and mainly serves as a symbol of sovereignty.[35] This tension derives from the displacement of Arabic from Arab culture to a symbolic status that signifies the rule. The move of excluding the nation from sovereign status and replacing it by Arabic has neutralised the latter and redefined it as a symbol.

The narrative structure of the Democratic Constitution is built on a comparison between international principles of individual and collective rights and the existing situation in the Zionist regime – in terms of its treatment of its Palestinian subjects. If universal values are the starting point, then the history of oppressive acts of government that prevent this national minority from exercising its rights in dignity leads to the conclusion that the nature of relations between the two national groups must be changed. As a solution for the existing situation, the Democratic Constitution proposes that the State of Israel and its governmental structure be retained, but where there is now one national group, it proposes the inclusion of another national group, the Arab minority, as the Constitution puts it, on an equal footing. However, as mentioned and for whatever extra-textual reasons, the Constitution avoids the term 'binational'.[36] The implications for the status of Arabic are highly significant. Translating bilingualism to a practical, procedural and constitutional level positions Arabic as a symbol. In this case, the symbol is blinding us from perceiving history as a process of both material and symbolic production: we see only the symbolic. This split causes the displacement of the settler-colonial conflict that is irresolvable (at a given historical moment) onto the legal-professional discourse and its procedural logic. When it reorganises the historical materials of the conflict, it turns the national community into a legal one with rights. For our purposes, the materials of 'Arabic' become symbolic and not communicative. The legal-professional discourse reduces the contradiction into an administrative procedure. However, the tension resulting from this move requires compensation, and that is the role of the symbol – a supreme, almost holy essence, detached from daily life and devoid of any real historical agency.

These vision statements reflect the changes in the relationships between the group of Palestinians and the Zionist regime since the early 1990s; at the same time, they try to intervene in those relationships. Some of the changes articulate global processes that have required a material-institutional level, NGOs instead of governmental and partisan institutions. These NGOs were founded on a legal-professional basis, by lawyers, academics and psychologists, among others, with a procedural logic, a logic that dominates civil society organisations. Due to this procedural logic, a gap has formed between what is apparent on the declarative level – realising the Palestinian collectivity as part of a transformed State of Israel – and the textual conceptualisation of the vision and the place of Arabic within it. When the Haifa Declaration proposes a return and repositioning that redefines 'Arabic' as a mechanism of producing a Palestinian national identity, it retains the function of 'Arabic', albeit changing its content. The Democratic Constitution, however, turns Arabic into a symbol that supposedly establishes the sovereignty of the Arab national minority, but as it is only a symbol, it cannot intervene in 'Arabic' and reorganise it as a site of producing a national identity, as the Haifa Declaration does. Thus, both vision statements propose a path of return and repositioning that essentially retains 'Arabic', whether on the functional level, or by turning Arabic into a symbol. In relating to 'Arabic' thus, they view Palestinians in Israel as a given body that has a language, and they argue that the relations between this Arabic and the sovereign state mechanisms must be examined, particularly its legal and constitutional status. The body of the language itself, however, need not.

The Language Academy Era: 'Arabic' as a Procedure

In contrast to the vision statements, which are materially detached from Arabic, the members of the Academy of the Arabic Language may be expected to be intimately familiar with the materiality of Arabic and its products. The following question arises: How have they structured their path of return and repositioning in 'Arabic' as an entire domain over which they claim a legal-professional monopoly? It is customary to tie the establishment of language academies in countries colonised by the Western nation-states together with processes of de- and recolonisation initiated by national liberation movements. It appears, however, that the unequivocal distinction between the colonial administration and the founders of language academies among colonised nations does not operate with regard to their particular historical building processes. I will set aside, for a moment, the charged issue of nationality itself being a derivative of the Western colonisation project.[37] In the case of many colonised peoples, the standard model that identifies nationality with language was conceived in the institutions producing knowledge/power in the metropole of the colonisers, only to be 'imported' subsequently to the colonised space and adopted by various social groups among the colonised people. Thus, we encounter various 'experts' from the colonising country as members of language academies of the colonised peoples, whether as consultants for 'renewing the language', or as various administrative officials.

The Palestinian case in Israel bears many of the hallmarks of this complex history, but also includes many elements that are not mentioned in academic case-studies, and this is partly due to its settler-colonial nature.[38] Although it is not a settler-colonial case, it appears that the case of the Academy of the Arabic Language in Cairo is most similar. Since the occupation of Egypt by the British in 1882, British officials employed in the colonial administration in Egypt actively and consistently intervened in linguistic affairs in Egyptian society.[39] Similar to the Cairo Academy, the Academy of the Arabic Language in Israel grew out of the knowledge/power of settler-colonial relations, in which the settler's intervention in the language of the natives was central to the management and shaping of them. This raises the following question: What is the type of return and repositioning in 'Arabic' that this academy enables or requires, and what is its structural position?

Chronological Framework: Constitutive Events

Before describing the establishment of the academy, I will present the chronological framework of its construction process in order to provide an initial point of reference to its complex relations with 'Arabic'. This will allow us to analyse its textual and public products from a more comprehensive perspective. The legal institutionalisation of the Academy of the Arabic Language in Israel was preceded by semi-institutional public initiatives. Their emergence in the public sphere began with a letter by three Arabic scholars – Farouk Mawasi, Fahd Abu Khadra and Elias Atallah – published in *Al-Jadid* in the October 1989 issue.[40] In this letter to the readership, the three declared the formation of a group aiming to develop Arabic among the Palestinians in Israel in line with modern sociocultural developments. These sociocultural developments included scientific knowledge and innovations, technologies and new means of communications, among others. The group consisted of academics, scholars, writers and educators. In the early 1990s, it began receiving support from the Ministry of Education's Arab Culture Division, at the time headed by Muwaffaq Khwry. At that stage, it began operating through the Christian Home Institute in Haifa, in order to be able to formally manage its budget and affairs. It also began the procedure of registration with the Israeli Registrar of Associations.[41]

At the same time and as part of the same dynamic in 'Arabic', Khawlah a-Saadi, Director of the Division of Planning and Developing Curricula for the so-called Arab Sector at the Ministry of Education, established the High Committee for the Arabic Language, whose members belonged to the same group formed around the letter. The High Committee was tasked with providing standard translation for lists of Hebrew words sent by professionals working on the Hebrew-Arabic translation of textbooks, both within and outside the ministry.[42] Their work on the committee made them view the need for establishing an academy for the Palestinians in Israel as even more acute.

More than ten years after publishing the first letter, the idea of starting an academy was born when the NGO was registered (a necessary step of protocol) and received the support of the Arab Culture Division. The academy's first public activity in this form was a conference dealing with various issues related to the modernisation of Arabic in the Palestinian context within Israel. The NGO was active as such until the *Supreme Institute of the Arabic Language* Law was passed in 2007, establishing the academy. The appointment of Palestinian parliamentarian Ghaleb Majadele as the Minister of Culture and Sports added to the official support of the academy. Even before this nomination, Majadele had collaborated with the group members on legislation to provide for an Arabic academy, whose status was to match that of its Hebrew counterpart.

The law was passed in March 2007, and ever since then the Academy of the Arabic Language has been operating by the power of the law, which requires direct funding by the state. Until then, the group members had worked together despite some differences, but the formalisation of this activity led to significant power struggles that reflected various sociopolitical conflicts within this group of Palestinians. The two declared main causes of disagreement concerned the questions who was to head the academy and where it should be located.[43]

Over a period of almost two decades, from 1989 to 2007, the academy underwent processes of organisation and institutionalisation, until it matured into a national institute by virtue of state law. The various forms of this organisation articulate different positions within 'Arabic' and are not external to its operational apparatuses. Most of the members were employees in the Israeli Arab education system, as teachers, principals and superintendents. What we have here is a dynamic of different positions that used to be polarised but began drawing closer. Academics, writers and intellectuals previously identified with one position began expressing different opinions. This rapprochement marks the end of one era and the beginning of another. The letter sent by the three 'Arabic' activists was the first public manifestation of these deep underground processes.

The Academy's Textual Corpus

Mawasi, Abu Khadra and Atallah, the authors of the *Al-Jadid* letter, had been involved in Arabic and its products since the mid-1960s and were considered leading figures in their areas of expertise: modern scientific knowledge about Arabic language and literature, as well as traditional knowledge imparted to them by Arab scholars from previous periods. By the late 1980s, *Al-Jadid* became the leading literary journal among the Palestinians in Israel, by then representing their mainstream political views as embodied in the Israeli Communist Party's agenda.[44] The publication of the letter by chief editor Malik Ibrahim indicates a profound change in the Palestinian public sphere in Israel. Ibrahim introduced the letter and explained its purpose – a call for establishing an Arabic institution – and called upon Arabic experts and enthusiasts to join this initiative. Next, the authors explained their motives:

> Many of us complain in our writings and conversations that our language does not meet our current daily needs, and that we find ourselves forced to turn to other languages and use their terms and expressions. And we – in this country – live with another language (Hebrew) that develops dynamically and keeps pace spontaneously with the modern era, courageously adopting words from other languages, with its experts electing alternative words, enabling this language to flow with the tongues and pens, keeping abreast with what is happening in the civilised world in terms of performance and implementation.[45]

The issue arising from this opening paragraph is that Arabic was not developing in step with modernity. The situation was exacerbated by the fact that, at least for the group of Palestinians in Israel, Arabic seemed to have failed where Hebrew had succeeded and was therefore abandoned for the latter. The authors described Hebrew as a role model and argued that Arabic should follow in its footsteps – to integrate into the global civilised sphere and develop according to the dictates of modernity.

This issue, however, was not new to Arabic speakers – since the early nineteenth century, the modernisation of Arabic had been a major goal of sociocultural and political movements. The authors addressed that issue by asking rhetorically: Why should we not adopt the recommendations of language academies in the Arab world instead of creating a new body of Arabic?[46] To justify their initiative, they referred to the stagnation in these academies and to the uniqueness of the group of Palestinians in Israel. Then they raised another question:

> And who are we to fill a fissure and close a hole?
>
> Let us put aside for a moment the disrespect for what we're publishing in this country. We, thank God, are concerned and willing to investigate and look deeply into what qualifies us for a very important mission. The three of us – Fahd Abu Khadra, Farouk Mawasi and Elias Atallah – have joined together to establish an NGO for language affairs that accepts whoever is willing to join it, willing to volunteer and feels responsible, in order for us to cooperate in the service of this language that we have dedicated ourselves to love and work for.[47]

The authors' reservations regarding their ability to pull through such a project, requiring as it does knowledge and expertise in Arabic and its products, attests to the importance that they assigned to their initiative and the fear that some readers would consider it pretentious. The act of declaring the establishment of the NGO and calling upon others to join it even before it had received establishment support was not unusual among Palestinian intellectuals in Israel. However, it was usually made under the aegis of some organisation or institute. What is unique here is that the NGO was initiated by professional experts on Arabic and its products, experts who have a passion for it.

At this point, the authors proceeded to describe the scientific method to be used in their work, asking readers to send them foreign words to translate into 'live and fresh' Arabic. The fact that scientific expertise here was considered a criterion for the legitimacy of the initiative constituted a turning point: hitherto, *Al-Jadid* and the authors themselves represented a position supportive of collective ownership of 'Arabic', while now they supported the professional authority of language experts. This shift brought those holding that position in 'Arabic' closer to the mediatory position described in the previous chapter, which relied on academic knowledge/power. Accordingly, when Khawlah a-Saadi, Director of the Division of Planning and Developing Curricula for the so-called Arab Sector at the Ministry of Education, established the High Committee for the Arabic Language, it was joined by most members of the group formed following the letter's publication.

Established in the mid-1990s, the High Committee for the Arabic Language included the three authors, as well as five other leading Arabic scholars. Its work primarily involved the standard translation of words from Hebrew and other languages into Arabic. The immediate context of its establishment was translating textbooks from Hebrew into Arabic for the Ministry of Education and the Arab education system in Israel. In the introduction to the committee's first publication, a Hebrew-English-Arabic glossary, its role was described as follows:

> The first and foremost area of this committee's activity is education and learning, which incorporates the foreign and Hebrew terms sent by the textbook translators of the Curriculum Division. It is our hope to come up with equivalent Arabic words and apply them as a standard. At this point, given the structure of the committee and its capabilities, its work is limited to the education and learning area and to [translating the] terms appearing in Hebrew [text]books the Division is translating and preparing [for print].[48]

This description indicates that Arabic and its products depend on events taking place in Hebrew and its products, at least in the area of education and learning, as emphasised by the committee members. The committee's specific focus on translating terms from Hebrew into Arabic and their standardisation according to the laws of Arabic required expert skills in both languages. Since fluency in Hebrew was taken for granted, the committee did not include Hebrew experts. Hebrew was hegemonic: the glossaries published by the committee were alphabetised according to Hebrew. Hence, the committee functions as mechanism that reproduces the knowledge/power relations in 'Arabic', by deepening the dependency of 'Arabic' and its inhabitants on Hebrew and its products.

This serves as an example of the compulsive literacy mode. The development here had little to do with the structure of knowledge/power relations and more with the attempt to professionalise and 'scientificise' compulsiveness as a mode through which the colonised native subject is constructed. The work of the group members on this committee, their meetings and the initiative that had started with the letter in *Al-Jadid* set in motion an important momentum that blazed the trail for the institutionalisation of the Academy of the Arabic Language in Israel.

The Palestinian researchers, academics and intellectuals who joined the registered association and took part in establishing the Academy of the Arabic Language in Israel held diverse views regarding the position of Palestinians in Israel and in relation to the Zionist regime.[49] Moreover, their positions within 'Arabic' until that time were diverse. They ranged from claiming ownership over Arabic and its products, as symbolic and semiotic means of producing the collective identity, to the establishment position that considered the Palestinians as 'Israeli Arabs'. Cooperation between them had been impossible in the earlier stages of the history of 'Arabic' – the academy certainly could not have been initiated. Suleiman Jubran, elected as the Head of the Academy of the Arabic Language in Israel when it was still a registered association, argued that it had been established in order to maintain Palestinian uniqueness in Israel by integrating into establishment apparatuses:

> For several years now, establishing an Academy of the Arabic Language in Israel was a dream for many writers and intellectuals. There were many attempts in this direction, some included meetings, but most of them failed due to the lack of material support for this distinguished project [. . .] Finally, several writers and intellectuals gathered in December 2001 and initiated concrete steps for establishing the academy in collaboration with the Division of Arab Culture at the Ministry of Education and Culture, in order to secure its material support. In that meeting, it was decided to consider its participants, most of whom are members of the High Committee for the Arabic Language appointed by the Division of Planning and Developing Curricula and are the founding members of the academy [. . .] Finally,

> after overcoming the procedural complications and obstacles, the academy obtained formal approval on 7 July 2001 and became an official 'registered association' designed to maintain, protect and develop the Arabic language in Israel.[50]

This description identifies the main participants in the process of establishing the Academy of the Arabic Language – the group that initiated the idea and the Israeli authorities, mainly those of the Ministry of Education. Note in particular the argument that the failure of previous attempts had been due to a lack of material support. It was the institutional-material basis provided by the Israeli ministry that eventually enabled the establishment of the academy. Jubran considered this a significant achievement, thereby positioning himself in the mediatory position of 'Arabic', even though this position was not static, but developed according to a professional expert discourse.

Contrary to this position, Hanna Abu Hanna called for dispensing with the symbolic dependency on the establishment, but at the same time retaining the material support. He argued:

> About fifteen years ago, the meetings to consider the establishment of an Academy of the Arabic Language in this country began. The reasons for that are many and profound [. . .] Language is one of the fundamental elements of individual and national identity. A person's dignity and right to identity are embodied in respect for his language, its maintenance and protection. Subservience and disrespect of one's national language express self-debasement and feeble submissiveness that relinquishes pride in one's cultural tradition, and certainly the relating to others from an equal rather than an inferior position.[51]

In contrast to Jubran, who came from Israeli academia, Abu Hanna had grown up in the Israeli Communist Party when it articulated the Palestinian national voice in Israel, and he was one of its leaders. The position he presented here claimed ownership of Arabic within 'Arabic', as the language of the Palestinian people in Israel. He pointed out the knowledge/power structure that placed Arabic and its owners at a position of severe inferiority *vis-à-vis* Hebrew and its national mechanisms. He called to break free of this inferiority and position Arabic as equal to Hebrew, and thereby Palestinian nationalism *vis-à-vis* Zionism. Abu Hanna's view of language's role in collective identity is almost essentialist: he did not focus on professionalism, but rather on a national revival that would transform the knowledge/power relations in the Israeli settler-colonial context.

Elias Atallah's position was similar to Abu Hanna's, but combined the national discourse with professionalism and expertise.[52] Atallah discussed the language situation of the Palestinians in Israel and claimed that language was a particular case of nationality. This argument implies that one of the ways of demolishing the general, nationality, is to destroy the particular, language. The reader could infer that the Zionist regime was not ingenuous in acting to distort the condition of Arabic among the Palestinians in Israel. Having located his analytic discourse in the history of the relation between the language of the coloniser and that of the colonised in the Arab World in various colonial periods, Atallah proceeded to describe the condition of Arabic in Israel:

> This reality is imbued with most theories of pure race cast into the religious and cultural dimension, and this is only made possible by highlighting the Other and its distancing from, or emptying of the elements that threaten the view and vision of the Jewish State, facilitating the series of activities of displacement from the homeland, expropriation of lands, settlement, Judaisation, Israelisation and most recently Hebraisation – and this is the most dangerous action in the experience of the Arab citizen of Israel, since it is directed at the heart of the particular [Arabic], which is the most sublime in the general national [Palestinian Arab nationality].[53]

Atallah presented two aspects here: the nature of the Zionist regime and its conduct in relation to Palestinians in Israel. The latter was a byproduct of the former. It was not incidental but consistent, and its intensity in relation to Arabic was growing. He argued that Arabic was a sublimative element of Palestinian Arab nationality, and it was therefore not surprising that the regime consistently invested in processes that would empty that element of all substance and thereby lead to the collapse of the national collective identity. Atallah pointed out two specific stages in that process: Israelisation, a process related to culture in general, and Hebraisation, a process related to language in particular. According to Atallah, the Hebraisation mechanism made Arabic redundant and replaced it with a hybrid language, a blend of spoken Arabic with a Hebrew that had undergone structural and other changes.[54]

Atallah proposed several ways of dealing with the present condition of Arabic. He suggested a path of return and repositioning that combined professional scientific knowledge/power and sought to enable a different kind of ownership of Arabic and its products in 'Arabic'. According to him, scientific professionalism and expertise would allow better ownership of Arabic, one that would enable it to become immune to the regime's attitude towards it. At this point, Atallah did not present the contradiction between 'Arabic' as part of the public domain enabled by the structure of the settler-colonial Zionist regime (and thereby also maintaining it) and Arabic and its products, as the embodiment of Palestinian Arab nationality.

The voices of Jubran, Abu Hanna and Atallah could have been sounded within the Academy of the Arabic Language in its first incarnation as an NGO supported by the Ministry of Education. When they sought political support, they met with both government representatives and Palestinian members of the Knesset, from both Arab and Zionist parties, including Ghaleb Majadele, as already mentioned. Majadele was willing to help the academy members. As a member of the Labour Party, he naturally had access to establishment funding, or so the academy members believed at the time. During the talks with him, they came up with the idea for a bill to regulate the academy's status, similar to that regulating the status of the Academy of the Hebrew Language, in order to ensure that it would be established on a strong footing with a permanent budget. The bill prepared by Majadele's parliamentary assistants was a carbon copy of the Law for the *Supreme Institute for the Hebrew Language*.[55]

Thanks to a fortunate coincidence, since Majadele's party at that time, in early 2007, was a member of the coalition in Ehud Olmert's government, he was appointed minister without portfolio. In March of that year, the Law for the *Supreme Institute for the Arabic Language* was enacted, and Majadele was appointed Minister of Culture and Sports. As the minister charged with implementing the law, he appointed members of the academy to manage its reestablishment, this time as a statutory body. Due to political disagreements, it was no surprise that Atallah was excluded from the founding members of the new academy. The candidates for the head of the academy were Mahmud Ghanayim and Fahd Abu Khadra. The composition of its members, appointed by the minister, ensured Ghanayim's election, and he served as the Head of the Academy of the Arabic Language until his death in 2021. Some members of the academy in its previous incarnation continued to serve in the new one as well, while others refused and proceeded to act in other channels within 'Arabic'. This split is highly significant, as it reflects different forces within the Palestinians in Israel. In what follows, I will focus on the academy's work and subsequently examine the alternative represented by Atallah.

From the time of its legal constitution onwards, the Academy of the Arabic Language has included most elements of its previous incarnations since the letter in *Al-Jadid* was published in October 1989. The founding core has remained unchanged, as have the chief purposes and courses of action. Crucially, however, the attitude to the Zionist regime has changed, since now the academy directly relies on establishment apparatuses. The academy's main activity is to determine standard Arabic renditions for non-Arabic, mostly Hebrew terms. It is active among students in the Arab education system in Israel, with a view to improve their literary Arabic and bring it closer to their daily life. Every year, it holds conferences on subjects related to Arabic and its products, with presentations by scholars and researchers from various disciplines. Since 2010, it has published a scientific journal and books on various aspects of Arabic and its products. The academy encourages the study of Arabic and grants scholarships to researchers and postgraduate students on a competitive basis.[56]

The academy's extensive activity has been enabled by its permanent budget from the state, which provides an institutional-material infrastructure that is maintained on an ongoing basis. I argue that the logic of these activities carries with it the return and repositioning in a more developed mediatory position in 'Arabic'. Unlike the mediatory position common in the previous era, the current one is active on two levels: the attempt to monopolise the domain of Arabic and its products by the Zionist regime, and the grounding of professionalism and expertise as criteria for entering that domain. These criteria are different from the one required in previous stages in the development of 'Arabic' – namely, professed loyalty to the State of Israel.

In summarising the first year of the academy's activity in its official incarnation, Ghanayim described the atmosphere during that time and positioned it in the developed mediatory position within 'Arabic':

> 'Our language is an easy, not a demanding language, and our command of it lacks nothing compared to the scholars of ancient times'.
>
> This statement, by the Dean of Arabic Literature, used to make us proud in our youth [. . .][57] This statement used to blind us, because it is deceptive and concealing. It is deceptive in that it is distant from the truth, and concealing since it conceals the challenges faced by our Arabic language [. . .] And in the context of the complexity of our cause, we the members of the Arab minority in Israel – the Academy of the Arabic Language in Israel was established with great excitement. This represents the maturation of the struggle by the intellectuals who have shown us the light throughout [. . .] We tried to be objective and practical, since we now have a historical opportunity that deserves a page of its own in the history of the Palestinian people and the Arab nation [. . .] By founding the academy, we are making history.[58]

To set aside for a moment Ghanayim's judgement of Hussein's statement, Ghanayim actually argued that the project of the revival of Arabic and its products in the Arab world had failed due to the inability of its reformers to recognise the real obstacles facing them. These obstacles were erected due to the ideological smoke-screen of Arab nationalism. The establishment of the academy in Israel, so Ghanayim maintained, represented 'maturity', the dispersal of that smoke-screen, by working within the existing 'reality', accepting the settler-colonial context inhabited by the Palestinians. It is precisely this maturity, so the argument runs, which is more national than other manifestations of Palestinian and Arab nationalism. Here, Ghanayim reintroduced the concept of year zero, but in a new way: not only was this group born with the establishment of the State of Israel, but it received its national Arab identity from what was enabled by the Zionist regime.

Ghanayim's words framed the discourse of the Academy of the Arabic Language and described the developed mediatory position as one that enabled this discourse. He went on to define the maturity referred to previously as the use of the scientific method and its criteria as the guiding principle in the academy's work.[59] He did not elucidate what he meant by 'scientific method', but used the term as if it were self-evident, despite the fact that it was not quite so in this context. This is because Arabic and the tradition of producing knowledge about it can stem from at least two sources: the knowledge accumulated over centuries of researching Arabic and its products by its speakers, and modern science and the body of knowledge that it has produced on Arabic and its products.

Unlike Ghanayim, his deputy Elinor Saiegh-Haddad was unequivocal. Upon marking the anniversary of the Academy's establishment, she wrote:

> This illustrious reality is epitomised by the establishment of a scientific institution, which is completely autonomous both intellectually and practically. The institution allocates its own budget and creates its own work plan – all on a completely democratic basis, and on the basis of free election and majority rule, far from spontaneity and nepotism in discussions and decision-making [. . .] In this general context, the Academy of the Arabic Language became a leading supporter in many studies, being a scientific institution whose primary objective is learning and research, and not only the protection and development of language.[60]

Saiegh-Haddad, a lecturer at the Department of English Literature and Linguistics at Bar Ilan University, highlighted two aspects in the logic of the academy's work: its scientific basis and democratic organisational culture. Compared to Ghanayim, whose discourse was hybrid in that he stressed both a scientific approach and developed mediation, Saiegh placed exclusive emphasis on science and the liberal values of managing a scientific institute. In this passage, as elsewhere in her article, she over-emphasised these two aspects on the declarative level, with no explicit attempt to engage with them critically. Strongly evident in her words is the almost complete absence of any reference to Arabic and its products. Although Arabic exists as an object of academic study, it is that study which provides it with its *raison d'être*. Although the position presented by Saiegh-Haddad was influenced by her scholarly endeavours of linguistics and language acquisition, clearly it is scientific professionalism and expertise that constitute the discursive formation organising the academy's work on the procedural level.

In order to examine the deep structure of the knowledge/power embodied in the developed mediatory position with regard to Arabic and its products, whose instances are represented by the head of the academy and his deputy, I will now analyse one of its main publications: Suleiman Jubran's *On the Margins of the Innovations and Limitations in the Modern Arabic Language*.[61] This book addresses the factors that enable the development of Arabic and its products – that is, the factors that enable its modernisation, along with the traditional factors that encumber it and prevent it from developing. This study was one of the first publications by the academy and to a significant extent may be seen as representing the position of the group that dominated it after the passage of the 2007 law. It discussed the basic issue of the possibility of reviving Arabic in the modern era, as well as both the intra-linguistic mechanisms that could facilitate such a revival and the extra-linguistic factors that could limit and delay the process. This issue has been one of the main axes of the discourse around Arabic and its products since almost the beginning of the nineteenth century, and it is strongly related to the socioeconomic and political history of the Arab peoples. Every position with regard to Arabic and its revival or preservation is part of a broader worldview regarding Arab society and culture in the modern era.

Jubran's basic argument is that Arabic and its products are sociohistorical phenomena that change across time and space. They must therefore be developed in step with modernity, in order to integrate into the modern quest for progress, based on developed Western civilisation. This modern perspective used to be shared by many intellectuals in the Arab world but, according to Jubran, failed due to social, religious and political reasons.[62] In order to reinforce his position and locate it within the intellectual discourse of the Arab world, Jubran prefaced his book with an introduction by Egyptian psychiatrist and philosopher Adel Mustafa. Modernist to the core, Mustafa argued that Arabic must be detached from the context of the sanctity of Islamic religious scriptures and repositioned, as proper from the modernist perspective, in the social history created by humans in a human society. He argued that language is not sacred, and that it is no miracle; by the same measure, no language was limited or inhibited in any way. According to Mustafa, the problems lie in the way in which a certain society uses its language.[63]

This framing of the modernist discourse positions Jubran among Arab intellectuals and researchers who have adopted Western modernity and tried to rebuild Arab culture, including language, according to the view that considers modern development and progress lofty, worthwhile aims. In order to understand Jubran's basic argument, let us examine some of the examples he offered as a model for reviving and modernising Arabic. This will allow us, in turn, to place these arguments in reference to the position structured by the academy within 'Arabic'.

First, Jubran argued that language changes throughout time, according to its users:

> The living language develops as its speakers develop and changes as their situation changes, with their passage from one period to the next, and from one intellectual cultural level to the next. This is also what happened to our Arabic language: it developed tremendously in the Middle Ages with the development of its speakers in the transition from a tribal desert society to a huge empire that inherited all of ancient civilisation, thereby eventually becoming the most advanced language; during the Ottoman period it deteriorated to the point of hitting bottom, and the threat of loss and extinction became painfully real.[64]

According to Jubran, the changes undergone by language are not free of value: it may progress or regress. The change over time can be a positive development that enhances the value of language and takes its speakers higher on the scale of development, or it can be a negative development that pushes the language and its speakers downwards.

The narrative he presented with regard to Arabic is that of a modern Arab nationalism that organised the history of the Arab nations according to the criterion stating that the Arabness of a political regime is a positive development, whereas non-Arabness, as in the Ottoman case, is negative. This linear view of the history of Arabic and Arab culture is designed to entrench the position of reviving contemporary Arab nationalism: the Arabness of the political regime is the present axis through which the past is organised. This makes Arabic the key mechanism in the project of structuring the Arabness of contemporary political regimes. Jubran went on to argue the following:

> In our age as well, our language has confronted a richer and more advanced civilisation. It had to develop lexically and grammatically, and fast, in order to keep up with the languages that have invaded it. Thus, our present language developed greatly thanks to the efforts of thousands of translators, journalists and authors, more than it developed thanks to the efforts of formal institutions, which did not exist at all initially, until it became significantly and distinctly different from the language of the ancient period.[65]

The contact with Western civilisation was the main motivating force behind the revival and renewal of Arabic, and with it also Arab national identity. Moreover, Jubran noticed that the group of professionals who used Arabic by virtue of their professional endeavours consisted of the group leading the development. He argued that official institutions either did not exist at all or delayed this positive development. To apply this pattern to the case of the Palestinians in Israel, this amounts to an adoption of the Israeli discourse: contact with Hebrew, which is supposedly richer and more advanced, led to the development of Arabic and its products among the Palestinians in Israel, as well to the development of their collective identity.

This argument by Jubran runs like a scarlet thread through his book. In the main chapter, titled 'Manifestations of Renewal and Limitation', he compared Arabic to Hebrew in order for the former to learn from the latter:

> A teacher colleague of mine who works on translating learning materials from Hebrew into Arabic asked me: How did Hebrew manage to develop, within a relatively short time, from a 'dead language' to a completely modern one, whereas our language barely staggers behind modern civilisation? I translate from Hebrew into Arabic and find tens if not hundreds of modern terms for which a Hebrew translation was found, which became commonly used among its speakers, and on the other hand I find it difficult, and sometimes impossible, to find an appropriate Arabic dictionary, despite using all existing dictionaries.[66]

Jubran's rhetorical exercise was designed to present his basic view that Hebrew should serve as a model for Arabic because it serves as a good example of what a modern language should be. Therefore, the contact of Arabic and its products with Hebrew can only promote the positive development of Arabic, which is straggling behind Western modernity. The evidence for Arabic's lagging is lexical – the lack of Arabic terms equivalent to Western terms, for which Hebrew has easily come up with equivalents.

In the second stage of his argumentation, Jubran let go of his teacher friend and continued in his own voice:

> We must admit that Hebrew has indeed developed more than Arabic over the past hundred years, as suggested by my friend. This is attested by the fact that translating from foreign languages such as English into Hebrew is much

> easier than into Arabic, whether in lexical or syntactical terms. We have no choice but to admit this fact if it is candour and objectivity that we seek.[67]

According to Jubran, there are three main reasons why Hebrew out-developed Arabic:

> The first reason for Hebrew's rapid development [. . .] is that Hebrew is more flexible. Indeed, Hebrew has long rid itself of the nunation and other markers of grammatical categories, as happened in our own spoken language [. . .] Moreover, the grammar of modern Hebrew is easy and easily adaptable: you can formulate your sentence almost any way you like to, without fear of falling into the 'forbidden' or deviating from the familiar [. . .] the second reason, which is more important for our purposes, is the human element. Those in Israel who attend to the Hebrew language, and scholarship in general, maintain direct contact with foreign languages and cultures and with Western civilisation [. . .] In this context, Israeli society is small and well-controlled by the various media, so that linguistic innovations become known in most sectors and quickly arrive to the man in the street. The third reason is that the Academy of the Hebrew Language is truly working, and its voice is heard in most educational, cultural and media institutions, despite the fact that its recommendations are not always mandatory, of course.[68]

This description of the reasons for Hebrew's success idealises the sociohistorical context of a living language. The first reason mentioned is the easy and fluent use of Hebrew – that is, an internal reason. But the claim that 'you can formulate your sentence almost any way you like' sounds very odd coming from a prominent linguist such as Jubran. It is highly problematic to attribute the elasticity of Hebrew to the lack of nunation, as every language has a set of rules that organises its use and the possible forms of the sentence structure and its elements. The question is, then, why did Jubran choose this phrasing?

The other two reasons for the success of Hebrew have to do with the human element and the Academy of the Hebrew Language. Here, too, Jubran's interpretation is problematic and idyllic. The human element responsible for the impact of Western civilisation is not an individual with this or that profession; it has to do with socioeconomic systems. Jubran's discourse, however, is not founded on diagnosing the working logic of these systems, but on the argument that Hebrew has positioned itself within Western progress. In his view, direct contact with the West is essential for rapid progress.

As for the Academy of the Hebrew Language, presenting it as 'truly' working and as having an influence on most relevant institutions is also an idealisation that derives from the claim that Arabic academies in the Arab world are failing and have gradually become irrelevant for most social, educational, cultural and media institutions. These arguments regarding the reasons for Hebrew's success and Jubran's idealisation of Hebrew under the Zionist regime are derived mainly from what he saw as problems and deficiencies in the situation of Arabic in its current, modern incarnation. For Jubran, Hebrew's imagined space was a construction of solutions he believed Arabic must adopt in order to modernise successfully.

In his book, Jubran is a perfect representative of the dominant group in the Academy of the Arabic Language. His intervention in 'Arabic' was built on return and repositioning in the developed mediatory position. The development he added to the mediation from the previous stage of 'Arabic' is the conscious adoption of the modernisation discourse and its systematic application to Arabic, particularly in the Palestinian context, by implementing the model of Hebrew's modernisation. Modernisation here is founded on a professional discourse of scientific expertise in Arabic, which operates according to a procedural logic applied to both the lexical level, the number of existing equivalent Arabic terms, and to the syntactic level, the pliability with which the sentence structure adjusts to the writer's wishes.

The three members of the Academy of the Arabic Language reviewed here – Ghanayim, Saiegh-Haddad and Jubran – represent variations on modernisation through the discursive formation of scientific professionalism and expertise, as they intervened in Arabic and its products by virtue of the institutional-material position afforded to them by the academy. They represent the dominance through which the academy operates within the arena of 'Arabic' in the present period of its development. As we have seen, the academy today includes elements of its previous incarnations ever since the publication of the letter in *Al-Jadid*. However, it did not adopt them in their previous form; it cast them into its institutional-material logic and its developed mediatory dominance. For example, the issue of reviving the language by way of modernisation exists in the *Al-Jadid* letter only in a preliminary and undeveloped form.

The institutional-material basis of the academy enabled the allocation of budgets for research in this field, and its publication and dissemination among a broad readership. Moreover, the academy sought to model the modernisation of Arabic after Hebrew under the Zionist regime, to the exclusion of other possibilities for reviving Arabic among the group of Palestinians in Israel. These moves were carried out by members of the academy, not only as members of the Palestinian Arab nation, but mostly as scientific professionals and experts on Arabic. These qualifications granted them the knowledge/power to perform comprehensive procedures in language, rather than isolated acts or a series of isolated acts. When examining the products of the academy, one finds conferences, books, a journal, newsletters, scholarships and so on – all these have nothing to do with what makes Arabic unique, but rather attest to an attempt to follow the example of the professionalism and expertise of the Hebrew procedure in the current stage in Zionist excessive literacy mode, which serves as an organising superstructure of the settler-colonial regime. Therefore, the position of developed mediation in 'Arabic' is one of compulsive literacy in the late settler-colonialist period, as manifested in the Zionist regime.

The Arab Culture Association: Liberating the Procedure from the Regime

The possibilities for modernising the language that were included in the letter of 1989 but excluded by the academy were embodied in various associations in the Palestinian public sphere in Israel, some working in parallel to the academy. One of these assciations was the Arab Culture Association. This NGO addressed Arabic and its products, but only after Elias Atallah had joined it – after Ghaleb Majadele had refused to appoint him as a member of the academy – did its intervention in Arabic and its products through 'Arabic' begin to develop rapidly and intensively.

The Arab Culture Association (hereafter ACA) was officially founded in 1998. It was one of the first NGOs that made a conscious and politically motivated decision to break free of Israeli government apparatuses and seek alternative sources of funding. It appears that this approach enabled it to develop a different discourse, one that opposed the Israeli government's mechanisms in the context of their oppressive acts against the Palestinians in Israel, their culture, their language and Palestinian Arab nationality. Moreover, the ACA initiated projects for promoting Arab culture beyond the boundaries enabled by the Zionist regime, and to a significant extent reconnected Palestinians with groups in the Arab world, especially groups for children and youth. Since the ACA's aim is to reinforce Arab culture and national belonging, reviving Arabic and its products has become one of its major axes of activity over the past two decades. This sub-section will examine its manner of return and repositioning in its efforts to own Arabic and its products – an action that became the main mechanism of the ACA in redesigning national Palestinian Arab identity in Israel.

Dealing with Arabic and its products represents one aspect of the ACA's various activities, distinguishing it from the sociocultural environment provided by the apparatuses of the government to Palestinians in Israel. The ACA's varied activities include: a campaign to encourage reading, cultural activities, creative activities, literary events, publication of research, art classes, exhibitions, a public library, a literary salon, a circle of Palestinian architects and projects for children and youth, mainly reconnecting them to the Arab world.[69] These activities appear to be similar to activities offered by any community club, but they are distinct by being based on Arabic and its products and designed to cultivate Arabic language and culture among the participants.

One prominent example is the 'My Language – My Identity' festival organised in the Old City of Acre on 11 September 2010, on the second day of Eid Al-Fitr. Because of the holiday, the Old City was full of Palestinians from the villages of Galilee and elsewhere in the country, and the festival itself attracted thousands. Festival workers wore black shirts with the dark-green inscription 'My Language – My Identity' in classic Arabic font. The festival included calligraphy displays, a book fair, plays for adults and children, stand-up comedy shows and Palestinian folksong performances – all in Arabic, of course. This day was a celebration of the link between Arabic and Palestinian Arab national identity – a celebration of Arabic and its products that reoccupied the Old City of Acre for at least a day. In the brochure produced for the festival, the ACA's director at the time, Rawda Atallah, wrote:

> Because of the importance of the Arabic language for forming the cultural identity and for the national existence, and by virtue of being the vessel of history and civilisation and creativity, and thanks to the importance of its roles in our communications and in our belonging, and in charting the path of the Arab nation to a society of knowledge, and its role in supporting cultural and social and economic growth, the Arab Culture Association invests its resources and energies in Arabic, out of a modern view of the effort to revive cultural production in the general national sphere.[70]

Thus R. Atallah clarified the roles of Arabic in the construction of the modern Arab nation, identifying both symbolic and practical ones. She even linked the pan-Arab nation with Palestinian national identity. This position accepts the basic assumption that there exists a relationship between language and nationality, and that language is a mechanism that constructs the subjectivity of the nation. In that, R. Atallah subscribed to the function of 'Arabic' based on the model determined by the Zionist regime. As in the above-mentioned Haifa Declaration, this discursive framing accepts the functional platform of 'Arabic', but struggles to revise its content and control it as a national group. R. Atallah proceeded with this line of argument:

> Naturally, our Arabic language is being deliberately attacked and colonised and perverted and destroyed. We must face a very serious question: can we make a decision and stand firm behind it – do we have the sense of belonging and the desire and power and right to choose how to treat our language and its products? Or are we a people who consume only what is presented to us so distorted and destroyed – even when it comes to language! Who is responsible for this Hebraisation – are only the Israeli authorities and ministries responsible, or are we too responsible for these failures?[71]

R. Atallah argued that, as a national collective, Palestinians must take responsibility for the actions of their language and the conditions of their national identity. According to her, while the conduct of the government apparatuses is well known and self-evident, the responsibility of the Palestinians is not, and it must be pointed out and acknowledged. Although the discourse that R. Atallah presented here is a hybrid discursive formation combining political and cultural activism on a national basis, she called for a return and repositioning that would lead to ownership of Arabic and its products as the symbolic and semiotic means of production of national collective identity.

One of the ACA's flagship projects was called 'Learn Arabic and Teach It to the People', the paraphrase of a hadith by the Prophet Muhammad.[72] The project's activity pattern embodied the ACA's manner of returning and repositioning. The first stage of the project was a review of the Arabic used in the textbooks of the Israeli Ministry of Education for its Arab sub-system. This included an examination of Arabic textbooks until second grade, as well as Arabic-language textbooks on history, geography and other subjects. It also included a representative sample of children's books published among the Palestinians in Israel, whether by bodies directly affiliated with or supported by the Ministry of Education. This review was conducted by a team of researchers and educators and took several years to complete. Based on its findings, a series of activities was initiated, focused on instilling scientific knowledge of Arabic and its products, as well as on providing guidelines for selecting and reading children's books for preschool and school children. Heba Amara, who coordinated this project for the ACA, described its working logic as follows:

> This project was initiated in order to correct the Arabic learned by our children [. . .] The project relies on the findings of a review of most problems in learning Arabic and a review of issues in the available textbooks. Based on these findings, a team of experts on Arabic, education and preschool education determined the priorities and courses of intervention, and these in turn led to the development of a specific school bag for the project. The school bag is made up of two courses. The first is on Arabic for teachers in the early classes in elementary school [. . .] and the second focuses on the literary, artistic and creative aspects of children's literature, as presented by a select group of lecturers.[73]

Amara tied the various elements of national identity together with the professional, expert discourse. The point of departure of the ACA and its employees is that national identity is being distorted through the mechanisms of the Israeli education system. As opposed to previous periods, this activity did not involve the promotion of the Palestinian national political discourse, but the use of a professional, expert discourse grounded in national identity.

The project employed teams of professional experts to identify and diagnose textual and pedagogical issues and to offer concrete, professional solutions. One such solution was the schoolbag with its lecture CDs, distributed among teachers and parents.

This raises the following question: What are the possible relations between the Palestinians' settler-colonial situation in Israel and the professional discourse? Most professionals have acquired their expertise in Israeli academia. Therefore, their knowledge/power, which enables them to intervene in Arabic and its products as taught in the Arabic education system in Israel, is part of the knowledge/power structure imparted by the academic regime – a sub-system of the general regime – to its Palestinian students. Thus, the relations between the professional and the expert, on the one hand, and the state apparatus, on the other, do not rely on knowledge but on a struggle to control the symbolic and semiotic means of production.

The project teams have continued reviewing the textbooks in the Arabic education system in Israel. Recently, they have published their findings in a book called *The Excluded: Critical Reading of Israeli Textbooks in Arab High Schools*.[74] The book consists of a collection of articles examining various content areas: literature, civics, history, sociology and, of course, Arabic. It concludes with a manifesto calling for educational autonomy of the Palestinians in Israel and argues that such autonomy is their right as a national collective. After describing the wrongs of the regime's policy of cultural control and oppression, the authors argued:

> We view the acceptance of this educational reality as unjustified surrender and consider the individual conditions [of Palestinians in Israel] and the objective conditions [socioeconomic and political conditions that do not depend on the Palestinians themselves] as suitable for making the initial serious and practical steps to demand educational and cultural autonomy for the Arab-Palestinian society within Israel as a collective right and strategic demand supported by most of our society.[75]

The issue of cultural autonomy of the Palestinians in Israel had entered the public discourse of the Palestinians by the early 1990s.[76] While at that time it was the purview of political activists and intellectuals, it is now being discussed in this NGO which combines national identity with a political discourse. What kind of return and repositioning in 'Arabic', as a structural site that mediates the relations between the group of Palestinians and the Zionist regime, does educational and cultural autonomy allow? On the one hand, there is no demand here to break away from the regime, but only to operate differently within it. On the other hand, the nature of this activity requires structural changes in the relationship between the Palestinians and the regime's mechanisms of supervision and control, including 'Arabic'. What, then, is the nature of the autonomy for which the authors call? They provide some clarification in regard to the proposed autonomy:

> Assuming responsibility requires that educational, cultural and community institutions, as well as professional and academic experts in the various areas, initiate the preparation and publication of alternative learning materials adopted by the parent committees, such that [the learning materials'] vision and objectives will seek to build a creative Palestinian Arab person, one who is aware of his/her identity and selfhood and history, who clings to his/her language, culture, values and human morality, and who is open to the cultures and civilisations of the world and the history of the sciences and the humanities. And at the same time, [institutions and professionals] must invest in creating training institutes for Arab teachers of various subjects and encourage them to take part in professional courses on proper Arabic and on subjects related to identity, critical thinking, and modern pedagogies and knowledge.[77]

The concept of cultural autonomy, as detailed above, is suggestive of a modern national revival based on the construction of an alternative system by sociocultural forces from among the Palestinians, at their own individual and collective initiative. This will make the Palestinians the owners of this system, the system of creating and managing a collective identity constructed on the 'Palestinian Arab person'. This subject, the core of the proposed autonomy, is an exceedingly modern one: the subject's main characteristic is awareness of his or her actions and positions in the sociohistorical environment.

NGOs and expert professionals, including academics and others, will be the ones to build this autonomous system and its subject. These operate according to the organising logic of professional expertise, which is a procedural logic. Therefore, the teachers must study Arabic and the standard elements of identity as part of their continuing education. The word 'standard' is key here: procedural logic requires standardisation, as it is essentially supportive of standardising subjectivity to the point of zero variation. Only in this way will ownership of the symbolic and semiotic means of production be enabled, a monopoly over an entire content area or domain – in this case, Palestinian national identity. Therefore, the autonomy proposed in this book requires autonomy from the Zionist regime and demands ownership of the symbolic and semiotic means of production of collective identity, an ownership that is essentially monopolistic, through a standardised procedure of structuring the national subjectivity. The return and repositioning proposed here claim ownership of 'Arabic', but do not deconstruct the mediatory structure as a platform for structuring the collective identity of the colonised native under the conditions of the Zionist regime. However, it is far from self-evident how to apply the procedural logic on Arabic and its products among the Palestinians in Israel, as this entails different dialectic layers of languages and histories that are interactive and interrelated.

Elias Atallah, a researcher specialising in Arabic and its products, decided to find the golden path in this matter. In a series of articles which he began publishing in 2005 in the local press and on websites of Palestinians in Israel, he proposed solutions for issues related to daily use of literary and spoken Arabic, as well as their interrelations. These articles were collated in a book called *If the Murdered Victim is Asked*, published by the Arab Culture Association in 2007.[78] In his articles, Atallah sought to find the root of words and expressions in spoken and literary Arabic, and to trace the phonetic, structural and semantic changes that they have undergone in the transition from literary Arabic to spoken Palestinian Arabic. In doing so, he sought to show the reader that the two levels of Arabic were alive and interactive, and he argued for their integration in a manner closer to the literary language. The word '(female) murdered victim' (*mawuda*) in the title refers to literary Arabic words that are deeply embedded in everyday speech but not recognised as such. When there are many 'murdered victims', their mother, the literary Arabic that Atallah wishes to protect, herself is in mortal danger.

The articles in the book are informed by the author's familiarity with the sociolinguistic situation in Palestinian society and in the Arab world in general, as well as his command of the history of literary Arabic. They are written in a casual and accessible style, often ironic and whimsical. Clearly, the author managed to remove the traditional obstacles between the reader and Arabic and its products. Atallah's aim was to recreate that sense of intimacy which is lacking between the Palestinian and his language and, by bridging the various elements of language – that is, literary and spoken Arabic – to reinforce the national Palestinian Arab identity.

In the article 'The Belly Remained a Womb . . .', Atallah discussed common expressions related to the family, the number of children in it and their relations with their parents. He traced the etymology of these daily expressions back to literary Arabic, as in the following example:

> Ahmad and Mahmoud [the equivalent of Tom, Dick and Harry] would not have burdened the women of our mothers' generation one bit – since when did the family make do with two? In the past, that 'modernity', grounded as it was in changed perceptions and socioeconomic developments, was of no consequence. It was opposed to the very nature of the social-familial structure. The house was supposed to be filled with children horsing around [the Palestinian colloquialism: *ur min al-awlad* – a bunch of children] [. . .] And *al-ur* is [the word] used by parents to describe the multiplicity of children: 'God help him . . . he has an *ur* of children'. It is not related to *al-aar* [shame] or other negative things [. . .] but comes from [the literary Arabic word] *al-ur*, meaning 'lad', and from *al-ura*, meaning 'female slave'. And *al-ur* is also one who is quick to fatten from breastfeeding, the latter in turn meaning that the infant has not been weaned yet, and we are left to count the *ur* of children in our home that are not yet weaned [. . .] And I'm not convinced I'm talking about our days, when the infant is weaned upon birth, or more precisely, is never weaned because it has never been breast-fed [. . .] Forget the reasons – this is a matter for clairvoyants, obstetricians and plastic surgeons.[79]

The main move here is returning spoken Arabic to its literary origins and, in fact, describing the spoken language as having branched off the literary mother tongue. There are additional, important dimensions to the way in which Atallah reconstructed the relationship between the languages, however. The textual constellation is modern and self-conscious. There are several voices here, dialoguing about Arabic and its layers in the context of Palestinian society and its current concerns. Nevertheless, clearly the issue of the nuclear family and its size is related to profound transformations undergone by Palestinian society, due to the intensive and coercive contact with the modern/settler-colonial project.

In order to examine the relation between the spoken and literary languages, Atallah set out to examine common expressions in the former. In that textual context, they sound warm and intimate, as they are related to the family and home. This enabled him to address present-day concerns related to transformation processes within society, linking the revival of the language to the redesign of the Palestinian subject and his collective identity. This is done by revitalising the language's past in the process of redesigning the collective identity of the group of Palestinians in Israel. However, this in turn relies on a professional logic that 'heals' or 'brings back to life' the 'murdered' literary language and, in a standard procedure of finding an equivalent in the ancient Classical Arabic dictionaries, actually drains the life out of spoken language, rendering it a mere offshoot of the literary language.

Particularly notable for our purposes is the fact that these are new moves never made in previous periods of 'Arabic': the bridging from spoken to literary language is made directly from the body of the language, without the mediation of establishment mechanisms, or at least without direct mediation. The relation between the two languages, as presented here, is derived from the language's internal structure and seems to have little to do with the regime. This move contradicts the structural relations of dependency, the knowledge/power hierarchy among those inhabiting the mediatory position within the Israeli academic establishment. In this book, Atallah realised the return and repositioning proposed by the ACA by combining the revival of Palestinian Arab national identity with a professional discourse, informed by a procedural logic of standardisation applied to an entire content area or domain – Arabic and its products.

In its concepts and projects, the ACA embodies the contradictions inherent in the relations between the Palestinians in Israel and the Zionist regime in the current period. Its various activities combine the discourse of revival of Palestinian Arab nationality with the professional discourse and its procedural logic. This combination enables the NGO and the socioeconomic and political basis that it represents – academic professionals and experts in various disciplines – to claim a path of return and repositioning, monopolising an entire sphere – that of the Palestinian collective. The call for educational-cultural autonomy is a claim to owning 'Arabic' itself, rather than any single position within the mediatory space. The claim to own that arena does not invalidate the superstructure of the Zionist regime but seeks to exclude it from the design of the collective identity of the Palestinians in Israel. This claim by the ACA has been accompanied by a call for collective action by the Palestinians in the area of Arabic and its products – a call answered by the ACA in its own activism.

In examining the ACA's activities, we have seen that the revival of the Palestinians' collective identity relies on professionalism and expertise acquired in Israeli academia, and that they follow a procedural logic of standardisation. Elias Atallah applied that logic in his textual intervention in the body of the Arabic language, both spoken and literary, and its products. The standard model that he constructed considers the former an offshoot of the latter. In that, Atallah 'corrected' the language, or in his terms, 'redeemed the potential murdered victim' and revived it in the late settler-colonial context requiring a standard procedure for sociocultural performances that may be distributed and consumed.

At this juncture, the question that needs to be answered is whether this type of compulsive reading/writing proposed by the NGOs concerns one event, or whether it tries to monopolise an entire domain, as required by the structural changes of the excessive literacy mode. I will also ask whether these developments of the compulsiveness mode, due to their global aspects, enable the opening of fissures in the stranglehold of the excessive literacy one. The following sub-section will paint a portrait of 'Arabic' in this final stage, based on the three positions presented heretofore – the vision statements, the Academy of Arabic Language in Israel and the Arab Culture Association.

The Late Moment of 'Arabic'

In the introduction to this chapter, I have argued that there exists a new spectrum of positions in 'Arabic', ranging between the two poles of the developed mediatory and the national declarative positions. These two poles and the three positions in 'Arabic' – that of the vision statement, the Academy of the Arabic Language and the Arab Culture Association – chart a bidirectional movement within 'Arabic' during that time, from the early 1990s until approximately 2018. One direction points to the body of the language – that is, grammar, its materiality and lingering on that materiality. This is represented, for example, in the translation of Hebrew terms into Arabic by the academy, without recommending the translation as anything but 'standardised'. Another example is invoked by Elias Atallah's model, which describes the body of spoken language descending from the motherly corpus of the literary language.

The second direction of this movement applies the standardisation procedure to the materiality of Arabic and its products, regardless of their particularity. One example is the restructuring of Arabic and its products by professional experts operating according to the procedural logic of standardisation in the Arab Culture Association. Another example is the defining of the relationship between the Palestinians in Israel as a national minority and Arabic as a legal right derived from its status as a constitutional entity, as embodied in the Haifa Declaration and Adalah's Democratic Constitution. Fascinatingly, both directions of the movement within 'Arabic' may be found in all its positions. More precisely, in order for a certain path of return and repositioning in Arabic to be possible and to constitute a position in 'Arabic', it must include both directions.

Based on these characteristics of 'Arabic' that arise from the analysis of the textual and public activities of the various positions in that arena, we may point to two spheres that constitute its current activity. One is the materiality of the body of the language and its organising principle, while the other is the procedure of translating the language into 'standardised' professional-legal matter, as well as its organising principle. The tension created between these two organising principles forms the outlines of the current portrait of 'Arabic'. The vision statements almost do not deal with the materiality of Arabic and its products in 'Arabic', but rather concentrate on the procedure of the standard right to Arabic and its products – but their call is a response to the distortion of the language's body by the government. Both the Academy of the Arabic Language and the Arab Culture Association combine the two principles in their activity, and usually it is the nature of the activity that determines which principle is to be prioritised. Moreover, the recurring argument of many of the Palestinian inhabitants of 'Arabic', to the effect that the regime and its mechanisms distort Arabic and its products, addresses the intervention in the materiality of the corpus of Arabic. On the other hand, the claim to own the symbolic and semiotic means of production of Arabic and its products is a claim to monopolise the standard procedure – that is, to monopolise the right to apply such a procedure to 'Arabic'.

This variation creates tension between the two spheres, mainly because each is a language in itself. Materiality is the language of the particular. The internal relations in Arabic and its products are unique to it, due to the history of the accumulation of work in this Arabic as objectified labour, a particular form of work, a kind of law organising the language work.[80] Yet, the language of the procedure of standardisation is a mechanism that erases the history of this accumulation of materiality by commodifying objective labour. In this sense, the materiality of Arabic cannot exist in its own right, but it must transform itself into a different form of social performance.[81] In the context of language, however – any particular language – erasure itself is impossible, as it would eliminate the criterion that defines it as a particular language, one that operates according to certain inner linguistic working laws. And in the context of Arabic and its products, the weight of accumulated objectified labour, the interventions in the body of Arabic at its different historical stages, as for example with its grammar, is considerable, compared to the weight of other layers of the language. This weight is due to the social history of Arabic, its centrality in traditional as well as modern Arab-Islamic culture.

Thus, the dialectics of erasing the accumulation, in the form of a certain working law, actually create considerable tension. This tension is caused by the movement attempting to retain Arabic and its products within 'Arabic' and, at the same time, to erase its Arabness. Most products labelled as a distortion of Arabic are actually what was created due to attempts to erase the uniqueness of Arabic and to subject it to the logic of the standardisation procedure. The tension between these two formative forces is real and dynamic: real because it represents real sociohistorical forces, NGOs and the Israeli establishment; dynamic because it is nothing but an irresolvable contradiction of settler and native, at this stage in its development at least.[82] The linking of the sociohistorical groups that join these formative forces in the current context of 'Arabic' is not only, or necessarily for that matter, inherent to Arabic and its products, or to its relation to this or that national identity, or even to these settlers and natives. The linking is partly contingent on the late capitalist moment, in its instantiation as the late settler-colonialism, as a conflict between local and global forces.[83] The struggle concerns control of symbolic and semiotic means of production made available by owning 'Arabic', whether it is owned by the settler or the native, or whether it is a compound of various differential ownerships.

The moment of late settler-colonialism requires the procedure as an organising superstructure of possible social performances, including language and its products – and 'Arabic' is a revealing example. In this moment, the materiality of social performances has attracted resistance to the organising superstructure, a polarisation resulting from the very structure of control in this late phase, rather than from a supposed resistance entailed in the materiality itself. 'Arabic' now operates according to the hegemony of the standardisation procedure, as represented by the vision statements, the academy and the ACA, but the materiality lies in the two poles or in the margins of this hegemony.

Whenever one seeks to challenge the ownership of this hegemony, as demonstrated by the ACA, or to reinforce it, as represented by the academy, one returns to the materiality of Arabic. By their very nature, power and control relations never stop: they are in constant movement. This movement gives birth to forms and configurations along the axes of time and space. The Zionist excessive literacy mode had to change its focus from single events to a whole domain of events, due to the rise of the procedure of standardisation to dominance in this late stage of the Israeli public sphere. Conversely, the Palestinian compulsive literacy mode, at this stage, is a move required by the status of the materiality of Arabic and its products in 'Arabic'. The excessiveness of this stage requires detaching the particularity of the group of Palestinians in Israel, as embodied in the materiality of Arabic. This is a belated variation on the act that resets the year zero of the group of Palestinians in Israel as contemporaneous with the establishment of the State of Israel.

Conclusion

This chapter has addressed the profound changes that occurred in the arena of 'Arabic' over the past three decades, changes that have led to modifications in its ways of operation. In order to trace these changes and elicit the paths that they offer for return and repositioning within 'Arabic', I have first characterised the period of late settler-colonialism among the group of Palestinians in Israel, in terms of their relation to the Zionist regime and contacts with global socioeconomic and political forces. The most significant change identified was the reorganisation of the Palestinian public sphere around civil society organisations. These have dealt with Arabic and its products in multiple ways, in public sites. Their treatment of 'Arabic' was informed by legal and linguistic professional discourse and expertise, operating subject to a procedural logic of standardisation.

In the next phase, I examined how this operation was manifested in various positions within 'Arabic'. This section reviewed the Haifa Declaration published by Mada al-Carmel, as well as Adalah's Democratic Constitution. These two documents conceive of the group of Palestinians in Israel as a national minority with legal status that grants it collective rights. One of its basic rights is the right to Arabic and its products. Arabic's transition from being an inherent characteristic of national collective identity to being a constitutional minority right relies on the translation of the relations between the Palestinians in Israel and the regime into a legal-professional discourse, operating according to a procedural logic. It is not Arabic and its products that are the issue here, but rather the right to own a language present side-by-side with Hebrew in the Zionist regime. With regard to 'Arabic', this means retaining the mediatory structure between the nation-state format and its subjects, and at the same time recreating a national Palestinian subjectivity instead of the 'Israeli Arab' produced by the settler-colonial state.

The Academy of the Arabic Language in Israel represents a mediatory position in 'Arabic' that is the development of the traditional mediatory position from previous periods. The academy operates on the textual and public levels in several spheres, but its working logic is based on the modernisation principle, through contact with the Hebrew language and its imagined model. This modernisation is the proper task of professionals specialising in Arabic and its products. That is, they accept the mediatory position and develop it in claiming ownership over an entire domain – Arabic and its products.

The third position analysed in this chapter is that of the Arab Culture Association. Since its establishment, this NGO has initiated projects dealing with Arabic and its products in order to revive Palestinian Arab identity. The path of return and repositioning claimed by the ACA relies on the combination of national identity and professional expert discourse, operating according to procedural logic. According to this position, national identity will be based on the work of professional experts on Arabic and its products. Implementing the procedure will lead to the revival of a standardised Arabic, a variant of the literary language. In its claim, the ACA does not deconstruct 'Arabic' or its role in the settler-colonial structure, but rather claims ownership of the symbolic and semiotic means used to produce the national collective identity of the Palestinians in Israel.

The portrait of 'Arabic' in this period is shaped by the tension between the materiality of the structure of 'Arabic' – that is, the body of Arabic and its products – and the procedural logic that involves the standardisation and commodification of this materiality. The procedural logic is required by late settler-colonialism, and resistance to this logic through materiality is derived from its structure. Therefore, in this phase of 'Arabic', the excessive literacy mode should be viewed as an attempt to control the materiality of Arabic and its products, whatever they may be, while the compulsive literacy mode should be viewed as a move required by the status of the materiality of Arabic and its products within 'Arabic'.

In this chapter, I have examined the current phase in the development of 'Arabic' and painted its portrait as reflected in the range of positions constituting it. In doing so, I have completed the presentation of the three main phases in the structural development of 'Arabic'. I will now examine the dynamics of this history beyond its specific phases and determine whether 'Arabic' includes an organising principle of narrating the history of relations between the Palestinians in Israel and the Zionist regime.

Notes

1. For more on this, see Uri Ram, *HaGlobalizatsiyah shel Israel: McWorld beTel Aviv, Jihad beYerushalayim* [The Globalisation of Israel: McWorld in Tel Aviv, Jihad in Jerusalem] (Tel Aviv: Resling, 2005); Adam Hanieh, 'From State-Led Growth to Globalization: The Evolution Israeli Capitalism', *Journal of Palestine Studies* 32, no. 4 (Summer 2003), 5–21; Assaf Razin, *Israel and World Economy: The Power of Globalization* (Cambridge, MA: MIT Press, 2018).

2. These relations and their transformation over the past two decades have been extensively reviewed in the literature, but this has tended to focus on particular aspects rather than the general picture. See Nashef, *Mi'māriyyat al-fuqdān*, 9–34.
3. For more on this issue in regard to the entire Palestinian society, see Benoit Challand, *Palestinian Civil Society: Foreign Donors and the Power to Promote and Exclude* (London: Routledge, 2008). For the group of Palestinians in Israel, see Amal Jamal, *Arab Minority Nationalism in Israel: The Politics of Indigeneity* (London: Routledge, 2011), 188–225; Shany Payes, *Palestinian NGOs In Israel: The Politics of Civil Society* (London: I. B. Tauris, 2005).
4. See Mandel, *Late Capitalism*; Fredric Jameson, *Postmodernism, or The Cultural Logic of Late Capitalism* (Durham, NC: Duke University Press, 1992). For more on late colonialism, see, for example, Mahmood Mamdani, *Citizen and Subject: Contemporary Africa and the Legacy of Late Colonialism* (Princeton: Princeton University Press, 1996). Regarding the Israeli case, see Arnon Degani, 'From Republic to Empire: Israel and the Palestinians after 1948', in *The Routledge Handbook of the History Settler Colonialism*, ed. Edward Cavanagh and Lorenzo Veracini (London: Routledge, 2017), 353–67.
5. For the impact of global capital movement on the West Bank and Gaza Strip, see, for example, Rex Brynen, *A Very Political Economy: Peacebuilding and Foreign Aid* (Washington: United States Institute for Peace, 2000). It appears that no study has hitherto examined the same impact among the Palestinians in Israel. For the politics of identity aspect though, see Dan Rabinowitz, 'Postnational Palestine/Israel? Globalization, Diaspora, Transnationalism, and the Israeli-Palestinian Conflict', *Critical Inquiry* 26, No. 4 (Summer 2000), 757–72.
6. For a critical analysis of this phenomenon among the Palestinians, see Nashif, 'Isn't It Good to Be Literate?'
7. A key activist in this context is Adv. Hassan Jabareen. See, for example, Hassan Jabareen, 'LiḲrat Gishot BiḲortiot shel haMiʿut haFalasṭini: 'Ezraḥut, Le'umiut veFeminisim baMishpaṭ haIsraeli' [Towards Critical Approaches of the Palestinian Minority: Citizenship, Nationality and Feminism in Israeli Law], *Plilim* 9 (2000), 53–93.
8. For more on the legal professional process among the Palestinians, see Ismail Nashef, 'Ḥawl imkāniyyat dirāsat al-nuẓum al-istiʿmāriyya: Filasṭīn namūdhajan' [On the Possibility of Studying the Colonial Systems: The Case of Palestine], in *Al-Nafī fī kitābat Isrā'īl: Abḥāth Filasṭīniyya ḥawl al-niẓām wa-l-mujtamaʿ wa-l-dawla fī Isrā'īl* [Negation in Writing Israel: Palestinian Studies on Regime, Society and

State in Israel], ed. Ismail Nashef (Ramallah: Madar, Palestinian Center for Israeli Studies, 2011), 8–27.

9. For the historical and legal aspects of these processes, see Hassan Jabareen, 'Hobbsian Citizenship: How the Palestinians Became a Minority in Israel', in *Multiculturalism and Minority Rights in the Arab World*, ed. Will Kymlicka and Eva Pfostl (Oxford: Oxford University Press, 2014), 189–218.
10. For more on the procedure's modus operandi in the contemporary Palestinian cultural context, see Nashef, *On Palestinian Abstraction*, 89–94.
11. During the period under study, four vision statements were published by three NGOs, all active in Haifa: Mada al-Carmel: Arab Centre for Applied Social Research; Adalah: Legal Centre for Arab Minority Rights in Israel; Musawa Centre for the Rights of Arab Citizens in Israel; and the High Follow-Up Committee for Arab Citizens of Israel. See Musawa Centre, *Dustūr mutasawin li-l-jamī'* [Equal Constitution for All] (Haifa: Musawa Centre, 2006); National Committee of Arab Mayors, *Al-Taṣawwur al-mustaqbalī li-l-'Arab fī Isrā'īl* [The Future Vision of the Arabs in Israel] (Nazareth: National Committee of Arab Mayors, 2006); Mada al-Carmel, *Wathīqat Ḥayfā* [Haifa Declaration] (Haifa: Mada al-Carmel, 2007); Adalah, *Al-Dustūr al-dīmuqrāṭī* [The Democratic Constitution] (Haifa: Adalah, 2007). These documents have attracted considerable attention from both Palestinians and Jews in Israel. See, for example, Khalil Nakhla (ed.), *Mustaqbal al-'aqaliyya al-Filasṭīniyya fī Isrā'īl* [The Future of the Palestinian Minority in Israel] (Ramallah: Madar, Palestinian Center for Israeli Studies, 2008); Uri Ram, 'Tensions in the "Jewish Democracy": The Constitutional Challenge of the Palestinian Citizens in Israel', *Constellations* 16, no. 3 (2009), 523–36.
12. This study addresses the period up until the instituting of the new Israeli law titled 'Basic Law: Israel as a Nation State of the Jewish People' on 19 July 2018. For more details on the impact of this law on the Palestinians in Israel, see Jabareen and Bishara, 'The Jewish Nation-State Law.'
13. On these events and their influence on the relations between Palestinians in Israel and the State of Israel, see, for example, Nimer Sultany, *Muwāṭinūn bi-lā muwāṭana: Taqrīr al-raṣd al-siyāsī al-sanawī 2000–2001* [Citizens without Citizenship: The Follow-Up Political Report 2000–2001] (Haifa: Mada Al-Carmel, 2003).
14. The key figures in formulating the declaration were Nadim Rouhana, Hassan Jabareen, Ramzi Suleiman, Muhamad Haj-Yahia and Nadera Shalhoub-Kevorkian. Apart from Jabareen, all held permanent academic positions. Rouhana has since moved to the United States, while the other three are still senior lecturers at Israeli universities.

15. For example, Nadim Rouhana established Mada al-Carmel, an NGO that focuses on applied social research on the Palestinians in Israel.
16. The development of this area may be indicated by a comparison of their publications from the early 1990s and shortly before and their publications in the 2000s.
17. The Palestinian academics in Israel, particularly those who pursued a career in Israeli academia, developed unique patterns of reading the corpus of texts published in Arabic in the Arab world. They concentrated on reading fiction and literature, and they read very few theoretical and research texts. For them, the language of science is mostly Hebrew or English.
18. Nakhla, *Mustaqbal al-'aqaliyya al-Filasṭīniyya.*
19. Mada al-Carmel, *Wathīqat Ḥayfā*, 4.
20. Mada al-Carmel, *Wathīqat Ḥayfā*, 7. The first emphasis is in the original, the second is by the author.
21. This approach is common among national movements and widely accepted in the research literature. See Yasir Suleiman, *The Arabic Language and National Identity: A Study in Ideology* (Washington, DC: Georgetown University Press, 2002).
22. Mada al-Carmel, *Wathīqat Ḥayfā*, 7–8. Author's italics.
23. For more on the authors' position on this issue, see Nadim Rouhana, 'Wathīqat Ḥayfā wa-l Filasṭīniyūn fī Isrā'īl: Min al-Hāmish al-siyāsī ilā l-markaz al-'akhlāqī' [The Haifa Declaration and the Palestinians in Israel: From the Political Margins to the Moral Centre], in *Mustaqbal al-'aqaliyya al-Filasṭīniyya fī Isrā'īl* [The Future of the Palestinian Minority in Israel], ed. Khalil Nakhla (Ramallah: Madar, Palestinian Centre for Israeli Studies, 2008), 76–103.
24. Mada al-Carmel, *Wathīqat Ḥayfā*, 15–16. Author's italics.
25. On the problem of sovereignty in the colonial context, in general, and in the Palestinian context, in particular, see Achille Mbembe, 'Necropolitics', *Public Culture* 15, no. 1 (2003), 11–40.
26. HCJ 4112/99, *Adalah and Co.* v. *Tel Aviv-Jaffa Municipality and Co* (2002).
27. Much has been written about the history and main issues of this discourse. See, for example, Lori Allen, *The Rise and Fall of Human Rights: Cynicism and Politics in Occupied Palestine* (Palo Alto: Stanford University Press, 2013).
28. Adalah, *Ad-Dustūr al-dīmūqrāṭī.*
29. Adalah, *Ad-Dustūr al-dīmūqrāṭī*, 3.
30. Adalah, *Ad-Dustūr al-dīmūqrāṭī*, 4.
31. Adalah, *Ad-Dustūr al-dīmūqrāṭī*, 4–5. Author's italics.
32. For the complete text of the declaration, see United Nations General Assembly, Resolution No. 47/135, 'Declaration on the Rights of Persons Belonging to

National or Ethnic, Religious and Linguistic Minorities' (18 December 1992), http://www.un-documents.net/a47r135.htm

33. Adalah, *Ad-Dustūr al-dīmūqrāṭī*, 5.
34. Adalah, *Ad-Dustūr al-dīmūqrāṭī*, 7–8.
35. For more on symbol work as opposed to other communication mechanism, see William F. Hanks, *Language and Communication Practices* (Boulder: Westview Press, 1996), 45–46.
36. For more on this issue, see Raef Zreik, 'Qirā'a fī l-naṣṣ' [Text Reading], in *Mustaqbal al-'Aqaliyya al-Filasṭīniyya fī Isrā'īl* [The Future of the Palestinian Minority in Israel], ed. Khalil Nakhla (Ramallah: Madar, Palestinian Centre for Israeli Studies, 2008), 105–19.
37. See Partha Chatterjee, *Nationalist Thought and the Colonial World: A Derivative Discourse?* (Minneapolis: University of Minnesota Press, 1986).
38. In most cases of settler-colonial regimes and as part of the symbolic and the material elimination of the native, the languages of the indigenous peoples were eliminated, or at least subjected to practices aiming at elimination. In this regard, the Palestinian case in Israel is different: the elimination has taken the shape of recreating a new 'register' of Arabic. The academy is one of the tools that produces this register. For practices of excavating the 'eliminated' languages of the natives, see, for example, Sarah Dowling, *Translingual Poetics: Writing Personhood under Settler Colonialism* (Iowa City: University of Iowa Press, 2018).
39. On the history of the Academy of the Arabic Language in Cairo, see Al-Jumaī', *Majma' al-lugha al-'Arabiyya.*
40. Fahd Abu Khadra, Farouq Mawasi and Elias Atallah, 'Bayān li-man yuhimmuhu 'amr al-lugha al-'Arabiyya' [Letter for Those to Whom the Arabic Language is Important], *Al-Jadid* 38, no. 10 (October 1989), 122.
41. See Suleiman Jubran, 'Kalima Ūlā' [Foreword], in *A'māl al-mu'tamar al-'awwal li-majma' al-lugha al-'Arabiyya* [Proceedings of the First Conference of the Academy of the Arabic Language], ed. Suleiman Jubran (Haifa: Academy of the Arabic Language, 2004), 5–8.
42. The committee published three such lists. See High Committee for the Arabic Language, *Al-Manhal fī l-muṣṭalaḥāt al-mu'āṣira* 1 [Al-Manhal: Contemporary Expressions 1] (Jerusalem: Ministry of Education, Division of Curricula Planning and Development, 1999), 1–3.
43. Following the struggle, the Al-Qasemi Academic College of Education in Baqa al-Gharbiyya established an academy of its own, and it was joined by several of the main group members, such as Fahd abu Khadra. Although it operates as

a language academy, it has failed to compete with the official one, functioning instead as a department within the college.

44. See Adel Manna, *Nakba wa-baqā': Ḥikāyāt Filasṭīniyīn ẓallū fī Ḥayfā wa-l-Jalīl, 1948–1956* [*Nakba* and Survival: The Story of Palestinians who Remained in Haifa and the Galilee, 1948–1956] (Beirut: Institute for Palestine Studies, 2016).
45. Abu Khadra, Mawasi and Atallah, 'Bayān'.
46. Abu Khadra, Mawasi and Atallah, 'Bayān', 122.
47. Abu Khadra, Mawasi and Atallah, 'Bayān', 122.
48. High Committee for the Arabic Language, *Al-Manhal*, 1:6.
49. For an overview of this diversity, see Suleiman Jubran (ed.), *A'māl al-mu'tamar al-'awwal li-majma' al-lugha al-'Arabiyya* [Proceedings of the First Conference of the Academy of the Arabic Language] (Haifa: Academy of the Arabic Language, 2004).
50. Jubran, 'Kalima Ūlā', 5.
51. Hanna Abu Hanna, 'Al-Ḥulm al-lādhī kāna janīnan yūladu basharan sawiyyan' [The Dream That Was a Fetus Was Born a Whole Human Being], in *A'māl al-mu'tamar al-awwal li-majma' al-lugha al-'Arabiyya* [Proceedings of the First Conference of the Academy of the Arabic Language], ed. Suleiman Jubran (Haifa: Academy of the Arabic Language, 2004), 9–15.
52. Elias Atallah, 'Wāqi' al-lugha al-'Arabiyya wa-taḥaddiyātuhā' [The Reality of Arabic and its Challenges], in *A'mal al-mu'tamar al-awwal li-majma' al-lugha al-'Arabiyya* [Proceedings of the First Conference of the Academy of the Arabic Language], ed. Suleiman Jubran (Haifa: Academy of the Arabic Language, 2004), 80–92.
53. Atallah, 'Wāqi' al-lugha al-'Arabiyya', 96–97.
54. Atallah, 'Wāqi' al-lugha al-'Arabiyya', 101–5.
55. For a comparison of the two laws, in Hebrew, see Law for the Supreme Institute for the Hebrew Language, 5713-1953, Law Book 135, 6 September 1953, pp. 168–69; Law for the Supreme Institute for the Arabic Language, 5767-2007, Law Book 2092, 28 March 2007, pp. 286–90.
56. For more on these activities, see Fuad Kan'ani (ed.), *Majma' al-lugha al-'Arabiyya fī Isrā'īl: Injāzāt wa-ṭumūḥāt – Kurāsa khāṣṣa bi-munāsabat murūr 'ām 'alā ta'sīs al-majma'* [Academy of the Arabic Language in Israel: Achievements and Aspirations – Special Booklet upon the First Anniversary of Its Founding] (Haifa: Academy of the Arabic Language, 2009).
57. Taha Hussein (1889–1973) was an Egyptian intellectual, one of the leaders of the revival of Arabic language and culture. In acknowledgment of his immense influence in this regard, he earned the sobriquet 'Dean of Arabic Literature'.

58. Kan'ani, *Majma' al-lugha al-'Arabiyya*, 1.
59. Kan'ani, *Majma' al-lugha al-'Arabiyya*, 2.
60. Kan'ani, *Majma' al-lugha al-'Arabiyya*, 7–8.
61. Suleiman Jubran, *'Alā hāmish al-tajdīd wa-l-taqyīd fi l-lugha al-'Arabiyya al-Mu'āṣira* [On the Margins of the Innovations and Limitations in the Modern Arabic Language] (Haifa: Academy of the Arabic Language, 2009).
62. Jubran, *'Ala hāmish al-tajdīd*, 28–33.
63. Jubran, *'Ala hāmish al-tajdīd*, 9–23.
64. Jubran, *'Ala hāmish al-tajdīd*, 37.
65. Jubran, *'Ala hāmish al-tajdīd*, 37.
66. Jubran, *'Ala hāmish al-tajdīd*, 96.
67. Jubran, *'Ala hāmish al-tajdīd*, 96.
68. Jubran, *'Ala hāmish al-tajdīd*, 96.
69. Arab Culture Association, *Lughatī huwiyyatī* [My Language is My Identity] (Nazareth: Arab Culture Association, 2010), 2.
70. Arab Culture Association, *Lughatī huwiyyatī*, 3.
71. Arab Culture Association, *Lughatī huwiyyatī*, 3.
72. Project participants received a schoolbag with a collection of short articles and abstracts, as well as some twenty CDs, half of them teaching a course in Arabic and half teaching a course on children's literature. See Arab Culture Association, *Ta'allamu l-'Arabiyya wa-'Allimuhā li-nās* [Study the Arabic Language and Teach It to People] (kit) (Nazareth: Arab Culture Association, 2009).
73. Arab Culture Association, *Lughatī huwiyyatī*, 5.
74. Eman Abu Hanna-Nahhas (ed.), *Al-Mughayyabūn: Qirā'a naqdiyya li-kutub al-manāhij al-Isrā'īliyya fi l-madāris al-'Arabiyya al-thānawiyya* [The Absented: Critical Reading of Israeli Textbooks in Arab High Schools] (Haifa: Association of Arab Culture, 2014).
75. Abu Hanna-Nahhas, *Al-Mughayyabūn*, back cover.
76. For more on cultural autonomy, see Bishara, *Al-'Arab fi Isrā'īl.*
77. Abu Hanna-Nahhas, *Al-Mughayyabūn*, back cover.
78. The title is borrowed from a Quranic verse that refers to a pre-Islamic Arab custom: a father who sired a daughter would bury her alive, so as to prevent her from becoming a weakness in inter-tribal strife. Atallah used this expression metaphorically: the murdered victim here is literary Arabic, now excluded from everyday speech. As a researcher, Atallah sought to reconnect spoken and literary language and, thereby, to reintroduce the assassinated literary language into the daily lives of Palestinians in Israel. See Elias Atallah, *Wa-Idhā l-maw'ūdatu*

su'ilat [And If the Murdered is Asked] (Nazareth: Arab Culture Association and Mawakib, 2007).

79. Atallah, *Wa-Idhā l-Maw'ūdatu su'ilat*, 108.
80. On materiality and its return as an analytic category in late capitalism, see Daniel Miller (ed.), *Materiality* (Durham, NC: Duke University Press, 2005).
81. On the political economy of language, see Rossi-Landi, *Language*.
82. For more on real social forces in the context of language, see Williams, *Marxism*, 21–44.
83. For an overview of the relations between language materiality and late capitalism, see Shalini Shankar and Jillian Cavanaugh, 'Language and Materiality in Global Capitalism', *Annual Review of Anthropology* 41 (2012), 355–69.

Conclusion: Narrating the History of the Non-historical

The possibility of a critical research gaze on the social history of the Palestinians in Israel is enabled by several structural changes. These structural changes affect the relationship of the Palestinians in Israel with the following: itself as a collective, the rest of Palestinian society, and the Zionist regime and the State of Israel. For our purposes, these changes manifest themselves in the historical narrative that the Palestinians generate about themselves. If this historical narrative of the Palestinian citizens of Israel is a collection of forms of compulsive reading and writing at work in different variations, then it is out of these variations that one must reverse-engineer the first and constitutive structural condition: the results of the 1948 war or *Nakba*. We must examine whether the status of constitutive condition of the total loss resulting from the war of 1948 has undergone changes, and whether these changes are being expressed as part of the Palestinians' historical narrative beyond a certain stage in the development of 'Arabic'. In this context, 'Arabic' reflects the developments in its enabling conditions – that is, the state apparatuses overseeing literary practices and ideologies in Israel and among its Palestinian citizens. Mainly, 'Arabic' expresses these conditions in its constituent materiality: literary Arabic and its associated symbolic and semiotic means of production.

The deep, all-Palestinian processes that have taken place over the past three decades have relocated the status of the total loss of 1948 to a new position, which is problematic and ambivalent from the point of view of the Palestinian national collective. These processes are related to the collective emotional structure concerning the *Nakba* – the last constitutive moment of the Palestinians in Israel as a historical group. Until the First Intifada (1987–93), this emotional structure relied on direct involvement with the total loss and on the various attempts to organise and deal with it through collective liberation, mainly on a national basis. With the end of the First Intifada and the influences of contemporary regional and global processes, a new attitude to the *Nakba* and the conditions of loss created thereby rose to the Palestinians' collective awareness. This attitude may be defined as second-degree loss. The Palestinians, as a collective, had failed to overcome their total loss resulting from the *Nakba*, according to the criteria of the national collective discourses.[1] In many respects, the Palestinians lost the ability to cope with the total loss and to remedy its tragic consequences.

Second-degree loss is embodied in the collective emotional structure among the Palestinians and expressed on various sociocultural and political levels. Mainly, it enables spatio-temporal distance from the total loss of 1948. Herein also lies the possibility of seeing it from an external viewpoint. Note that the contradictions of the first loss have not been resolved. What we have here is a Freudian *deferred action*, which enables a reorganisation of the *Nakba* and the total loss, so as to perceive them from a temporal distance.[2] To a large extent, the contemporary research gaze on the social history of the Palestinians in Israel and particularly on 'Arabic' is enabled by this deferred action, which was made possible by this second-degree loss.

This development in regard to the status of the total loss of 1948 enables the research gaze to shift from following discrete events along the temporal sequence to following a chain of events beyond a certain point in time. Take, for example, scholars focusing on a certain communicative event in 'Arabic', such as the publication of a poetry collection. During the period of direct involvement with the total loss, the scholarly research gaze was limited to the event itself, because the scholars themselves were overwhelmed by the temporal proximity to the total loss. Involvement through second-degree loss enables a research perspective that can examine a chain of communicative events – such as multiple collections by the same poet or several poets. I argue that it is the contemporary moment (since the mid-1990s) in the development of 'Arabic', in the context of second-degree loss, that enables us to talk about a historical narrative that organises the chain of events presented in the previous chapters.

One of the main characteristics of the transition to second-degree loss is the change in how the Palestinians in Israel relate to themselves as a national collective. During the first stage of the loss, this relation was grounded in a view that bordered on the essentiality and sanctity of the collective identity. Various sociocultural spheres of action were subordinated to this, including literary Arabic and its products. Conversely, in the second stage, the relation changed; it is now built on a blending of approaches, characterised by a dynamic of construction and deconstruction.

Let us consider an example of that change. In the first stage, if one had acquired a profession, that profession was subject to the 'essentialist' mode of the collectivity, since as a professional, one contributed to reinforcing and maintaining the collectivity. In the second stage, however, the profession exists in its own right, and sometimes the profession and expertise redefine and change the Palestinian collectivity. This characteristic applies to literary Arabic and its products, producing new contexts that enable the reading and writing of its social history in a new light. We can read it now as a transition from language, as a signifier of essentialist collectivity – framing literary Arabic as sacred – to a state of no single dominant view of national collectivity, thereby freeing the sign of its sacred essentiality. This process is not linear and unequivocal; it is ambivalent and affected by sociopolitical forces that channel it in directions derived from their position within 'Arabic'. Perhaps the most salient example of this is the Academy of the Arabic Language in Israel and its call for modernisation, combined with its maintenance of the standardisation of literary Arabic developed within the arena of 'Arabic'.

Through this book, we have seen that between 1948 and around 1990, the main mode among the Palestinians consisted of compulsive reading/writing of communicative events in 'Arabic': these events were read and written as isolated events, even though they were sometimes part of a chain of events. In the recent period, however, that of second-degree loss, analysis of the public textual activities in 'Arabic' reveals the formulation of a demand by different agents, such as the Academy of Arabic Language in Israel, to monopolise the domain of literary Arabic and its products. This raises the question whether these claims for monopoly reposition compulsive literacy, producing changes in 'Arabic' itself. To address this issue, I will now review the general historical narrative of 'Arabic' in light of the insights of second-degree loss and the deferred action of the research gaze enabled thereby.

The Biography of 'Arabic'

One of the characteristics of the biography of 'Arabic' is its ability to undergo socioeconomic and political changes and reposition itself as the structural arena that handles literary Arabic and its products. Despite those changes, the structural position of 'Arabic' has consistently played its role as the site where the relations between the Palestinians in Israel and the state and its mechanisms are organised. The relation between these changes and the structurality of 'Arabic' produces tension: these changes are not the outcome of an event that is internal to the arena, but they depend on socioeconomic and political factors that are external to it. This relationship operates according to organising principles different from those that organise the arena of 'Arabic' internally and enable its continuity as a mediating site. To this day, no event in the materiality of literary Arabic and its products has yet occurred in 'Arabic' which has led to any change in the arena or its subordinate spheres in the State of Israel. The general historical narrative of 'Arabic' begins with it echoing events from different spheres, which may be seen as a meta-narrative of the settler-colonial context. Such a narrative of 'Arabic', however, may lead to a narrow and even problematic view of the issue: if we accept the secondary status of 'Arabic', we accept, in fact, the logic of Zionist excessiveness. Therefore, I will try to liberate this narrative from that excessiveness and trace our steps back to its materiality.

After the destruction of the social-material infrastructure of the Palestinians in Israel, the excessive literacy mode was identified as essential and was bounded in a structural arena that operated according to the mechanisms of the nation-state format: this is how 'Arabic' was formed. The analysis tracing the development of 'Arabic' since then suggests the accumulation of three main portraits that have developed within it. Since 1948, these portraits have gradually come to constitute the materiality of the arena of 'Arabic'. These portraits have three layers: the institutional-material infrastructure, the sign used as an exchange value and the discursive formations that apply the sign to communicative events in the realities of 'Arabic'. These layers interact to produce the profile of the work of the arena of 'Arabic' at any given moment.

I have connected these layers and their interactions to their embodiment in literary Arabic – that is, in the nature of the textual structure manifested in the public activity of the compulsive literacy mode.

The first portrait of 'Arabic', which represents a stratum in the structural accumulation of subsequent forms of work, is made up of three positions: that of the state mechanism, that of the *Al-Jadid* group and that of the *Al-Mujtama* group. The literary critical articles of each position indicate that literary Arabic, which is a collective signifier of the Palestinians, became a material that had to be cast in order to shape the Palestinian collective through it. The state's position disconnected literary Arabic from all that had preceded 1948 and declared that year as zero, as the moment of constituting the group of its Palestinian citizens. The state also disconnected literary Arabic spatially, by distancing it from the modern cultural Arab tradition. The *Al-Jadid* group presented the opposite intervention: the Palestinians own literary Arabic, in continuation of what preceded 1948, according to both their relations with modern Arab culture and their unique positioning in Israel. Conversely, *Al-Mujtama* accepted the conditions of 'Arabic' dictated by the relevant state mechanisms and translated them into literary Arabic texts, but it made an additional step that the state may not have predicted: it believed that the Zionist regime would accept it – as part of the regime – if only it acted according to the conditions of 'Arabic' dictated by the state.

Already at this point in the history of 'Arabic', it seems to have inhered contradictions focused on other areas, mainly socioeconomic and political. The coalescence of these contradictions was initially characterised by immediacy and was largely transparent: the relation between the attitude towards the state and the characteristics of the text was causal and even direct. Accepting the conditions dictated by the state to the Palestinians was manifested directly in the literary reviews written and read in a certain position in 'Arabic'. Its mechanisms of causality and transparency, which determined the linkage between various social areas and 'Arabic', changed significantly in the second portrait of 'Arabic', when the academic mask was cast into the literary Arabic body of literary criticism.

The transparent causality of the first portrait was derived mainly from the primary institutional-material infrastructure of 'Arabic' in this period. The institutionalisation of 'Arabic' in literary Arabic occurred mainly through the academisation of textual and public activities. The academisation of the materiality of this arena paralleled the modernisation of the Palestinians in Israel through state apparatuses. Behind the academic mask, the mediatory position demanded not only a declaration of loyalty to the State of Israel, but also a reframing of the settler-colonial context, as an expression of national renewal. This is in fact the peak of the development of compulsive literacy, which structurally adopts Zionist excessiveness in the sociocultural areas of the Palestinian collective in Israel.

This process of institutionalisation through academisation, however, created an accumulation of symbolic capital – scientific academic knowledge on literary Arabic – among a group of Palestinians, granting it a distinct status among the Palestinians in Israel. This led to a sharp split between the institutional-material infrastructure, derived from the state, and the mobile symbolic capital in the context of the late settler-colonial moment. This characteristic of the group of Palestinian academics in Israel developed into a sharp contradiction, which, towards the end of the academisation period, blurred the boundaries between the traditional positions in 'Arabic', leading to a call to organise a group of experts in literary Arabic and establish an Arabic academy among the Palestinians in Israel.

In the early 1990s, the academisation processes and the accumulation of symbolic capital among Palestinian academics in Israel coincided with local, regional and global changes. As result, the institutional-material infrastructure developed, civil society organisations flourished, and the Academy of the Arabic Language was founded. These events led to significant changes in the type of exchange sign and the structure of discursive formations that organised the communicative events within 'Arabic'. The Palestinian NGOs that dealt with literary Arabic and its products translated the Palestinian national discourse into a professional language of experts, mainly that of lawyers and social scientists. The Academy of the Arabic Language also operates on the basis of professional expertise in literary Arabic, but its activity is based on a procedural principle of standardisation and is limited to translating the model of Hebrew and its products into the body of literary Arabic and its products. This is a development of the mediatory model presented by the academisation position from the previous period. Particularly noteworthy in this context is the position of the NGOs, which is opposed to that of the academy. The NGOs try to combine Palestinian Arab national identity with professionalism and expertise in literary Arabic and its products. This position expresses standardisation that claims ownership of Arabic and its products in 'Arabic' in order to shape the Palestinian collectivity in Israel and claim ownership of it. This portrait of 'Arabic' is built on professionalism and expertise, with a procedural organising principle that does not transgress the boundaries of the arena, but rather claims various types of ownership of it.

The materiality of 'Arabic', which has been shaped by the three portraits, tells a modern settler-colonial story. It begins with isolated initial events, proceeds with the institutionalisation of those events through academisation and ends with the accumulation of mobile symbolic capital in a global era when professionalism and expertise dominate 'Arabic'. From this perspective, we see a historical narrative in which 'Arabic' has been serving as a marginal structural site on which the regime has projected one of its fundamental contradictions – its settler-colonial relations with the Palestinians in Israel – in order to examine these relations in a controlled manner that would enable it to reposition them as subjects who accept the existing social order through the subjectivity of 'Israeli Arabs' – that is, the symbolic elimination of the Palestinian collective.[3] We must now ask, however, whether this narrative, like other modern narratives of settler-colonialism that contain irresolvable contradictions, includes the possibilities of resisting and deconstructing it.

The Trap

In opposition to Gramsci's argument that every structure of coercion and oppression includes a structure of resistance to it, 'Arabic' includes no such structure.[4] This is a structural arena that exists in the Israeli settler-colonial context, where the Palestinians in Israel are characterised by the loss of the ability to lose, which is part of the processes of their elimination as natives. In terms of the social-material infrastructure, Palestinians are unable to constitute an opposing structure at this point in their history. This aspect is sharpened even further when examining the position of 'Arabic' in the excessive literacy mode of Zionism, which serves as a superstructure that reads/writes the Palestinians in Israel. Here, the structurality of 'Arabic' is a byproduct of the compulsive literacy mode, and this does not enable a structural level of resistance because it maintains the loss of the ability to lose as the basis for the settler-colonial relations in the Zionist regime. Therefore, if we rely on Gramsci's argument, we must deny 'Arabic' its structurality because it blocks the structure of resistance to symbolic elimination. Denying that structurality leads us to events along the time axis in spaces external to 'Arabic'. We must ask, then, which events in literary Arabic and its products can derive from its materiality, beyond 'Arabic', among the Palestinians in Israel.

Two such event loci are still spaces that cannot be subject to the compulsive principles of the arena of 'Arabic'. One is the Quran, and the classical interpretive corpus thereof. This is a source of events in literary Arabic that have a formative power, which acts on a large section of the Palestinians in Israel as an Islamic collective.[5] In the course of the social history of 'Arabic', institutional-material infrastructures have been formed in an attempt to create an exchangeable sign and discursive formations of such events. These include the Israeli Sharia courts responsible for marital law among the Muslim Palestinians, learning materials about Islam in the Arab education system, Sharia colleges, the appointment of mosque officials and radio and television broadcasts on Islam. Nevertheless, there still has been no public textual activity related to the Quran and its interpretive corpus, similar to the activity in the area of modern poetry and prose.[6] To a large extent, part of the Palestinian Islamic community has managed to hold on to the source of communicative events in literary Arabic that define its collectivity. This aspect of the social history of the Palestinians in Israel has yet to be examined in depth – paradoxically, most available studies focus on the group's attitude towards the Zionist project and its regime.

The second locus of communicative events in literary Arabic consists of public textual activities that occur in the Arab world and are not related to the structural arena of 'Arabic', and these are quite extensive. In previous periods, state apparatuses have applied various regulations to control the flow of these communicative events. A prime example is the censorship of literary Arabic texts before they reach the Palestinians in Israel. Public textual activities in 'Arabic' have also framed such texts as negative communicative events in certain aspects. Today, with the development of information technologies and the establishment of transnational communications, it is doubtful whether the same mechanisms of censorship and control may be applied.

Still, there is no institutional-material infrastructure among the Palestinians in Israel that can provide a basis for communicative events occurring in the Arab world. These events, however, have an exchangeable sign that operates among the Palestinians in Israel, even if they do not reproduce a collectivity with a clear and homogeneous character.[7]

These loci of communicative events can provide a starting point for an exit from 'Arabic' but cannot negate the structural arena. This is because they themselves emerged as a negation from the social history of 'Arabic', as presented in the previous chapters. Moreover, modern Arab nationalism and the Islamic community are in a bind, similar to that of the Palestinians in Israel, in terms of their relations with other Western colonial powers. They are part of the structural arena of 'Arabic' by way of exclusion and should be positioned as part of its historical narrative.

This concluding discussion indicates that the historical narrative of 'Arabic' has several characteristics. The first is that 'Arabic' serves the regime as a site for projecting its fundamental contradictions with the Palestinians in Israel in order to work them through the materiality of literary Arabic and its products. The second characteristic is that the structural opening of the arena has required for Palestinians in Israel a new mode of literacy that would allow them to work through contradictions, according to the position of this structure in the settler-colonial regime. This mode is the compulsiveness derived from the Zionist excessive literacy mode and, therefore, constitutes the social agency of the Palestinians in Israel, enabled by the Zionist regime. The third characteristic is that the various positions in 'Arabic' have gone through three stages, all variations on the modern development of the fields of the nation-state format: events, institutionalisation and professionalism. The difference between the modern and its settler-colonial variation in this context lies in the latter's echo of the former, in terms of the locus of the social event. The fourth characteristic is the development in the Palestinians' relation to the loss of the ability to lose, a development that has led to second-degree loss, thereby enabling deferred action on the temporal axis. This characteristic has enabled us to reflect back on the historical narrative of 'Arabic' and to notice that it marks a general movement which has excluded two loci of communicative events, the Islamic and the pan-Arab.

These characteristics describe a structure that does not enable a negating counter-structure, which according to Gramsci is necessarily derived from the structure of coercion and oppression. Nor does the structure of the Israeli settler-colonial order operate mainly as a dominance without hegemeony, to use R. Guha's reading of Gramsci and others in the Indian colonial context. Rather, the over-determined relations in our case indicate a dominance without history as the main defining characteristic of this settler-colonial regime.[8] The aim of material and symbolic elimination of the natives by the settlers is terminating their sociohistorical agency. While this characteristic of dominance without history is shared with other settler-colonial cases – such as the United States, Australia and Canada – what seems to be particular to the Palestinians in Israel is that the over-determined relations of elimination are instantiated in the body of the natives' language, Arabic.

The Station That Will Not be Reached

These characteristics of the (non-)historical narrative of 'Arabic' operate as a single dynamic movement. This movement is embodied in literary Arabic and its products, as it has developed in 'Arabic', and orbits around the central axis of the relationship between language and loss in the structure of settler-colonial relations. More precisely, this narrative may be organised according to the order of its events: the loss of the ability to lose, followed by the recharging of language as a substitute for the lost object, followed by the settler-colonial power relations that enforce an alternative chain of events. The first two events were used as a platform for the Palestinians in Israel as a collective, while the settler's event denies them and replants an event that occurred in a different place and time – that is, European modernity/coloniality – in their stead. In negating the first two events, however, it binds the Palestinians in Israel to an event that is related to them only in being imposed on them coercively in order to eliminate them. The historical narrative of 'Arabic' denies the loss of the ability to lose and the option for dealing with it collectively through language. It imposes an external event on the group that has lost, describing it as a constitutive event, despite the fact that this group is originally unrelated to it. The group's only relation to this event is the violent relations of power imposed upon it. We can therefore call this narrative 'the narrative of a history of the non-historical' – one that is devoid of structural events.

What is the next station of 'Arabic', the one it has yet to reach? In the modern discourse of liberation, the conscious insight, both individual and collective, is supposed to blaze the trail to liberation from relations of power and coercion. In the discourse of late modernity, insight, consciousness and liberations are procedures of delay, ballroom masks from times gone by. On the stage of late settler-colonialism, which is that same history of the non-historical in its more mature form, a new drama is unfolding – a split between procedural violence and purely physical, material violence. It appears that the text, including the literary text, has temporarily died at the gap between procedure and physical matter.[9]

Notes

1. For an extensive and critical discussion of those processes, see Nashef, *Miʿmāriyyat al-fuqdān*, 9–34.
2. On the application of 'deferred action' in sociocultural contexts, see Hal Foster, *The Return of the Real* (Cambridge, MA: MIT Press, 1996), 1–35.
3. See Wolfe, 'Settler Colonialism and the Elimination of the Native'.
4. See Antonio Gramsci, *Prison Notebooks*, transl. Quentin Hoare and Geoffrey Nowell Smith (New York: International Publishers, 1971).
5. For more on the Palestinian Islamic community in Israel, see Eli Rekhess and Arik Rudnitzky, *Mi'uṭim Muslemim biMdinot Rov Lo-Muslemi: HaTnu'ah haIslamit biIsrael keMiḳreh Boḥan* [Muslim Minorities in Non-Muslim Majority Countries: The Islamic Movement in Israel as a Test Case] (Tel Aviv: Moshe Dayan Center for Middle Eastern and African Studies, 2011).
6. Noteworthy in this regard are the recent developments of some associations that address literacy among Palestinian Islamic activists; see, for example, Ayman Agbaria and Muhanad Mustafa, 'The Case of Palestinian Civil Society in Israel: Islam, Civil Society, and Educational Activism', *Critical Studies in Education* 55, no.1 (2013), 44–57, https://doi.org/10.1080/17508487.2014.857360
7. There is no definitive study on the relations between the Palestinians in Israel and the Arab world that covers the entire period since 1948. In most available studies, these relations are referred to in the context of the outcomes of the 1967 war, as well as the relations that developed between the Palestinians in Israel and those in the Occupied Territories (and, through them, the relations

with the Arab world). For the earlier periods of these relations, see, for example, Nassar, *Brothers Apart.*

8. For different variations on these power relations that deny the natives and the colonised sociohistorical agency, see, for example, Eric R. Wolf, *Europe and the People without History* (Berkeley: University of California Press, 1982); Depish Chakrabarty, *Provincializing Europe: Postcolonial Thought and Historical Difference* (Princeton: Princeton University Press, 2000).
9. For more on this death of the text, see Nashef, *Mawt al-naṣṣ.*

References

Abassi, Mahmoud. *Taṭawwur al-riwāya wa-l-qiṣṣa al-qaṣīra fī l-adab al-'Arabī fī Isrā'īl* [The Development of the Novel and the Short Story in Arabic Literature in Israel]. Haifa: Kull Shay', 1998.

'Abbas, Ihsan, and Mohamad Yousuf Nijim. *Al-Shi'r al-'Arabī fī l-mahjar* [Arab Poetry in the Diaspora]. Beirut: Dar Sadir, 1967.

Abu Al-Sa'ud, 'Adnan. 'Thaqāfat al-Muwāṭinīn al-'Arab fī l-mujtama' al-Isrā'īlī' [The Culture of Arab Citizens in Israeli Society]. *Al-Mujtama'* 2, no. 1 (January 1955): 6–10.

Abu Hanna, Hanna. 'Al-Ḥulm al-lādhī kāna janīnan yūladu basharan sawiyyan' [The Dream That Was a Fetus Was Born a Whole Human Being]. In *A'māl al-mu'tamar al-'awwal li-majma' al-lugha al-'Arabiyya* [Proceedings of the First Conference of the Academy of the Arabic Language], edited by Suleiman Jubran, 9–15. Haifa: Academy of the Arabic Language, 2004.

———. *Ṭalā'i' al-nahḍa fī Filasṭīn: Khirījū l-madāris al-Rūsiyya, 1862–1914* [The Pioneers of the Renaissance in Palestine: Graduates of Russian Schools, 1862–1914]. Beirut: Markaz al-Dirasat al-Filastiniyya, 2005.

Abu Hanna-Nahhas, Eman, ed. *Al-Mughayyabūn: Qirā'a naqdiyya li-kutub al-manāhij al-Isrā'īliyya fī l-madāris al-'Arabiyya al-thānawiyya* [The Absented: Critical Reading of Israeli Textbooks in Arab High Schools]. Haifa: Association of Arab Culture, 2014.

Abu Khadra, Fahd, Farouq Mawasi and Elias Atallah. 'Bayān li-man yuhimmuhu amr al-lugha al-'Arabiyya' [Letter for Those to Whom the Arabic Language is Important]. *Al-Jadid* 38, no. 10 (October 1989): 122.

Abu-Manneh, Bashir. *The Palestinian Novel: From 1948 to the Present.* Cambridge: Cambridge University Press, 2016.

Abu-Manneh, Butrus. 'Jerusalem in the Tanzimat Period'. *Die Welt des Islams* 30, no. 1/4 (1990): 1–44.

Abu-Remaileh, Refqa. 'The Afterlives of *Iltizam*: Emile Habibi through a Kanfanisque Lens of Resistance Literature,' In *Commitment and Beyond: Reflection on/of the Political in Arabic Literature since 1940s*, edited by Friedrike Pannewick and George Khalil, 171–84. Wiesbaden: Reichert Verlag, 2015.

——. 'Three Enigmas of Palestinian Literature'. *Journal of Palestine Studies* 48, no. 3 (Spring 2019): 21–25.

Abu-Saad, Ismael. 'Palestinian Education in Israel: The Legacy of the Military Government'. *Holy Land Studies* 5, no. 1 (2006): 21–56.

Abu Saleh, Saif al-Din. *Al-Ḥaraka al-'adabiyya al-'Arabiyya fī Isrā'īl: Ẓuhūrhā wa-taṭawwurhā min khilāl al-mulḥaq al-thaqāfī li-jarīdat Al-Ittiḥād bayn al-sanawāt 1948–2000* [The Arab Literary Movement in Israel: Its Origin and Development Seen from the Literary Supplement of *Al-Ittihad* 1948–2000]. Haifa: Academy of the Arabic Language, 2010.

Adalah. *Al-Dustūr al-dīmuqrāṭī* [The Democratic Constitution]. Haifa: Adalah, 2007.

Agamben, Giorgio. *Homo Sacer: Sovereign Power and Bare Life.* Translated by Daniel Heller-Roazen. Palo Alto: University of Stanford Press, 1998.

Agbaria, Ayman, ed. *Hakhsharat Morim baḤevrah haFalasṭinit biIsrael: Prakṭikot Mosadiyot uMediniyut Ḥinukhit* [Teacher Training in the Palestinian Society in Israel: Institutional Practices and Educational Policy]. Tel Aviv: Resling, 2013.

Agbaria, Ayman, and Mustafa, Muhanad. 'The Case of Palestinian Civil Society in Israel: Islam, Civil Society, and Educational Activism'. *Critical Studies in Education* 55, no.1 (2013): 44–57, https://doi.org/10.1080/17508487.2014.857360

Agbaria, Ayman, and Hellali Pinson. 'Navigating Israeli Citizenship: How Do Arab-Palestinian Teachers Civicize Their Pupils?' *Race, Ethnicity, and Education* 22, no. 3 (2019), 391–409, https://doi.org/10.1080/13613324.2018.1511527

Ahmad, Aijaz. 'Jameson's Rhetoric of Otherness and the "National Allegory"'. *Social Text* 17 (Autumn 1987): 3–25.

Ahmed, Leila. *Women and Gender in Islam: Historical Roots of a Modern Debate.* New Haven: Yale University Press, 1992.

Al-Eid, Youmna. *Fī ma'rifat al-naṣṣ* [On Knowledge of the Text]. Beirut: Dar Al-Adab, 1983.

Al-Ghadhami, Abdallah. *Al-Mar'a wa-l-lugha* [Woman and Language]. Casablanca: Al-Markaz Al-Thaqafi Al-Arabi, 1997.

Al-Haj, Majid. *Education, Empowerment, and Control: The Case of the Arabs in Israel.* Albany: State University of New York Press, 1995.

Al-Huṣrī, Satti'. *Fī l-lugha wa-l-'adab wa-'alāqathum bi-l-qawmiyya* [On Language and Literature and their Relation to Nationalism]. Beirut: Dar Al-Tali'ah, 1966.

Al-Jumaī', 'Abd Al-Mun'im Al-Dasūqī. *Majma' al-lugha al-'Arabiyya: Dirāsa tā'rīkhiyya* [Academy of the Arabic Language: A Historical Study]. Cairo: Al-Hay'a al-'Amma Lil-Kitab, 1983.

Allen, James S. *In the Public Eye: A History of Reading in Modern France, 1800–1940.* Princeton: Princeton University Press, 1991.

Allen, Lori. *The Rise and Fall of Human Rights: Cynicism and Politics in Occupied Palestine.* Palo Alto: Stanford University Press, 2013.

Al-Qāsim, Nabīh. *Al-Ḥaraka al-Shi'riyya al-Filasṭīniyya fi bilādinā min khilāl majallat Al-Jadīd, 1953–1985* [Palestinian Poetry in Our Country through *Al-Jadid*, 1953–1985]. Kufr Qara', Israel: Dar al-Huda, 2003.

Althusser, Louis. *For Marx.* Translated by Ben Brewster. London: Verso, 1996.

——. *Lenin and Philosophy and other Essays.* Translated by Ben Brewster. New York: Monthly Press Review, 2001.

Amara, Muhammad. *Al-Lugha al-'Arabiyya fi Isrā'īl: Siyāqāt wa-taḥaddiyāt* [The Arabic Language in Israel: Contexts and Challenges]. Umm al-Fahm, Israel: Markaz Dirasat wa-Dar al-Huda, 2010.

——. *Arabic in Israel: Language, Identity, and Conflict.* London: Routledge, 2017.

'Amel, Mahdi. *Muqaddimāt naẓariyya* [Theoretical Introductions]. Beirut: Dar Al-Farabi, 1990.

Amin, Samir. *Three Essays on Marx's Theory of Value.* New York: Monthly Review Press, 2013.

Amit, Geish. 'Bet haSfarim haLeumi ṿhaUniversiṭayi 1945–1955: Mif'al Ha'varatam shel Sifre Ḳorbanot haSho'ah, 'issuf haSifriyot haFalasṭiniyot beMilḥmet 1948, ṿe'ssuf Sifre Mehagrim miArtsot haIslam' [The National and Academic House of Books 1945–1955: The Project of Gathering the Books of the Holocaust Victims, Collecting the Palestinian Libraries from the War of 1948 and Collecting the Books of the Immigrants from Islamic Countries]. PhD diss., The Hebrew University of Jerusalem, 2011.

——. 'Salvage or Plunder? Israel's "Collection" of Private Palestinian Libraries in West Jerusalem'. *Journal of Palestine Studies* 40, no. 4 (2011): 6–23.

Anderson, Benedict. *Imagined Communities: Reflections on the Origins and Spread of Nationalism.* London: Verso, 1983.

Anidjar, Gil. *The Jew, the Arab: A History of Enemy*. Palo Alto: Stanford University Press, 2003.

Arab Culture Association. *Lughatī huwiyyatī* [My Language is My Identity]. Nazareth: Arab Culture Association, 2010.

——. *Ta'allamu l-'Arabiyya wa-'Allimuhā li-nās* [Study the Arabic Language and Teach It to People] (kit). Nazareth: Arab Culture Association, 2009.

Ashrawi, Hanan. 'The Contemporary Palestinian Poetry of Occupation'. *Journal of Palestine Studies* 7, no. 3 (Spring 1978): 77–101.

Assaf, Michael. 'Hishtalvut ha'Aravim beIsrael' [The Integration of Arabs in Israel]. *HaMizraḥ HaḤadash* 1 (1949): 2–7.

Atallah, Elias. *Wa-Idhā l-maw'ūdatu su'ilat* [And If the Murdered is Asked]. Nazareth: Arab Culture Association and Mawakib, 2007.

——. 'Wāqi' al-lugha al-'Arabiyya wa-taḥaddiyātuhā' [The Reality of Arabic and its Challenges]. In *A'mal al-mu'tamar al-awwal li-majma' al-lugha al-'Arabiyya* [Proceedings of the First Conference of the Academy of the Arabic Language], edited by Suleiman Jubran, 80–92. Haifa: Academy of the Arabic Language, 2004.

Ayalon, Ami. *Reading Palestine: Printing and Literacy, 1900–1948*. Austin: University of Texas Press, 2004.

Azoulay, Ariella. *'Alimut Mekhonenet, 1947–1950: Gene'alogiyah Ḥazutit shel Mishṭar veHafikhat ha'Ason le'Ason miNḳudat Mabaṭam'* [Constituent Violence: Visual Genealogy and the Turning of the Catastrophe into a Catastrophe in Their Eyes, 1947–1950]. Tel Aviv: Resling, 2009.

Baalbaki, Ramzi, ed. *Al-Lugha wa-l-huwiyya fī l-waṭan al-'Arabī: Ishkāliyyāt Tā'rīkhiyya wa-thaqāfiyya wa-siyāsiyya* [Language and Identity in the Arab Homeland: Historical, Cultural and Political Issues]. Doha: Arab Center for Research and Policy Studies, 2013.

Badawi, Al-Said Muhammad. *Mustawayāt al-'Arabiyya al-mu'āṣira fī Miṣr: Baḥth fī 'alāqat al-lugha bi-l-ḥaḍāra* [The Levels of Contemporary Arabic in Egypt: A Study on Language-Culture Relations]. Cairo: Dar al-Ma'arif, 1973.

Badawi, M. M. *A Critical Introduction to Modern Arabic Poetry*. Cambridge: Cambridge University Press, 1975.

Badr, 'Abd al-Muhsin Taha. *Taṭawwur al-riwāya al-'Arabiyya al-ḥadītha fī Miṣr, 1870–1938* [The Development of the Modern Arabic Novel in Egypt, 1870–1938]. Cairo: Dar al-Ma'arif, 1963.

Ballas, Shimon. *HaSifrut ha'Aravit beTsel haMilḥamah* [Arabic Literature under the Shadow of War]. Tel Aviv: Am Oved, 1978.

Barthes, Roland. 'The Death of the Author'. In *Image Music Text.* Translated by Stephen Heath, 142–48. London: Fontana Press, 1977.

——. 'Myth Today'. In *Mythologies.* Translated by Annette Lavers, 109–64. New York: Farrar, Straus & Giroux, 1972.

Bataille, Georges. *The Accursed Share: An Essay on General Economy.* Vol. 1: *Consumption.* Translated by Robert Hurley. New York: Zone Books, 1991.

Beck, Marie Rose. 'Language as Apparatus: Entanglements of Language, Culture and Territory and the Invention of Nation and Ethnicity'. *Postcolonial Studies* 21, no. 2 (2018): 231–53, https://doi.org/10.1080/1388790.2018.1462085

Benrabah, Mohamed. *Language and Conflict in Algeria: From Colonialism to Post-Independence.* Bristol: Multilingual Matters, 2013.

Bernstein, Deborah. *Constructing Boundaries: Jewish and Arab Workers in Mandatory Palestine.* Albany: State University of New York Press, 2000.

Bhabha, Homi K. *The Location of Culture.* London: Routledge, 1994.

Bishara, Azmi. *Al-'Arab fī Isrā'īl: Naẓarah min al-dākhil* [The Arabs in Israel: A View from Within]. Beirut: Markaz Dirasat al-Wihda al-Arabiyya, 2000.

——. 'Al-'Arabī al-Isrā'īlī: Al-Khiṭāb al-siyāsī al-mabtūr' [The Israeli Arab: The Disjointed Political Discourse]. *Majallat al-Dirasat al-Filastiniyya* 24 (1995): 26–54.

Blanchot, Maurice. *The Writing of the Disaster.* Translated by Ann Smock. Lincoln: University of Nebraska Press, 1986.

Block, David. *Political Economy and Sociolinguistics.* New York: Bloomsbury Academic, 2018.

Bloom, Harold. *The Anxiety of Influence: A Theory of Poetry.* Oxford: Oxford University Press, 1973.

Bourdieu, Pierre. *Language and Symbolic Power.* Translated by Gino Raymond and Mathew Adamson. Cambridge, MA: Harvard University Press, 1991.

——. *Outline of a Theory of Practice.* Translated by Richard Nice. Cambridge: Cambridge University Press, 1977.

Brenner-Feldhay, Rachel. *Inextricably Bonded: Israeli Arab and Jewish Writers Re-Visioning Culture.* Madison: University of Wisconsin Press, 2010.

Brynen, Rex. *A Very Political Economy: Peacebuilding and Foreign Aid.* Washington, DC: United States Institute for Peace, 2000.

Budeiri, Musa. 'Iqrār bi-l-dhanb: 'Īmīl Tūma wa-l-taqsīm alladhī lam yaḥduth' [Acknowledging Guilt: Emile Tuma and the Division that Did Not Happen]. *Bidayyat,* 18–19 (2017–18): 201–25.

——. *The Palestine Communist Party 1919–1948: Arabs and Jews in the Struggle for Internationalism.* Chicago: Haymarket Books, 2010.

Campos, Michelle. *Ottoman Brothers: Muslims, Christians, and Jews in Early Twentieth-Century Palestine*. Palo Alto: Stanford University Press, 2011.

Cavanagh, Edward, and Lorenzo Veracini, eds. *The Routledge Handbook of the History of Settler Colonialism*. London: Routledge, 2017.

Césaire, Aimé. *Discourse on Colonialism*. New York: Monthly Review Press, 2001.

Chakrabarty, Depish. *Provincializing Europe: Postcolonial Thought and Historical Difference*. Princeton: Princeton University Press, 2000.

Challand, Benoit. *Palestinian Civil Society: Foreign Donors and the Power to Promote and Exclude*. London: Routledge, 2008.

Chatterjee, Partha. *Nationalist Thought and the Colonial World: A Derivative Discourse?* Minneapolis: University of Minnesota Press, 1986.

Cleary, Joe. *Literature, Partition and the Nation-State: Culture and Conflict in Ireland, Israel and Palestine*. Cambridge: Cambridge University Press, 2004.

Cohen, Bernard. *Colonialism and Its Forms of Knowledge: The British in India*. Princeton: Princeton University Press, 1996.

Cohen, Hillel. *The Good Arabs: The Israeli Security Agencies and the Israeli Arabs, 1948–1967*. Berkeley: University of California Press, 2010.

Coombes, Annie E., ed. *Rethinking Settler Colonialism: History and Memory in Australia, Canada, Aotearoa New Zealand, and South Africa*. Manchester: Manchester University Press, 2006.

Darraj, Faisal. *Bu's al-thaqāfa fī l-mu'assasa l-Filasṭīniyya* [The Wretchedness of Culture in the Palestinian Establishment]. Beirut: Dar al-Adab, 1996.

——. 'Muthaqqaf ḥadāthī fī mujtama' taqlīdī' [A Modern Intellectual in a Conservative Society]. In *Tārīkh 'ilm al-'adab 'ind al-Ifranj wa-l-'Arab wa-Fīktūr Hūjū* [History of the Science of Literature among Westerners and the Arabs and Victor Hugo], by Muhammad Ruhi al-Khalidi, 7–20. Doha: Kitab al Dawha, 2013.

Degani, Arnon. 'From Republic to Empire: Israel and the Palestinians after 1948'. In *The Routledge Handbook of the History Settler Colonialism*, edited by Edward Cavanagh and Lorenzo Veracini, 353–67. London: Routledge, 2017.

Deleuze, Gilles. *Difference and Repetition*. Translated by Paul Patton. New York: Columbia University Press, 1995.

De Saussure, Ferdinand. *Course in General Linguistics*. Translated by Wade Baskin. New York: Columbia University Press, 2011.

Doumani, Beshara. *Rediscovering Palestine: Merchants and Peasants in Jabal Nablus, 1700–1900*. Berkeley: University of California Press, 1995.

Dowling, Sarah. *Translingual Poetics: Writing Personhood under Settler Colonialism*. Iowa City: University of Iowa Press, 2018.

Eagleton, Terry, Frederic Jameson and Edward Said. *Nationalism Colonialism and Literature*. Minneapolis: University of Minnesota Press, 1990.

Elad-Buskila, Ami. *Moledet Niḥlemet, 'Erets 'Avudah: Shishah Praḳim baSifrut haFalasṭinit haḥadashah* [Dreamt-of Homeland, Lost Country: Six Chapters in Modern Palestinian Literature]. Or Yehuda, Israel: Maariv, 2001.

El-Eini, Roza. 'The Impact of British Imperial Rule on the Landscape of Mandate Palestine, 1929–1948'. PhD diss., The Hebrew University of Jerusalem, 2000.

Ellison, David. *Ethics and Aesthetics in European Modernist Literature: From the Sublime to the Uncanny*. Cambridge: Cambridge University Press, 2001.

Eqeiq, Amal. 'Writing the Indigenous: Contemporary Mayan Literature in Chiapa, Mexico and the Palestinian Literature in Israel'. PhD diss., University of Washington, 2013.

Eshed, Haggai. *Reuven Shiloah, the Man Behind the Mossad: Secret Diplomacy in the Creation of Israel*. Translated by David and Leah Zinder. London: Frank Cass, 1997.

Esmeir, Samera. *Juridical Humanity: A Colonial History*. Palo Alto: Stanford University Press, 2012.

Eyal, Gil. *Hasarat haḲesem min haMizraḥ: Toldot haMizraḥanut be'Idan haMizraḥiyut* [Disenchanting the Orient: The History of Orientalism in the Mizrahi Era]. Tel Aviv: Hakibbutz Hameuchad and Van Leer Jerusalem Institute, 2005.

Fairclough, Norman. *Critical Discourse Analysis: Critical Study of Language*. London: Routledge, 2010.

Fanon, Frantz. *Black Skin, White Masks*. Translated by Charles Lam Markmann. New York: Pluto, [1952] 1991.

——. *The Wretched of the Earth*. Translated by Richard Philcox. New York: Grove Press, 1967.

Farag, Joseph. *Politics and Palestinian Literature in Exile: Gender, Aesthetics, and Resistance in the Short Story*. London: I. B. Tauris, 2017.

Fayāḍ, Tawfiq. *Al-Mushawwahūn* [The Deformed]. Haifa: Kull Shay', [1963] 2008.

Ferguson, Charles. 'Diglossia'. *Word* 15 (1959): 325–40.

Fortna, Benjamin C. *Imperial Classroom: Islam, the State, and Education in the Late Ottoman Empire*. Oxford: Oxford University Press, 2003.

Foster, Hal. *The Return of the Real*. Cambridge, MA: MIT Press, 1996.

Foucault, Michel. *The Archeology of Knowledge*. Translated by A. M. Sheridan Smith. London: Routledge Classics, 2002.

——. 'The Order of Discourse'. In *Untying the Text: A Post-Structural Reader*, edited by Robert J. C. Young, 48–78. London: Routledge, 1981.

Freud, Sigmund. 'Mourning and Melancholia'. In *The Standard Edition of the Complete Psychological Works of Sigmund Freud*, Vol. 14, translated by J. Strachey, 237–58. London: The Hogarth Press and the Institute of Psychoanalysis, 1955.

——. 'The Uncanny'. In *The Standard Edition of the Complete Psychological Works of Sigmund Freud*, Vol. 17, translated by J. Strachey, 217–52. London: The Hogarth Press and the Institute of Psychoanalysis, 1958.

Gebauer, Gunter, and Christoph Wulf. *Mimesis: Culture, Art, Society*. Translated by Don Reneau. Berkeley: University of California Press, 1995.

Ghanayim, Mahmud. *Al-Madār al-ṣa'b: Riḥlat al-qiṣṣa al-Filasṭīniyya fī Isrā'īl* [The Difficult Path: The Journey of the Palestinian Story in Israel]. Haifa: Haifa University, 1995.

——. 'Al-Mawḍūʿāt al-ijtimāʿiyya fī l-qiṣṣa l-qaṣīra l-maḥaliyya' [Social Themes in Local Short Stories]. *Al-Sharq* 7, no. 5–7 (1977): 9–23.

——. 'Al-Tajārib al-ʿarūḍiyya fī shiʿrnā l-ḥurr: Dīwān fī Intiẓār al-qiṭār li-Fārūq Mawāsī' [Experiments in Classical Meters in Our Free Verse Poetry: 'Waiting for the Train' by Farouq Muwasi]. *Al-Sharq* 2, no. 3 (1971): 15–20.

——. *Bayn al-rafḍ wa-l-iltizām: Dirāsa fī shi'r 'Abd al-Raḥīm Maḥmūd* [Between Refusal and Commitment: A Study of Abd al-Rahim Mahmoud's Poetry]. Jerusalem: Abu-'Arafa, 1980.

——. 'Dirāsāt fī l-qiṣṣa l-qaṣīra l-maḥaliyya' [Studies on the Local Short Story]. *Al-Sharq* 9, no. 4 (1979): 17–41.

——. *Fī mabnā al-naṣṣ: Dirāsa fī riwāyat 'Imīl Ḥabībī 'Al-waqā'i' al-gharība fī ikhtifā' Sa'īd Abī al-Naḥs al-Mutashā'il'* [Structure of the Text: A Study of Emile Habibi's Novel 'The Extraordinary Chronicle of the Disappearance of Said Abu al-Nahas the Pessoptimist']. Jat, Israel: Al-Yasar, 1987.

——. *Tayār al-wa'ī fī l-riwāya al-'Arabiyya al-ḥadītha: Dirāsa uslūbiyya* [Stream of Consciousness in the Modern Arabic Novel: A Stylistic Study]. Beirut: Dar al-Jil, 1992.

Ghanem, Asʿad. *The Palestinian-Arab Minority in Israel, 1948–2000*. New York: State University of New York Press, 2001.

Gottesfeld, Dorit. *HaEtsba'ot haNistarot: Siporet Nashim Falasṭiniot* [The Hidden Fingers: The Prose of Palestinian Women]. Tel Aviv: Resling, 2013.

Gramsci, Antonio. *Prison Notebooks*. Translated by Quentin Hoare and Geoffrey Nowell Smith. New York: International Publishers, 1971.

Greenberg, Ela. 'Majjallat Rawdat al-Maʿarif: Constructing Identities within a Boy's School Journal in Mandatory Palestine'. *British Journal of Middel Eastern Studies* 35, no. 1 (April 2008): 79–95.

Guha, Ranajit. *Dominance without Hegemony: History and Power in Colonial India*. Cambridge, MA: Harvard University Press, 2011.

Habib, Rafey M. A. *A History of Literary Criticism and Theory: From Plato to the Present*. London: Blackwell, 2007.

Habibi, Emile. *Sarāya bint al-ghūl: Khurāfiyya* [Saraya, the Ogre's Daughter: A Fairytale], London: Riyad al-Rayyis, 1992.

Haddad, Michel. "Alāqat al-udabā' bi-mujtamaʿihim' [The Relationship of Authors to their Society]. *Al-Mujtamaʿ* 2 (October 1954): 1–3.

——. 'Al-Fuṣḥā wa-l-ʿāmiyya' [Literary and Spoken Arabic]. *Al-Mujtamaʿ* 2, no. 9 (September 1955): 3–4.

——. 'Ḥawla l-qiṣṣa' [On the Story]. *Al-Mujtamaʿ* 2, no. 12 (December 1955): 9–11.

——. 'Ḥikāyat al-mujtamaʿ' [The Story of Society]. *Al-Mujtamaʿ* 3 (November 1954): 1–2.

——. 'Naḥwa madrasa 'adabiyya' [Towards a Literary School]. *Al-Mujtamaʿ* 2, no. 12 (December 1955): 3–4.

Haddad, Michel, ed. *Alwān min shiʿr al-ʿArabiyya fī Isrāʾīl* [Colours of Arabic Poetry in Israel]. Nazareth: Al-Hakim, 1955.

Haeri, Niloofar. 'Form and Ideology: Arabic Sociolinguistics and beyond'. *Annual Review of Anthropology* 29 (2000): 61–87.

Hafez, Sabri. *The Genesis of Arabic Narrative Discourse: A Study in the Sociology of Modern Arabic Literature*. London: Al Saqi Books, 1993.

Hammoudi, Abdellah. *Master and Disciple: The Cultural Foundation of Moroccan Authoritarianism*. Princeton: Princeton University Press, 1997.

Hanieh, Adam. 'From State-Led Growth to Globalization: The Evolution of Israeli Capitalism'. *Journal of Palestine Studies* 32, no. 4 (Summer 2003): 5–21.

Hanks, William F. *Language and Communication Practices*. Boulder: Westview Press, 1996.

Hassan, Wail. 'Postcolonialism and Modern Arabic Literature: Twenty-First Century Horizon'. *Interventions* 20, no. 2 (2017): 157–73, https://doi.org/10.1080/1369801X.2017.1391711

——. 'Post Colonial Theory and Modern Arabic Literature: Horizons of Application'. *Journal of Arabic Literature* 33, no. 1 (2002): 45–64.

Hawker, Nancy. *Palestinian Israeli Contacts and Linguistics Practices*. London: Routledge, 2018.

Hawkes, Terence. *Structuralism and Semiotics*. Berkeley: University of California Press, 1977.

Heller, Monica, and Bonnie McElhinny. *Language, Capitalism, Colonialism: Toward a Critical History*. Toronto: Toronto University Press, 2017.

Herzog, Hanna and Eliezer Ben-Rafael, eds. *Language and Communication in Israel.* New Brunswick: Transaction Publishers, 2001.

Hever, Hannan. *HaSipur vehaLe'om: Kri'ot Biḳortiot beḲanon haSiporet ha'Ivrit* [The Story and the Nation: Critical Readings in the Canon of Hebrew Prose]. Tel Aviv: Resling, 2007.

High Committee for the Arabic Language. *Al-Manhal fi l-muṣṭalaḥāt al-mu'āṣira* 1 [Al-Manhal: Contemporary Expressions 1]. Jerusalem: Ministry of Education, Division of Curricula Planning and Development, 1999.

Hussein, Mahmoud. *Class Conflict in Egypt, 1945–1970.* Translated by Alfred Ehrenfeld and Michel Chirman. New York: Monthly Review Press, 1973.

Hymes, Dell. 'Introduction: Toward Ethnographies of Communication'. *American Anthropologist* 66, no. 6 (1964): 1–34.

Jabareen, Hassan. 'Hobbsian Citizenship: How the Palestinians Became a Minority in Israel'. In *Multiculturalism and Minority Rights in the Arab World*, edited by Will Kymlicka and Eva Pfostl, 189–218. Oxford: Oxford University Press, 2014.

——. 'LiḲrat Gishot BiḲortiot shel haMiʿut haFalasṭini: 'Ezraḥut, Le'umiut veFeminisim baMishpaṭ haIsraeli' [Towards Critical Approaches of the Palestinian Minority: Citizenship, Nationality and Feminism in Israeli Law]. *Plilim,* 9 (2000): 53–93.

Jabareen, Hassan, and Suhad Bishara. 'The Jewish Nation-State Law: Antecedents and Constitutional Implications'. *Journal of Palestine Studies* 48, no. 190 (2) (Winter 2019): 46–55.

Jabra, Jabra I. 'The Palestinian Exile as Writer'. *Journal of Palestine Studies* 8, no. 2 (Winter 1979): 77–87.

Jacquemond, Richard. *The Conscience of the Nation: Writers, State, and Society in Modern Egypt.* Translated by David Tresilian. Cairo: The American University in Cairo Press, 2008.

Jamal, Amal. *Arab Minority Nationalism in Israel: The Politics of Indigeneity*. London: Routledge, 2011.

Jameson, Fredric. *The Political Unconscious: Narrative as a Socially Symbolic Act.* Ithaca, New York: Cornell University Press, 1981.

——. *Postmodernism, or The Cultural Logic of Late Capitalism.* Durham, NC: Duke University Press, 1992.

——. 'Third World Literature in the Era of Multinational Capitalism'. *Social Text* 15 (Autumn 1986): 65–88.

Jubran, Suleiman, ed. *A'māl al-mu'tamar al-'awwal li-majmaʿ al-lugha al-'Arabiyya* [Proceedings of the First Conference of the Academy of the Arabic Language]. Haifa: Academy of the Arabic Language, 2004.

——. 'Kalima Ūlā' [Foreword]. In *A'māl al-mu'tamar al-'awwal li-majma' al-lugha al-'Arabiyya* [Proceedings of the First Conference of the Academy of the Arabic Language], edited by Suleiman Jubran, 5–8. Haifa: Academy of the Arabic Language, 2004.

——. *'Alā hāmish al-tajdīd wa-l-taqyīd fī l-lugha al-'Arabiyya al-Mu'āṣira* [On the Margins of the Innovations and Limitations in the Modern Arabic Language]. Haifa: Academy of the Arabic Language, 2009.

Kabha, Mustafa, ed. *Al-'Aqaliyya al-Filasṭīniyya fī Isrā'īl fī ẓill al-ḥukm al-'askarī wa-irthuhu* [The Palestinian Minority in Israel in the Shadow of the Military Government and its Legacy]. Haifa: Mada al-Carmel, 2014.

——. 'Al-Ṣaḥāfa al-'Arabiyya fī ẓill al-ḥukm al-'askari, 1948–1966' [The Arab Press under the Military Government, 1948–1966]. In *Al-'Aqaliyya al-Filasṭīniyya fī Isrā'īl fī ẓill al-ḥukm al-'askarī wa-irthuhu* [The Palestinian Minority in Israel in the Shadow of the Military Government and its Legacy], edited by Mustafa Kabha, 123–70. Haifa: Mada al-Carmel, 2014.

——. *'Itonut be'En haSe'arah: ha'Itonut haFalasṭinit keMakhshir le'Itsuv Da'at haḲahal, 1929–1939* [Press in the Eye of the Storm: The Palestinian Press as a Shaper of Public Opinion, 1929–1939]. Jerusalem: Yad Ben-Zvi, 2004.

Kabha, Mustafa, and Dan Caspi. 'MiYerushalayim haḲedoshah 'ad haMa'ayan: Megamot ba'Itonut ha'Aravit beIsrael' [From Jerusalem to the HaMaayan: Trends in the Arabic Press in Israel]. *Panim* 16 (2001): 44–55.

Kan'ani, Fuad, ed. *Majma' al-lugha al-'Arabiyya fī Isrā'īl: Injāzāt wa-ṭumūḥāt – Kurāsa khāṣṣa bi-munāsabat murūr 'ām 'alā ta'sīs al-majma'* [Academy of the Arabic Language in Israel: Achievements and Aspirations – Special Booklet upon the First Anniversary of Its Founding]. Haifa: Academy of the Arabic Language, 2009.

Kassem, Fatma. *Palestinian Women: Narrative Histories and Gendered Memory*. London: Zed Books, 2011.

Khazzoom, Eliyahu. 'Shirah 'Aravit BiIsrael' [Arabic Poetry in Israel]. *HaMizraḥ HaḤadash* 7, no. 3 (1956): 232.

Kimmerling, Baruch. 'Ideology and Nation-Building: The Palestinians and their Meaning in Israeli Sociology'. *American Sociological Review* 57, no. 4 (1992): 446–60.

Kimmerling, Baruch, and Joel S. Migdal. *Palestinians: The Making of a People*. Cambridge, MA: Harvard University Press, 1998.

Laor, Yitzhak. *Anu Kotvim Otakh Moledet: Massot 'al Sifrut Israelit* [We Write You, Homeland: Essays on Israeli Literature]. Tel Aviv: Hakibbutz Hameuchad, 1995.

Lubani, 'Isa. 'Al-Mushawwahūn li-Tawfīq Fayāḍ' [Al-Mushawwahun by Tawfiq Fayad]. In *Dirāsāt fī l-adab al-Filasṭīnī al-maḥalī* [Studies in Local Palestinian Literature], edited by Nabih al-Qassim, 34–37. Acre: Dar al-Aswar, [1964] 1984.

Lustick, Ian. *Arabs in the Jewish State: Israel's Control of a National Minority*. Austin: University of Texas Press, 1980.

Mada al-Carmel. *Wathīqat Ḥayfā* [Haifa Declaration]. Haifa: Mada al-Carmel, 2007.

Mamdani, Mahmood. *Citizen and Subject: Contemporary Africa and the Legacy of Late Colonialism*. Princeton: Princeton University Press, 1996.

Mandel, Ernest. *Late Capitalism*. Translated by Joris de Bres. London: Verso, 1998.

Manna, Adel. *Nakba wa-baqā': Ḥikāyāt Filasṭīniyīn ẓallū fī Ḥayfā wa-l-Jalīl, 1948–1956* [Nakba and Survival: The Story of Palestinians who Remained in Haifa and the Galilee, 1948–1956]. Beirut: Institute for Palestine Studies, 2016.

Mansour, Atallah. *BeOr Ḥadash* [In a New Light]. Tel Aviv: Karni, 1966.

——. *In a New Light*. Translated by Abraham Birman. Elstree, Herts.: Vallentine Mitchell Publications, 1969.

Marion, Jean-Luc. *In Excess: Studies of Saturated Phenomena*. Translated by Robyn Horner and Vincent Ber Bronx. New York: Fordham University Press, 2004.

Marquez, J. Bayley, and Juliet Rose Kunkel. 'The Domestication Genocide of Settler Colonial Language Ideologies'. *American Quarterly* 73, no. 3 (2021): 461–82.

Massad, Joseph. *Desiring Arabs*. Chicago: University of Chicago Press, 2007.

Massalha, Nur. *The Politics of Denial: Israel and the Palestinian Refugee Problem*. London: Pluto Press, 2003.

Mazawi, Andre. 'University Education, Credentialism, and Social Stratification among Palestinian Arabs in Israel'. *Higher Education* 29 (1995): 351–68.

Mbembe, Achille. 'Necropolitics'. *Public Culture* 15, no. 1 (2003): 11–40.

McCrea, Barry. *Languages of the Night: Minor Languages and Literary Imagination in Twentieth-Century Ireland and Europe*. New Haven: Yale University Press, 2015.

Mendel, Yonatan. *The Creation of Israeli Arabic: Political and Security Considerations in the Making of Arabic Language Studies in Israel*. London: Palgrave, 2014.

Metzer, Jacob. *The Divided Economy of Mandatory Palestine*. Cambridge: Cambridge University Press, 2002.

Mignolo, Walter. *Local Histories/Global Desgins: Coloniality, Subaltern Knowledges, and Border Thinking*. Princeton: Princeton University Press, 2000.

Miller, Daniel, ed. *Materiality*. Durham, NC: Duke University Press, 2005.

Mitchell, Timothy. *Colonising Egypt*. Berkeley: University of California Press, 1991.

Moreh, Shmuel. 'HaSifrut baŚafah ha'Aravit beMedinat Israel' [Arabic Literature in the State of Israel]. *HaMizraḥ HaḤadash* 9, no. 1–2 (1958): 26–39.

Morris, Benny. *The Birth of the Palestinian Refugee Problem Revisited*. Cambridge: Cambridge University Press, 2004.

Muhammad, Zakariyya. *Qaḍāyā fī l-thaqāfa al-Filasṭīniyya* [Issues in Palestinian Culture]. Ramallah: Muwatin, Palestinian Institute for the Study of Democracy, 2002.

Musawa Center. *Dustūr mutasawin li-l-jamī'* [Equal Constitution for All]. Haifa: Musawa Center, 2006.

Muwasi, Faruq. *Fī intiẓār al-qiṭār* [Waiting for the Train]. Nablus: The Association of Print Houses Cooperative, 1971.

Nahas, Habib Dunia. *The Israeli Communist Party*. London: Croom Helm, 1976.

Nakhla, Khalil, ed. *Mustaqbal al-'aqaliyya al-Filasṭīniyya fi Isrā'īl* [The Future of the Palestinian Minority in Israel]. Ramallah: Madar, Palestinian Center for Israeli Studies, 2008.

Nashef, Ismail. 'A Deconstruction of Collusion'. *Jadal* 12 (2012): 1–7.

——. 'Ḥāl al-tawāṭu" [On Complacency]. *Jadal Mada* 12 (February 2012): 1–10.

——. 'Ḥawl imkāniyyat dirāsat al-nuẓum al-isti'māriyya: Filasṭīn namūdhajan' [On the Possibility of Studying the Colonial Systems: The Case of Palestine]. In *Al-Nafi fi kitābat Isrā'īl: Abḥāth Filasṭīniyya ḥawl al-niẓām wa-l-mujtama' wa-l-dawla fi Isrā'īl* [Negation in Writing Israel: Palestinian Studies on Regime, Society and State in Israel], edited by Ismail Nashef, 8–27. Ramallah: Madar, Palestinian Center for Israeli Studies, 2011.

——. 'Mawt al-Naṣṣ' [The Death of the Text]. *Majallat al-Dirasat al-Falastiniyya* 96 (Autumn 2013): 96–117.

——. *Mi'māriyyat al-fuqdān: Su'āl al-thaqāfa al-Filasṭīniyya al-mu'āṣira* [The Architecture of Loss: The Question of Contemporary Palestinian Culture]. Beirut: Dar al-Farabi, 2012.

——. *On Palestinian Abstraction: Zohdy Qadry and the Geometrical Melody of Late Modernism*. Haifa: Raya Publications, 2014.

Nashif, Esmail. 'Isn't It Good to Be Literate?' *Mediterranean Historical Review* 21, no. 1 (2006): 105–14.

Nassar, Maha. *Brothers Apart: Palestinians Citizens of Israel and the Arab World*. Palo Alto: Stanford University Press.

National Committee of Arab Mayors. *Al-Taṣawwur al-mustaqbalī li-l-'Arab fi Isrā'īl* [The Future Vision of the Arabs in Israel]. Nazareth: National Committee of Arab Mayors, 2006.

Omri, Mohamed-Salah. 'History, Literature, and Settler Colonialism in North Africa'. *Modern Language Quarterly* 66, no. 3 (2005): 273–98.

Ozacky-Lazar, Sarah. 'Hitgabshut Yaḥase haGomlin ben Yehudim ṿe'Aravim beMedinat Israel: ha'Aśor haRishon, 1948–1958' [The Crystallisation of Mutual Relations between Jews and Arabs in the State of Israel: The First Decade, 1948–1958]. PhD diss., Haifa University, 1996.

Pappe, Ilan. *The Ethnic Cleansing of Palestine*. Oxford: Oneworld Publications, 2006.

Payes, Shany. *Palestinian NGOs In Israel: The Politics of Civil Society.* London: I. B. Tauris, 2005.

Qaʿwar, Jamal. *Salmā: Majmūʿat aqāṣīṣ shiʿriyya* [Salma, a Collection of Poetic Stories]. Nazareth: Al-Hakim, 1956.

Qaʿwar-Farah, Najwa. *ʿābirū sabīl* [Passers-By]. Beirut: Dar al-Rihani, 1956.

——. *Durūb wa-maṣābīḥ* [Lanes and Lanterns]. Nazareth: Al-Hakim, 1956.

Rabinowitz, Dan. 'Postnational Palestine/Israel? Globalization, Diaspora, Transnationalism, and the Israeli-Palestinian Conflict'. *Critical Inquiry* 26, No. 4 (Summer 2000): 757–72.

Ram, Uri. *HaGlobalizatsiyah shel Israel: McWorld beTel Aviv, Jihad beYerushalayim* [The Globalisation of Israel: McWorld in Tel Aviv, Jihad in Jerusalem]. Tel Aviv: Resling, 2005.

——. 'Tensions in the "Jewish Democracy": The Constitutional Challenge of the Palestinian Citizens in Israel'. *Constellations* 16, no. 3 (2009): 523–36.

Rancière, Jacques. *The Politics of Aesthetics.* Translated by Gabriel Rockhill. New York: Continuum, 2004.

Razin, Assaf. *Israel and World Economy: The Power of Globalization.* Cambridge, MA: MIT Press, 2018.

Rekhess, Eli, and Arik Rudnitzky. *Miʿuṭim Muslemim biMdinot Rov Lo-Muslemi: HaTnuʿah haIslamit biIsrael keMikreh Boḥan* [Muslim Minorities in Non-Muslim Majority Countries: The Islamic Movement in Israel as a Test Case]. Tel Aviv: Moshe Dayan Center for Middle Eastern and African Studies, 2011.

Reshef, Yael. *HaʿIvrit biTkufat haMandaṭ* [Hebrew in the Mandate Period]. Jerusalem: Ha-Akademiyah la-Lashon haʿIvrit, 2015.

Rossi-Landi, Ferrucio. *Language as Work and Trade: A Semiotic Homology for Linguistics and Economics.* New York: Praeger, 1983.

Rouhana, Nadim. 'Wathīqat Ḥayfā wa-l Filasṭīniyūn fī Isrā'īl: Min al-Hāmish al-siyāsī ilā l-markaz al-'akhlāqī' [The Haifa Declaration and the Palestinians in Israel: From the Political Margins to the Moral Centre]. In *Mustaqbal al-'aqaliyya al-Filasṭīniyya fī Isrā'īl* [The Future of the Palestinian Minority in Israel], edited by Khalil Nakhla, 76–103. Ramallah: Madar, Palestinian Center for Israeli Studies, 2008.

Rouhana, Nadim, and Areej Sabbagh-Khoury. 'Settler-Colonial Citizenship: Conceptualizing the Relationship between Israel and its Palestinian Citizens'. *Settler-Colonial Studies* 5, no. 3 (2015): 205–25, https://doi.org/10.1080/2201473X.2014.947671

Sa'di, Ahmad. *Thorough Surveillance: The Genesis of Israeli Policies of Population Management Surveillance and Political Control towards the Palestinian Minority.* Manchester: Manchester University Press, 2013.

Sa'di, Ahmad, ed. *Nadwa ḥawl kitāb al-duktūr 'Imīl Tūma 'Mukhtārāt fi l-naqd al-'adabī'* [A Workshop on Dr Emil Tuma's Book 'Selected Essays in Literary Criticism']. Haifa: Emil Tuma Institute for Social and Political Research, 1993.

Sa'di, Ahmad, and Lila Abu-Lughod (eds). *Nakba: Palestine, 1948, and the Claims for Memory*. New York: Columbia University Press, 2007.

Said, Edward. *Culture and Imperialism*. New York: Vintage, 1994.

Salaita, Steven. *Inter/Nationalism: Decolonizing Native America and Palestine*. Minneapolis: University of Minnesota Press, 2016.

Scholch, Alexander. *Palestine in Transformation, 1856–1882: Studies in Social, Economic, and Political Development*. Washington, DC: Institute for Palestine Studies, 1993.

Seikaly, Sherene. *Men of Capital: Scarcity and Economy in Mandate Palestine*. Palo Alto: Stanford University Press, 2015.

Shankar, Shalini, and Jillian Cavanaugh. 'Language and Materiality in Global Capitalism'. *Annual Review of Anthropology* 41 (2012): 355–69.

Sharabi, Hisham. *Neopatriachy: A Theory of Distorted Change in Arab Society*. Oxford: Oxford University Press, 1993.

Sheehi, Steven. *Foundations of Modern Arab Identity*. Gainesville: University Press of Florida, 2004.

Shihade, Magid. 'Settler Colonialism and Conflict: The Case of Israel and its Palestinian Subjects'. *Settler Colonial Studies* 2, no. 1 (2012): 108–23, https://doi.org/10.1080/2201473X.2012.10648828

Shohat, Ella. *On the Arab-Jew, Palestine, and Other Displacements: Selected Writings*. New York: Pluto Press, 2017.

Somekh, Sasson. 'Al-'Adab al-'Arabī wa-l-qāri' al-'Ibrī'' [Arabic Literature and the Hebrew Reader]. *Al-Sharq* 3, no. 1–2 (1972): 49–58.

——. 'Fī intiẓār al-qiṭār' [Waiting for the Train]. *Al-Sharq* 1, no. 2 (1971): 8.

——. 'Al-Ḥaraka wa-l-iyqā' fī Mārsh al-ghurūb' [Movement and Pace in Sunset March]. *Al-Sharq* 2, no. 8 (1972): 5–9.

——. 'Al-'Alāqāt al-naṣṣiyya fī l-niẓām al-'adabī al-wāḥid' [The Textual Relations in One Literary System]. *Al-Karmel* 7 (1986): 109–29.

——. *Bagdad Etmol* [Bagdad Yesterday]. Tel-Aviv: Hakibbutz Hameuchad, 2004.

——. *Lughat al-qiṣṣa fi adab Yūsuf Idrīs* [The Language of the Story in Yusuf Idris's Literature]. Tel-Aviv, Acre: Tel-Aviv University, Srouji Publications, 1984.

——. 'Masraḥ Mahmūd Taymūr: Lughat al-ḥiwār fī ṣiyāghatayn' [Mahmoud Taymour's Theatre: A Dialogue in Two Versions]. In *Abḥāth fi l-lugha wa-l-uslūb* [Studies in Language and Style], edited by Sasson Somekh, 24–27. Tel-Aviv: Tel-Aviv University, The Arab Publishing House, 1980.

——. 'Naḥwā l-ma'nā l-murakkab' [Toward A Complex Meaning]. *Al-Sharq* 10, no. 1 (1980): 26–29.

——. 'Ṣīghat al-ḥadātha fī shi'r Michel Haddad' [Modernist Form in Michel Haddad's Poetry]. *Al-Karmel* 4 (1983): 49–66.

——. *The Changing Rhythm: A Study of Najib Mahfuz's Novels*. Leiden: Brill, 1973.

——. *Yamim Hazuyim: Ḳorot Ḥayim 1951–2000* [Call it Dreaming: Memoirs, 1951–2000]. Tel-Aviv: Hakibbutz Hameuchad, 2008.

Suleiman, Camelia. *The Politics of Arabic in Israel: A Sociolinguistic Analysis*. Edinburgh: Edinburgh University Press, 2018.

Suleiman, Yasir. *Arabic in the Fray: Language Ideology and Cultural Politics*. Edinburgh: Edinburgh University Press, 2013.

——. *A War of Words: Language and Conflict in the Middle East*. Cambridge: Cambridge University Press, 2004.

——. *The Arabic Language and National Identity: A Study in Ideology*. Washington, DC: Georgetown University Press, 2002.

Sultany, Nimer. *Muwāṭinūn bi-lā muwāṭana: Taqrīr al-raṣd al-siyāsī al-sanawī 2000–2001* [Citizens without Citizenship: The Follow-Up Political Report 2000–2001]. Haifa: Mada Al-Carmel, 2003.

Swirski, Shlomo. *Mḥir haYohorah: haKibush – haMḥir shelsrael Meshalemet* [The Price of Vanity: The Occupation – The Price that Israel Pays]. Tel-Aviv: Adva Center, Mapah, 2005.

Tamari, Salim. *Mountain against the Sea: Essays on Palestinian Society and Culture*. Berkeley: University of California Press, 2008.

Tatour, Lana. 'Citizenship as Domination: Settler Colonialism and the Making of Palestinian Citizenship in Israel'. *Arab Studies Journal* 27, no. 2 (2019): 8–39.

Thiong'o wa, Ngugi. *Decolonising the Mind: The Politics of Language in African Literature*. Nairobi: Heinemann, 1986.

Thompson, John B. *Studies in the Theory of Ideology*. Berkeley: University of California Press, 1984.

Tuma, Emile. *Al-A'māl al-kāmila* [Collected Writings]. 5 vols. Haifa: Emile Tuma Institute of Social and Political Studies, 1995–97.

——. *Mukhtārāt fī al-naqd al-adabī* [Selected Writings in Literary Criticism]. Haifa: Emile Tuma Institute of Social and Political Studies, 1993.

United Nations General Assembly. Resolution No. 47/135. 'Declaration on the Rights of Persons Belonging to National or Ethnic, Religious and Linguistic Minorities'. 18 December 1992. http://www.un-documents.net/a47r135.htm

Veracini, Lorenzo. *Israel and Settler Society*. London: Pluto Press, 2006.

———. *Settler Colonialism: A Theoretical Overview*. New York: Palgrave, 2010.
———. 'The Other Shift: Settler Colonialism, Israel, and Occupation'. *Journal of Palestine Studies* 42, no. 2 (2013): 26–42.
———. 'Understanding Colonialism and Settler Colonialism as Distinct Formations'. *Interventions* 16, no. 5 (2014): 615–33, https://doi.org/10.1080/1369801X.2013.858983
Volosinov, V. N. *Marxism and the Philosophy of Language*. Translated by Ladislav Matejka and I. R. Titunik. Cambridge, MA: Harvard University Press, 1986.
Williams, Raymond. *Marxism and Literature*. Oxford: Oxford University Press, 1977.
Wolf, Eric R. *Europe and the People without History*. Berkeley: University of California Press, 1982.
Wolfe, Patrick. 'Purchase by Other Means: The Palestine Nakba and Zionism's Conquest of Economics,' *Settler Colonial Studies* 2, no. 1 (2012): 133–71, https://doi.org/10.1080/2201473X.2012.10648830
———. 'Settler Colonialism and the Elimination of the Native'. *Journal of Genocide Research* 8, no. 4 (2006): 387–409, https://doi.org/10.1080/14623520601056240
———. *Settler Colonialism and the Transformation of Anthropology: The Politics and Poetics of an Ethnographic Event*. London: Cassell, 1999.
Yāghi, ʿAbd al-Raḥmān. *Ḥayāt al-ʾadab al-Filasṭīnī al-ḥadīth: Mundhu bidāyat al-Nahḍa wa-li-ghāyat al-Nakba* [The Life of Modern Palestinian Literature: From the Beginning of the National Revival to the Nakba]. Beirut: Dar al-Afaq, 1981.
Young, Robert. *Colonial Desire: Hybridity in Theory, Culture, and Race*. London: Routledge, 1995.
———. *Postcolonialism: An Historical Introduction*. Oxford: Blackwell Publishers, 2001.
———. 'Postcolonial Remains'. *New Literary History* 43, no. 1 (2012): 12–42.
Yu, Wang, and Hillel Cohen. 'Marketing Israel to the Arabs: The Rise and Fall of *al-Anbaa* Newspaper'. *Israel Affairs* 15, no. 2 (2009): 190–210.
Zreik, Raef. 'Qirā'a fī l-naṣṣ' [Text Reading]. In *Mustaqbal al-ʾAqaliyya al-Filasṭīniyya fī Isrāʾīl* [The Future of the Palestinian Minority in Israel], edited by Khalil Nakhla, 105–19. Ramallah: Madar, Palestinian Center for Israeli Studies, 2008.

Legislative Sources

HCJ 4112/99, *Adalah and Co.* v. *Tel Aviv-Jaffa Municipality and Co* (2002).
Law for the Supreme Institute for the Arabic Language, 5767-2007, Law Book 2092, 28 March 2007, 286–90.
Law for the Supreme Institute for the Hebrew Language, 5713-1953, Law Book 135, 6 September 1953, 168–69.

Index

al-Abassi, Issam, 66
Abassi, Mahmoud, 137
  Novel and Short Story in Arabic Literature in Israel, The, 137
'Abiru sabil' (Passers By) essay (Tuma, Emile), 67
Abu Hanna, Hanna, 57, 66, 187–8, 189
Abu Khadra, Fahd, 181, 183–5, 189
Abu al-Saud, Adnan, 89–90
  'Culture of Arab Citizens in Israeli Society, The' 89–90
ACA (Arab Culture Association), 167, 198–204, 206–8, 211–12
academics
  Israeli, 117, 132, 151
  Palestinian, 112–14, 151, 152, 163–4, 169
  see also Ghanayim, Mahmud; Somekh, Sasson
academisation, 15–16, 103, 111, 112–13, 153, 163, 225–6
  mediatory position, 114–18, 133–47
  mimesis, 115
  see also Somekh, Sasson; Ghanayim, Mahmud,
Academy of the Arabic Language, Egypt, 181
Academy of the Arabic Language, Israel, 166, 167, 180, 181, 208, 211, 207–8, 211, 222, 225
  Abu Hanna, Hanna, 187–8, 189
  activities, 190–1
  Atallah, Elias, 181, 183–5, 188–9, 204
  chronological framework of construction, 181–3
  diverse views, 186, 190
  Ghanayim, Mahmud, 189–92
  Jubran, Suleiman, 186–7, 189, 192–7
  Majadele, Ghaleb, 182, 189
  Saiegh-Haddad, Elinor, 192
  textual corpus, 183–98
Academy of the Hebrew language, 196, 197
Adalah: Legal Centre for Arab Minority Rights in Israel, 174–5
  Democratic Constitution, 168, 169, 174–80, 208, 211
Al-Anba newspaper, 63, 120
Al-Eid, Youmna, 115–16
Amara, Heba, 201
Ar-Raid, 81
Arab Culture Association (ACA), 167, 198–204, 206–8, 211–2
Arab custom, 218n
Arab-Islamic culture 25, 39
Arab Literature under the Shadow of War (Ballas, Shimon), 137
Arabic, 64
  ACA, 167, 198–204
  academy, 16
  civil society organisations, 162–5, 211, 225
  Democratic Constitution, 174–5, 176–80

Arabic (*cont.*)
desire for, 149
dialects, 2, 90–2
diglossia, 90–1
elimination of, 29–31
equality, 172–3, 174–5
etymology, 204, 205
expropriation and closure, 6–7, 85
Haddad, Michel, 90–2
Haifa Declaration, 170–4, 180
Hebrew, subordination to, 33
materiality, 208–10
modernisation, 183–4
mother, symbolic equivalence, 148–9, 151–2
national identity, 6, 36–7, 55, 57, 170–1, 173, 174
nationalism, 56–7
political sovereignty, 173
settler-colonial condition in Israel, 29–31
social history of, 3–5
spoken, 10, 90–2, 127, 133, 204–6
translation, 185, 195–6, 208
writing, 59
see also Academy of the Arab language; literary Arabic; literature; NGOs
'Arabic' (arena), 14–17, 35–6, 47, 102–3, 207–12
Assaf, Michael, 61–4, 98
biography of, 223–6
constitution 55–60, 97–101
declarative national position, 166–7
developed mediatory position, 166–7
education, 62–3
formalisation, 58
Haddad, Michel, 86–97
historical narrative, 223–30
institutionalisation, 224–5
Israeli Arabs, 86–97
Khazzoom, Eliyahu, 74–6, 98
legal-professional process, 167
literacy criticism, 60–97, 111
literature, 60–1
Moreh, Shmuel, 77–86, 98
NGOs, 180
orientalists, the 73–86, 102
Palestinian academics, 112, 113, 114
press, the, 60–1
return and repositioning, 66–7
Somekh, Sasson, 117, 118–30
structurality, 226–8
Tuma, Emile, 65–77, 98, 102
see also academisation; mediatory position
artistry, 128–9, 133, 145–7, 150
Assaf, Michael, 61–4, 98
'Integration of Arabs in Israel, The' 61–2, 63
Atallah, Elias, 181, 183–5, 188–9, 204–6, 207, 208
ACA, 198
If the Murdered Victim is Asked, 204–5
Atallah, Rawda, 200–1
Azzam, Samira, 121–2

Badr, Abdel-Muhsen Taha, 138
Ballas, Shimon, 137
Arab Literature under the Shadow of War, 137
Palestinian Stories, 121
Basic Law – The Nation State of the Jewish People, 5
Bataille, Georges, 27
bilingualism, 175, 177–8
binationalism, 175, 179
Bishara, Azmi, 106n
Bloom, Harold, 149
Bourdieu, Pierre, 28
British Mandate, 4, 37, 39, 40
literature during, 77–8
bureaucracy, 165–6

capitalism, 28; *see also* print capitalism
Al-Carmel newspaper, 124
censorship 227
citizenship, 7; *see also* national identity
civil society organisations, 162–5, 211, 225; *see also* NGOs
collective memory, 164, 165
colonialism, 3
bidirectional dependency, 27
co-presence of two languages, 2
Egypt, 181
language academies, 180–1
language enforcement, 2
language, 10
modernity/coloniality, 28

new syntheses of languages, 2
power, 3
resistance 134–5
sociolinguistic relations, 2, 8–13
communicative events 3, 8–9, 14, 221, 222, 225
literary Arabic, 227–8
settler-colonialism, 1
communist literature, 80, 81
community, the, and the state, 25
compulsive literacy, 14, 27, 28, 31–6, 40, 42, 43, 60, 101
High Committee for the Arabic Language, 186
knowledge/power framework, 119
NGOs, 207, 210
Palestinian fragmentariness, 46
Somekh, Sasson, 119, 130
compulsiveness, 28; *see also* compulsive literacy
control and surveillance mechanisms, 150
cultural autonomy, 202–4
cultural memory, 21n
culture, 74–5
Arab, 25, 89, 95
Haifa Declaration, 170
Somekh, Sasson, 121
'Culture of Arab Citizens in Israeli Society, The' (Abu al-Saud, Adnan) 89–90

Darraj, Faisal, 149
Darwish, Mahmoud, 66, 133, 150
declarative communication, 147
declarative national position, 166–7
Deformed, The (Fayad, Tawfiq), 112, 138
Democratic Constitution (Adalah), 168, 169, 174–80, 208, 211
desire, 116–17, 149
developed mediatory position, 166–7
dialects, 2, 90–2
Difficult Path: The Journey of the Palestinian Story in Israel, The (Ghanayim, Mahmud), 138, 143–4, 145
discursive formations, 35
Dreamt-of Homeland (Elad-Buskila, Ami), 137
'Durub wa-masabih' (Lanes and Lanterns) essay (Tuma, Emile), 67
Dwairy, Marwan, 175

education, 7, 32, 60–1
ACA, 201–3
Assaf, Michael, 62
autonomy, 203
corrective, 62
expropriation and closure, 65
Hebrew, 62
High Committee for the Arabic Language, 185
languages under Ottoman rule, 36
mediatory position, 115
mimesis, 115
newspapers, 63–4
Palestinian academics, 113–14
pre-statehood period, 62
segregation, 33, 34, 57
standardisation, 9
state control, 97
Egypt
Academy of the Arabic Language, Cairo, 181
novels, 138
Elad-Buskila, Ami
Dreamt-of Homeland, 137
emigration, 74–5, 78–9
Equal Constitution for All (Musawa Centre), 168
equality, 172–3, 174–5, 177–9
etymology, 204, 205
excessive literacy, 14, 27–8, 31–6, 37, 42–3, 60, 101, 223
expenditure, 41
knowledge/power framework, 119
mediatory position, 151
Moreh, Shmuel, 82
NGOs, 207, 210
Palestinian fragmentariness, 46
social domains, 165–6
Somekh, Sasson, 119, 130, 151
excessiveness, 27; *see also* excessive literacy
Excluded: Critical Reading of Israeli Textbooks in Arab High Schools, The (Abu Hanna-Nahhas, Eman), 202
expropriation and closure, 56, 57, 60, 67, 100, 101
Arabic, 6–7, 85
Atallah, Elias, 188
education, 65

expropriation and closure (*cont.*)
Haddad, Michel 96
Military Government, 64, 65
poetry, 77, 85
press, the, 65

family, 205–6
Fayad, Tawfiq, 112, 138
Deformed, The, 112, 138
Ghanayim, Mahmud, 138
Future Vision of the Arabs in Israel (High Follow-Up Committee for Arab Citizens of Israel), 168

genres, 11–12
Ghanayim, Mahmud, 15–16, 117–18, 133–4, 153–4, 167
Academy of the Arabic Language, 189–92
artistry, 145–7, 150
Difficult Path: The Journey of the Palestinian Story in Israel, The, 138, 143–4, 145
Gottesfeld, Dorit, 118
Habibi, Emile, 135–7, 138, 139–42, 143, 145–6
language, 139–42, 149–50
literary system, 142–5, 150
literature, divorced from reality, 134–9, 146, 149–50
Mahmoud, Abdelrahim, 134–5, 142–3
mediatory position, 149–50
Muwasi, Faruq, 131–2
Somekh, Sasson, 118, 130, 145
'Studies on the Local Short Story', 133
Textual Structure in Emile Habibi's The Pessoptimist, The, 135–7, 139–42, 143
globalisation, 162–3
human rights, 169
see also late settler-colonialism
Gottesfeld, Dorit, 118
Gramsci, Antonio, 226, 227, 229

Habibi, Emile, 57
Pessoptimist, The, 135–7, 138, 139–42, 143
Saraya, the Ogre's Daughter, 145–6
Haddad, Michel, 15, 60, 74, 75, 81, 86–97, 129
'Literary and Spoken Arabic', 90–2
Al-Mujtama journal 15, 60, 81, 86–97
'Relationship of Authors to Their Society, The', 87–9
Somekh, Sasson, 128–9
'Towards a Literary School', 93–5
Haifa Declaration (Mada al-Carmel), 168–74, 208, 211
Haj-Yahia, Muhamad, 214n
HaMizrah HaHadash journal see *New Orient, The* journal
Hammoudi, Abdellah, 149
Haqiqat al-Amr newspaper, 4, 63, 73, 79, 81
'HaSifrut baSafah haAravit beMedinat Israel' (Moreh, Shmuel), 77
Hebraisation, 188
Hebrew, 24, 25, 64, 172–3, 183–4
Democratic Constitution, 174–5, 176
education, 62
High Committee for the Arabic Language, 185–6
Iraqi Jews, 80
Jubran, Suleiman, 195–7
national identity, 37
Ottoman rule, 36
poetry, 74
High Committee for the Arabic Language, 182, 185
High Follow-Up Committee for Arab Citizens of Israel
Future Vision of the Arabs in Israel, 168
history, role of, 122–3
human rights, 169, 176–7, 179, 211
humanity, total loss of, 44; *see also* total loss
Hussein, Rashid, 82–3, 85
'Our Poets', 82–3
Hussein, Taha, 217n

Ibrahim, Hanna, 66
Ibrahim, Malik, 183
identity, 32
Israeli Arabs, 110n, 171–2
Palestinian collective, 206, 207, 222
see also national identity
Idris, Yusuf, 126–7, 128
If the Murdered Victim is Asked (Atallah, Elias), 204–5
In a New Light (Mansour, Atallah), 111
influence, anxiety of 149, 152

Institute for Oriental Studies, 4
institutions of the state *see* state institutions
'Integration of Arabs in Israel, The' (Assaf, Michael) 61–2, 63
intertextuality, 146
Iraqi Jews, 77, 78–80
ironic intertextuality, 146
Islam, 227
Israel, State of, 2, 35, 86
  Arabic elimination in, 29–31, 37
  Basic Law – The Nation State of the Jewish People, 5
  bureaucracy, 165–6
  construction market, 152
  Democratic Constitution, 175–8
  language control, 3, 25
  loss of literacy, 37–8, 39
  loyalty to, 47–8
  Military Government, 56, 63–4, 65
  print capitalism 47–8
  as settler-colonial regime, 6, 8, 18n, 24, 33
  sociopolitical order, 5–6
  state apparatuses, 6
  see also Israeli academics; Palestinians in Israel; Zionist regime
Israeli academics, 117, 132; *see also* Somekh, Sasson
Israeli Arabs, 98–9
  Assaf, Michael, 62
  Democratic Constitution, 175
  Haddad, Michel, 86–97
  identity, 110n, 171
  literary criticism, 60
  literary school, 92–5
  literature, 92–6
  poetry, 75, 84, 85
  society, 88, 89–90, 95
  see also Palestinians in Israel
Israeli Communist Party, 59
Israelisation, 188
Al-Ittihad newspaper, 4, 65, 81

Jabareen, Hassan, 214n
Jabra, Jabra Ibrahim, 110n
Al-Jadid journal 15, 65–7, 70, 81, 181, 183–5, 224
Jubran, Khalil Jubran, 138
Jubran, Salem, 66
Jubran, Suleiman, 117
  Academy of the Arabic Language, 186–7, 189
  On the Margins of the Innovations and Limitations in the Modern Arabic Language, 192–7

Kanafani, Ghassan, 121, 122
Kayal, Mahmoud, 117
Khazzoom, Eliyahu, 59, 74–7, 98
knowledge/power framework, 119, 123, 124–30, 134–47; *see also* mediatory position

Landau, Jacob M., 74
Lanes and Lanterns (Qawar-Farah, Najwa), 70–2
language, 2, 64
  Atallah, Elias, 204–6
  bilingualism, 175, 177–8
  British Mandate, 37
  bureaucracy, 165
  Democratic Constitution, 174–5, 176–7
  dialogue, 141
  domain of, 32, 34
  eliminated, 216n
  equality, 172–3, 174–5, 178–9
  genres, 140–1
  Ghanayim, Mahmud, 139–42, 149–50
  Haddad, Michel, 90–2
  hierarchy, 2, 30, 37, 63–5, 91, 95
  human rights, 176–7
  infrastructure, 9, 29, 30
  institutional separation, 4
  Jubran, Suleiman, 193–4
  in literary texts, 126–7
  of loss, 31
  material-institutional sphere of, 33–4
  Mustafa, Adel, 193
  national identity, 36, 37, 38
  nationality, 180, 187–8
  of one's own, 165
  Ottoman rule, 36
  separation, 37
  Somekh, Sasson, 126–7
  standardisation, 9
  state institutions, 32
  see also Arabic

language academies, 180–1
language infrastructure, 9, 29, 30
  destruction, 29
late settler-colonialism 163, 164
'Learn Arabic and Teach It to the People' project, 201–2
legal procedures, 165–6
legal-professional process, 164–5, 166, 167
Levi, Ovadia, 63–4
literacy, 5, 11–12
  'Arabic' (arena), 58
  history of the loss of, 36–41
  Palestinian, 14, 36–41
  Zionist, 14
  see also compulsive literacy; excessive literacy
'Literary and Spoken Arabic' (Haddad, Michel), 90–2
literary Arabic, 10–11, 13–16, 25–6, 56–7, 224–5
  Atallah, Elias, 204–6
  communicative events, 227–8
  Ghanayim, Mahmud, 133
  Haddad, Michel, 90–2
  Islam, 227
  mediatory position, 116
  Quran, the, 227
  reappropriation of, 31
  settler-colonial version, 31
  sexual desire, 116–17
  Somekh, Sasson, 126–7
literary criticism, 12, 13, 15, 59, 60–5, 97–8, 100, 224
  academics, 117
  academisation, 15–16, 111, 112–18
  Assaf, Michael, 61–4
  in Europe, 125–6
  Haddad, Michel, 60, 74, 75, 81, 86–97
  Israeli Arabs, 60
  Israeli Communist Party, 59
  Jubran, Suleiman, 117
  Kayal, Mahmoud, 117
  Khazzoom, Eliyahu, 59, 74–7
  Landau, Jacob M. 74
  literature of life, 60–5
  mediatory position, 114–18, 148–53
  Moreh, Shmuel, 74, 77–86, 117, 132
  orientalists, 59, 73–86, 102
  ownership, 152
  Qawar-Farah, Najwa, 67–72
  Semah, David, 117
  Tuma, Emile, 59, 65–73, 102
  see also Ghanayim, Mahmud; Somekh, Sasson
literary events, 84, 93–5, 100–1, 151
  academisation, 15–16, 103, 111
  history, role of, 122–3
  see also literary criticism
literary system, 127–8, 142–5, 150
literature, 59, 97–8, 100
  British Mandate, 77–8
  communist, 80
  Ghanayim, Mahmud, 138, 144
  Haddad, Michel, 87, 93–5
  infrastructures, 81
  Israeli Arab, 92–6
  modes of, 82–4
  Moreh, Shmuel, 77–86
  Al-Mujtama, 87
  non-communist, 80–1
  Qawar-Farah, Najwa, 67–72
  reality, divorced from, 125–6, 134–9, 146–7, 149–51
  religious, 80, 81
  secular, 80, 81
  short stories, 132–3
  Somekh, Sasson, 120–1, 125–6, 134–9
  statehood, 78
  Tuma, Emile, 72
  see also literary criticism; poetry
loss 43, 44
  ability to lose, 44–5, 226–7, 229
  language of, 31
  of literacy, 36–41
  Nakba, 43–7, 220–1
  second-degree, 221–3
  total, 44, 220–1
Loubani, Issa, 66
loyalty, 62

Mada al-Carmel: Arab Centre for Applied Social Research
  Haifa Declaration, 168–74, 208, 211
Mahfouz, Naguib, 122
al-Mahjar poets, 74
Mahmoud, Abdelrahim, 134–5, 142–3
Majadele, Ghaleb, 182, 189

al-Malaika, Nazik, 79
Mansour, Atallah
In a New Light, 111
Marion, Jean-Luc, 27
Marx, Karl, 27
mass media, 9, 32, 97; *see also* press, the
master-disciple pattern, 149, 151
material-institutional sphere, 33–4, 35
Mawasi, Farouk, 181, 183–5
mediatory position, 113, 114–18, 124–30, 153–5
Academy of the Arabic Language, 190–1
settler-colonial mimesis, 130–47, 148–53
Mendel, Yonatan, 18n
Military Government, 56, 63–4, 65
mimesis, 115
settler-colonial, 130–47
Ministry of Education
Arab Culture Division, 181, 182, 186
'Modernist Form in Michel Haddad's Poetry' (Somekh, Sasson), 129
modernity/modernism, 39, 146–7, 152
Academy of the Arabic language, 197–8
Arabic, 183–4
coloniality, 28
Ghanayim, Mahmud, 136–9, 145–6
Jubran, Suleiman, 193–7
Mustafa, Adel, 193
Somekh, Sasson, 128, 129
Moreh, Shmuel, 74, 77–86, 98, 117, 132
'HaSifrut baSafah haAravit beMedinat Israel', 77
mother, symbolic, 148–9, 151–2
'Movement and Pace in Sunset March' (Somekh, Sasson), 128
Al-Mujtama journal, 15, 60, 81, 86–97, 224
Musawa Centre for the Rights of Arab Citizens in Israel
Equal Constitution for All, 168
Mustafa, Adel, 193
Muwasi, Faruq, 130–2
Waiting for the Train, 131
'My Language – My Identity' festival, 199–200
mysticism, 69–70

Nahda, 3
Nakba, 40, 43–7, 220–1
Naqara, Hanna, 57, 65
nation-states *see* state, the
national identity, 32, 102, 164–5, 180, 203–4
ACA, 201, 212
Arabic 6, 36–7, 55, 57, 170–1, 173, 174
dialects, 91–2
Haifa Declaration, 170–1, 173
language, 36, 37, 38
nationalism, 56–7, 194
nationality, 172–3, 180, 187–8, 200
natives, elimination of, 29
New Orient, The journal, 15, 61, 73, 74
NGOs (non-government organisations), 48, 167, 169, 180–2, 225–6
ACA, 167, 198–204, 206–7, 211–12
Democratic Constitution, 168, 169, 174–80, 208, 211
Haifa Declaration, 168–74, 180, 208, 211
vision statements, 167, 168–80, 207–8
see also Academy of the Arabic Language, Israel
1948 war see *Nakba*
1967 war, 111–12
non-communist literature, 80–1
non-government organisations *see* NGOs
Novel and Short Story in Arabic Literature in Israel, The (Abassi, Mahmoud), 137

On the Margins of the Innovations and Limitations in the Modern Arabic Language (Jubran, Suleiman), 192–7
orientalists, 59, 61, 63, 64, 88, 96–7, 102
literary criticism, 59, 73–86
Ottoman rule, 36–7
'Our Poets' (Hussein, Rashid), 82–3

Palestine, 3–4
local history, 38–9
loss of literacy 36–41
poetry, 82, 83, 84
resistance culture, 134
settler-colonial order, 47
Palestine Liberation Organisation (PLO) 134
Palestinian academics, 112–14, 152, 163–4, 169; *see also* Ghanayim, Mahmud
Palestinian Stories (Ballas, Shimon), 121

Palestinians, 174
Arab-Islamic tradition, 39
collective memory, 38–9, 44
culture, 57
fragmentation of society, 45–6
integration, 110n
intellectuals, 4, 15, 16, 57, 65, 90, 110n
life-cycle, 44
literacy, 14
loss of literacy 36–41
modernity, 39
Nakba, 43–6
national identity, 203–4
physical elimination, 29
Somekh, Sasson, 121–2
written discourse, 41–2
see also Palestinians in Israel
Palestinians in Israel, 3, 4, 5, 6–8, 36, 41–2
and the Arab world, 228
Arabic, 25, 37, 48, 55, 174–5, 176–7
Arabic, elimination of, 29–31, 37–8
'Arabic' (arena), 58
Arabic literature, 59
Assaf, Michael, 61–4
civil society organisations, 162–5, 211
collective identity, 206, 207, 222
collective memory, 38–9, 44
community, creating, 55
construction market, 152
control of, 56
critical discourse, 164
cultural autonomy, 202–3
elimination of, 29, 226
fragmentariness, 46
Haifa Declaration, 170–2
historical narrative, 220
human rights, 176–7, 179, 211
as indigenous minority, 176–7
integration, 62, 64, 111
isolation of, 29–30, 56
legal status, 168
legal-professional process, 164–5, 166, 167
literary Arabic, 31, 56
loss of literacy 36–41
loyalty to the state, 47–8
Military Government, 56, 63–4, 65
Nakba, 40, 43–7, 220–1
1967 war, 111–12
Palestinian subject, the 112
poets, 74–5
political economy, 99
print capitalism, 48
reading Zionist texts, 41–2
resistance, 226–7
sociolinguistic fields, 2, 8–13
Somekh, Sasson, 121–2
sub-contractors, 152
written discourse, 41–2
see also compulsive literacy; Israeli Arabs; Palestinian academics
Passers By (Qawar-Farah, Najwa), 68
Pessoptimist, The (Habibi, Emile), 135–7, 138, 139–42, 143
PLO (Palestine Liberation Organisation) 134
poetry, 74–85
classical metres, 131
colonisation resistance and, 134–5
Haddad, Michel, 129
Muwasi, Faruq, 130–2
political, 82–5
politician-intellectual relationships, 149
postcolonialism, 2
press, the, 60–73
Arab-language, 63
bans, 65
expropriation and closure, 65
print capitalism, 11, 24–5, 28
destruction of Palestinian, 38
settler-colonial context, 46–8
Zionist regime, 46–8
production, means of, 33, 152–3
NGOs, 48
ownership, 48, 114–15, 152–3, 154, 164
semiotic, 6–7, 15, 28, 32, 48
symbolic, 32, 48, 98, 100, 113, 115, 152–3, 154, 164
public textual activities, 11

Al-Qasemi Academic College of Education, 216n
Qawar, Jamal, 74, 76
Qawar-Farah, Najwa, 57, 67–72, 74, 83
Ghanayim, Mahmud, 138
Lanes and Lanterns, 70–2
Passers By, 68
Quran, the, 227

reading, 5, 11–12
'Arabic' (arena), 58
Arabic elimination, 31
commodification, 46–8
modes, 24–5
Palestinians in Israel, 41–2
see also literacy
'Relationship of Authors to Their Society, The' (Haddad, Michel), 87–9
religious literature, 80, 81
return and repositioning, 15, 56, 66–7
ACA, 199, 201, 206, 208
academisation, 114
Academy of the Arabic Language, 180, 181, 190, 208, 212
'Arabic', 15, 16, 59, 99, 115, 203, 204
Atallah, Elias, 189, 206
Haifa Declaration, 173–4, 180
Israel-Arab literary school, 93
Jubran, Suleiman, 197
mediatory position, 152–3
Al-Mujtama, 95
orientalists, 73–7
Qawar-Farah, Najwa, 68, 71
revolution, 90, 168
Rouhana, Nadim, 214n, 215n
Russian formalism, 122, 123, 124, 125

a-Saadi, Khawlah, 182, 185
Said, Ahmad Tawfiq, 75
Saiegh-Haddad, Elinor, 192
Saraya, the Ogre's Daughter (Habibi, Emile), 145–6
saturation, 27–8
second-degree loss, 221–3
secular literature, 80, 81
segregation, 33, 34, 57
Semah, David, 117
semiotics, 34–5
settler-colonialism, 1–2, 5, 8, 29, 226, 229–30
Arabic, 29–31, 148–9
contradictions, 73, 99–100, 103, 113
dominance without history, 229
hegemony, 30
hierarchy,14, 26, 30, 32, 37, 63–5, 114, 115, 154, 206
language elimination, 216n
language, 181
late, 209
literary practices, 46–8
mediatory position, 114–15, 124–47, 148–53
mimesis, 130–47, 148–53
modernity, 39
oppression, 171–2
Palestine 45–7
political economy, 99, 100
print capitalism, 46–8
settlers' identity, 32
sexual desire, 116–17
Shalhoub-Kevorkian, Nadera, 214n
Shammas, Anton, 150
Sharet, Moshe, 86–7
Al-Sharq journal, 120, 124
short stories, 132–3
sign (semiotics), 34
social groups, 32–3
fragmentation, 45
social history, 3–5
society, 87
Israeli, 95
Israeli Arabs, 88, 89–90, 95
literature, 87–8
socioeconomic class, 2, 96, 151, 164
sociolinguistic fields, 8–9, 24, 27, 48
determining factors, 32
literacy modes, 14
Palestinian, 39, 40
Palestinians in Israel, 2, 8–13
sociopolitical order, 5–6
Somekh, Sasson, 117, 118–30, 153–4, 167
artistry, 128–9
Ghanayim, Mahmud, 118, 130, 145
history, role of, 122–3
Idris, Yusuf, 126–7, 128
influence, 149
knowledge/power framework, 123, 124–30
language 126–7
literary system, 127–8
literature, divorced from reality, 125–6
Mahfouz, Naguib, 122
mediatory position, 124–31
'Modernist Form in Michel Haddad's Poetry', 129

Somekh, Sasson (*cont.*)
'Movement and Pace in Sunset March', 128
Muwasi, Faruq, 130–1
Russian formalism, 122, 123, 124, 125
'Toward a Complex Meaning', 128–9
sovereignty, 178–9
standardisation, 9, 13, 208–10
state, the, 32, 175, 224
and the community, 25
control, 3, 25, 56, 57, 61, 97
language, 173, 178
literature, 78
loyalty to, 47
state apparatuses/institutions, 6, 8, 12–13, 25, 32, 35
duality, 6
institutional separation, 4
'Studies on the Local Short Story' (Ghanayim, Mahmud), 133
Suleiman, Ramzi, 214n
Supreme Institute of the Arabic Language Law, 16, 166, 182, 189
surplus, 27
al-Syyab, Badr Shakir, 79

Taha, Muhammad, Ali, 133
Tanzimat of 1841, 3
Tel Aviv University (TAU), 117, 118, 119–20
Shiloah Institute, 120
Department of Arab Language and Literature 118
texts, 5, 11
genres, 11–12
Textual Structure in Emile Habibi's The Pessoptimist, The (Ghanayim, Mahmud), 135–7, 139–42, 143
total loss, 44, 220–1
'Toward a Complex Meaning' (Somekh, Sasson), 128–9
'Towards a Literary School' (Haddad, Michel), 93–5
traditionalism, 128, 131–2
translation, 185, 195–6, 208
Tuma, Emile, 15, 57, 98, 102
'Abiru sabil' (Passers By), 67
'Durub wa-masabih' (Lanes and Lanterns), 67
literary criticism, 59, 65–73
Tuqan, Ibrahim, 135

Waiting for the Train (Muwasi, Faruq), 131
war, 111–12
writers, 66–72, 93, 96
secular, 81
society, 88
see also literature; poetry
writing, 5, 11–12
Arabic, 59
'Arabic' (arena), 58
'Arabic' communication, 25
Arabic elimination, 31
commodification, 46–8
modes, 24–5
post-1948 void, 41
Zionist, 41–2
see also literacy

Al-Yawm newspaper, 15, 33, 63–4, 73, 79, 81, 120

Ziad, Tawfiq, 66
Zionist regime, 7–8
academics, 132
'Arabic' (arena), 58
Arabic literature, 59
binary classification system, 26, 106n
critical discourse, 164
hierarchy,14, 26, 30, 32, 37, 63–5, 114, 115, 154, 206
literacy, 14, 39, 40
print capitalism, 46–8
as settler-colonialist regime, 43
Somekh, Sasson, 119, 123
state control, 57, 61
writing, 41–2
see also excessive literacy; Israel, State of

EU representative:
Easy Access System Europe
Mustamäe tee 50, 10621 Tallinn, Estonia
Gpsr.requests@easproject.com

www.ingramcontent.com/pod-product-compliance
Lightning Source LLC
Chambersburg PA
CBHW051120160426
43195CB00014B/2269
* 9 7 8 1 3 9 9 5 1 2 0 2 2 *